Beyond Mass Higher Education

SRHE and Open University Press Imprint

Current titles include:

Beyond Mass Higher Education

Building on Experience

Edited by
Ian McNay

The Society for Research into Higher Education
& Open University Press

Open University Press
McGraw-Hill Education
McGraw-Hill House
Shoppenhangers Road
Maidenhead
Berkshire
England
SL6 2QL

email: enquiries@openup.co.uk
world wide web: www.openup.co.uk

and Two Penn Plaza, New York, NY 10121–2289, USA

First published 2006

A catalogue record of this book is available from the British Library

ISBN-13: 978 0335 21857 8 (pb)   978 0335 21858 5 (hb)
ISBN-10: 0335 21857 1 (pb)   0335 21858 X (hb)

Library of Congress Cataloging-in-Publication Data
CIP data has been applied for

Typeset by RefineCatch Limited, Bungay, Suffolk
Printed in Poland by OZGraf SA.
www.polskabook.pl

Contents

Acknowledgements

Most of the chapters in this collection derive from presentations to seminars in a series 'From mass to universal higher education: building on experience'. This was part funded by the Economic and Social Research Council, Award Number R451265231. Other funding came from the Society for Research into Higher Education and, through the editor, the Open University.

The idea for the seminar series came originally from Michael Shattock and Richard Pearson, who were co-coordinators of the project, with Ian McNay. It was then adopted by the Society through its Research and Development Committee. The formal submission was made through the University of Greenwich, where the editor was based.

Thanks are due to other contributors to the series – there were 26 presenters in total, and so not enough room for them all – and to nearly 200 people who participated in the seminars and contributed to the development of thinking. A full list of sessions, with titles of presentations and details of presenters was included in the Society's Annual Report, 2004.

Material used in presentations, and included in Part Four, was also used, with permission, as the basis for articles in *Higher Education Quarterly* Volume 58, No. 4.

Contributors

Gráinne Conole is Professor of Educational Innovation in Post-Compulsory Education at the University of Southampton, with research interests in the use, integration and evaluation of Information and Communication Technologies and e-learning and their impact on organizational change. She was previously Director of the Institute for Learning and Research Technology at the University of Bristol.

Stephen Court is Senior Research Officer at the Association of University Teachers. He has published widely on aspects of higher education policy.

Jim Gallacher is a professor at Glasgow Caledonian University, and joint Director of the Centre for Research into Lifelong Learning, a joint initiative with the University of Stirling.

Peter T. Knight is Director of the Institute of Educational Technology at the Open University. He has taught in primary and secondary schools, and has previously worked at Lancaster University and St Martin's College, Lancaster. He is the author, with Mantz Yorke, of *Assessment, Learning and Employability* (SRHE/Open University Press).

Dr Carole Leathwood is a senior research fellow in the Institute for Policy Studies in Education, London Metropolitan University. She specializes in research in post-compulsory education, particularly issues of gender, class and 'race', including widening participation in HE, managerialism and marketization in FE, and critical analyses of policy. She is the Ireland/Britain editor for *Women's Studies International Forum*.

Brenda Little is a senior policy analyst with the Open University's Centre for Higher Education Research and Innovation. Her main research interests lie in work-based and vocational aspects of HE policy and practice and the changing nature of the student experience.

Dr Lisa Lucas is a lecturer in the Graduate School of Education, University of Bristol, and a former winner of the SRHE Newer Researcher award. Her main research interests are in the organization, funding and development of national systems of HE in a global context. Recent studies have been on comparative systems of funding and evaluating university research, and on the links between research and teaching within academic work. She is the author of *The Research Game in Academic Life* (SRHE/Open University Press).

Ian McNay is Emeritus Professor of Higher Education and Management, University of Greenwich. His career spans roles as administrator, policy advisor, researcher, staff developer and consultant based in four European countries and working in some 22 around the world.

Bob Osborne is Professor of Applied Policy Studies and Acting Director of the Social and Policy Research Institute at the University of Ulster. He has acted as adviser to committees at Westminster and Stormont. He was a member of the Northern Ireland Equality Commission from 1999 to 2004. He was joint editor of *Fair Employment in Northern Ireland: A Generation On* (Blackstaff Press).

Dr Richard Pearson is an independent consultant and was previously Director of the Institute for Employment Studies. He has over thirty years of experience in research and consultancy relating to HE, to student demand and the labour market for professionals, to graduates and mobility, and to workforce planning and corporate performance.

Dr Wendy Saunderson lectures in the School of Policy Studies at the University of Ulster. Her specific focus on academic identity and equal opportunities in the university sector is part of her wider research interest in the conceptualization, 'measurement' and analysis of identity development and dynamics (using ISA) in relation to policy change.

Michael Shattock, after many years as Registrar at the University of Warwick, is now Visiting Professor at the Institute of Education, London University, where, with Gareth Williams, he developed and directed the MBA in Higher Education Management. He is the author of *Managing Successful Universities* (SRHE/Open University Press).

Marilyn Wedgwood is Pro-Vice-Chancellor and Director of External Relations at Manchester Metropolitan University. She has been active for over fifteen years in the development and delivery of 'third stream' policy at the DTI, the University of Sheffield and MMU. She chairs and serves on national and regional committees relating to HE and society. Advisory roles have included work with the House of Lords' Science and Technology Committee on Science and the RDAs, and as a consultant on regional strategy for Yorkshire and Humberside.

Celia Whitchurch is Senior Assistant College Secretary, King's College, London. Previous posts were at Cambridge, Kent and Birmingham. She was the founding editor of *Perspectives: Policy and Practice in Higher Education,* the journal of the Association of University Administrators. Her PhD is on the changing roles and identities of professional managers in UK higher education.

Mantz Yorke is Professor of Higher Education at Liverpool John Moores University. He has researched, reflected and published on various aspects of the student experience, including assessment, student retention and employability.

Abbreviations

AGR	Association of Graduate Recruiters
API	Age Participation Index
AUT	Association of University Teachers
CAA	Computer Assisted Assessment
CPD	continuing professional development
EMA	Education Maintenance Allowance
EO	equal opportunities
FE	further education
FEC	further education college
GCSE	General Certificate of Secondary Education
HE	higher education
HEFCE	Higher Education Funding Council for England
HEFCW	Higher Education Funding Council for Wales
HEI	higher education institution
HEIF	Higher Education Innovation Fund
HESA	Higher Education Statistics Agency
HNC	higher national certificate
HND	higher national diploma
ICT	information and communications technology
IER	Initial Entry Rate
LEA	local education authority
MLEs	managed learning environments
OECD	Organisation for Economic Co-operation and Development
PSA	Public Service Agreement
QAA	Quality Assurance Agency
RAE	research assessment exercise
SCQF	Scottish Credit and Qualifications Framework
SFEFC	Scottish Further Education Funding Council
SHEFC	Scottish Higher Education Funding Council
SMEs	small and medium sized enterprises
TQA	teaching quality assessment

UGC	University Grants Committee
UOA	unit of assessment
VLEs	virtual learning environments
WBL	work-based learning

Part One

Introduction

1

Delivering Mass Higher Education – The Reality of Policy in Practice

Ian McNay

Introduction

Between 1987–8 and 1997–8, the Age Participation Index (API) for UK higher education (HE) rose from 14.5 per cent to 33.4 per cent (HoC, 26.10.2004). After a decade when the figure had hardly changed, there was a sudden surge to put the UK clearly within Trow's (1974) category of mass provision. The New Labour administration, coming in to office in 1997, made a commitment to moving towards an Initial Entry Rate (IER) of over 50 per cent, though the timetable for achieving this, and even the definitions employed, kept changing. Upward movement in the figure was sluggish, and may be in reverse, particularly for men. Scotland saw a 2 per cent drop in 2004, mainly in the further education (FE) college-based provision. In England there was a slight fall in the API, with the IER roughly constant. Applications for 2005 entry through UCAS suggest that male participation rates will continue to fall after any leap caused by early applications from those seeking to avoid higher fees.

This chapter looks at reasons for the first surge and considers how far the conditions are in place for any second surge towards 'universal' levels of access. It then reviews Trow's ideas, drawing on Brennan's analysis (Brennan, 2004), and Scott's framework (Scott, 1995), which have provided the two main reference points for discussion of mass higher education. There is a need for redefining the meaning of the term, if only to help institutions, staff and students in finding clear identities and defined roles. Those themes recur through this book. The chapters that follow examine aspects of provision in some detail to draw out lessons for policy makers, institutional leaders and over 300,000 staff who work in the sector.

Elite to mass and more – contributory factors

A confluence of factors led to the steep curve in the API after 1988. Not all applied equally to all four countries in the UK, which currently have different levels of participation (Court, 2004). UK figures conceal these variations because of the dominance of England, which has the slowest rate of improvement. Note that the API applies only to *young* people (under 21) entering *full-time* higher education. The IER covers students up to the age of 30, in any mode of participation. The percentage growth in full-time undergraduate degree study by young home students over this period was lower than for part-time study, for postgraduate study and for international students. That shift from a dominant conception of a higher education student has not often been seen in ministerial pronouncements, despite commitment to diversity. Nor did the Dearing Report (NCIHE, 1997) develop its implications significantly.

For the group covered by the API, the size of the age group was falling at that time. The size of the 15–24 age group in the UK changed as follows (ONS, 2004, Table 1.4):

1981	9019m
1991	8168m
2001	7261m

This allowed upward movement in the index (a percentage figure) without necessarily growth in the student headcount. This decline in the size of the cohort was not evenly distributed, so that there was a shift in class profile. More school leavers were from those classes that had a record of higher participation in higher education, particularly because those involved in the expansion in the 1960s now had children coming up to HE entry. The decline was also higher in Scotland, which has a lower fertility rate than the rest of the UK.

There had been changes to curriculum and assessment at 16 and 18, though this had less impact in Scotland after the reviews under Munn and Dunning. Elsewhere, the cap on pass rates at A level was lifted and the norms for grade distribution abolished. A levels were modularized, and coursework was recognized as contributing to the final grade. Pass rates went up, particularly for girls, and passes at higher levels increased. Feeding these developments, the General Certificate in Secondary Education (GCSE) was introduced, incorporating the previous two-tier qualifications at 16+ – CSE and GCE 'O' level. The proportion of successive cohorts achieving the equivalent of 5 'good' passes increased substantially in the years following this reform. In further education, rationalization under the National Council for Vocational Qualifications, set up in 1986, led to fuller recognition of what became 'vocational A levels' for HE entry, similar to the earlier Action Plan in Scotland.

Those shifts in attainment, mainly in the comprehensive schools, while private and grammar schools moved little, may have led to shifts in attitude and aspiration and to increased demand for HE. They may have been reinforced by perceptions of the changing labour market in a period of high unemployment, with government emphasizing the, then, challenge from the high technology tiger economies of Asia, with their higher participation rates. The challenge now is more to the unskilled underclass, as jobs are outsourced to the Asian subcontinent with its lower labour costs. The concept of the 'knowledge economy' was emerging, and higher education institutions (HEIs) were seen as the repositories of knowledge, and now have a new role in 'knowledge transfer' in a mode different from teaching (see Wedgwood, this volume).

Government support for unemployed young people through social services was withdrawn, increasing pressure to stay in education. The introduction of loans to displace grants for full-time HE study did not appear to act as a deterrent to demand.

That may have been because of changes on the supply side. The 1988 and 1992 Acts had given corporate status to polytechnics and colleges, with independence from local education authorities (LEAs). The 1992 Acts abolished binary lines across the UK and brought all HEIs under the same financial regimes, though these differed in the four countries. The reduction in the unit of resource – government payment per student – continued for the former polytechnics. The traditional universities, whose funding levels per student had been protected by the University Grants Committee (UGC) through the 1980s, by reduction in home student numbers, were now subject to similar 'efficiency measures'. The pressure was, therefore, to recruit more students, at lower 'prices' just to maintain overall institutional budget levels. This, alongside a growing commitment to wider access, drove up student numbers beyond those covered by the API. As Court (this volume) records, there was a consequent deterioration in the student:staff ratio. Growth in participation rates in other European countries was not accompanied by such reductions in the unit of resource (Mayhew *et al.*, 2004).

Bekhradnia (2004) claims that the government plan was for a decrease of 17 per cent in the unit of resource, but that institutions 'offered up' a 34 per cent cut. Dearing (NCIHE, 1997, Tables 3.15 and 3.16) records a drop in average public funding per student of 42 per cent between 1976 and 1995. As a result, the percentage of GDP spent on HE was at the same level in both years despite a near tripling of student numbers and improvement in research performance. At 1.1 per cent overall, 0.8 per cent of public money, it remains one of the lowest in the Organisation for Economic Co-operation and Development (OECD) group of countries (OECD, 2004). Yet cost to the public purse has been cited as the reason for the introduction of loans, the 'consolidation' of student numbers in the late 1990s, with penalties for over-recruiting, the abolition of grants and the introduction of, and later increase in, fees. Kenneth Baker, in a 1989 speech to mark the twenty-fifth anniversary of Lancaster University, did claim gleefully to have put a time bomb under the Treasury by the commitment to a move to an API of 30 per cent in ten years. Even the achievement of that target in half the time, though, cannot be claimed to have demanded a higher proportion of the nation's wealth. The reasons for reductions in funding were ideological, part of the continuing neo-conservative agenda to reform the post-war settlement and the welfare state. When higher education was for an elite it was funded by general taxation on the mass of the population; now the masses are participating, the tax burden on the elite to fund them would allegedly be electorally unacceptable. The Scandinavian countries, where social democracy and the welfare state continue, have no fees and have higher participation rates, though there is no consistent correlation between these two factors across other countries. Australian participation is at 70 per cent, alongside Finland, but with a very different fee regime.

Finally, the figures need conditioning. Part of the apparent increase in participation results from a structural adjustment – incorporation of provision for nurses and allied professions following the implementation of Project 2000. That brought its own financial regime, with payment, on a customer-contractor basis, by local arms of the NHS. And . . . the census for 2001 suggested that the numbers of young people, especially men, in the population had been overestimated, allowing participation rates to be revised upwards against this lower base.

So, a combination of demographic shifts, changes to the school curriculum, financial sticks and carrots, perceptions of employment prospects and incorporation of higher education as an entry route to an extended group of occupations fed shifts in demand for participation. Weaver (1982) identified four policy domains and all were involved. They can be seen in particular initiatives of that period and in the contemporary scene. Was Project 2000, on nurse education and training, about *access* – who gains entry, how many and how; or *curriculum* – the changed balance between theory and clinical based practice; or *structure* – the base for provision and integration into mainstream institutions; or *resources* – the level and source of funding? Similar questions can be asked currently about foundation degrees – a device for access by a new group of students, a curriculum based on employment, structural location in FE colleges, or just a cheaper, shorter route to qualification? All four elements interact, of course.

Bekhradnia (2004), after 12 years with the Higher Education Funding Council for England (HEFCE), is hesitant to suggest that policy was a factor in growth in access: it 'enabled, but certainly did not cause the changes'. He concludes that:

> Supply side policies are really rather blunt. The only really effective policy action is demand-side, and this is long-term. Supply must follow, when demand rises, to enable demand to be met. But until demand is there, there is no point in increasing supply.
>
> (Bekhradnia 2004: 14)

Mayhew *et al.* (2004: 68) disagree: 'in large part, the expansion in higher education was a matter of government decision', particularly through financial formulae, where 'Say's Law' (supply creates its own demand) may have operated. They note also that an increasing proportion of applicants was accepted (84 per cent in 2002), so that more of the demand was satisfied.

Do those factors, then, feature currently in perceptions of the future, in the planned move to a 50 per cent IER?

There is a demographic parallel. In Scotland, the number of people aged 16–24 starts to decline in 2006 and the funding councils foresee a drop of 8 per cent in ten years and 20 per cent in 20 years (SFCs, 2004). In the UK overall, the number of live births fell from 792,000 in 1991 to 669,000 ten years later, so the 18+ cohort will shrink from the end of the present decade. There will be some moderation of this fall because of inward migration. There is also a demographic shift to ethnic minority groups who, in the main, participate and succeed better then white Britons, especially men. Twenty per cent of UK domiciled applicants accepted on to full-time undergraduate courses in 2003 were non-white (HoC, 21.12.2004). The proportion of school-leavers with graduate parents will also increase, given the growth in participation levels just described.

The school curriculum is in constant flux as government seeks to meet its targets. There is now a Welsh baccalaureate; the Scots have moved 'higher still', and in England another major report (Working Group on 14–19 Reform, 2004), though not accepted, has led to further proposals for reform of the 14–19 curriculum (DfES, 2005). It is worth noting, however, that the countries with higher APIs have contrasting school systems. Scotland is mainly comprehensive with a broader, more integrated, range of study after 16; Northern Ireland still has a selective, sectarian system with a mainly traditional curriculum. England is moving back to a selective, stratified system, which has previously led to lower progression rates through to HE.

Employment is high and unemployment low, which may be a factor in current sluggishness in API increase. The research findings on graduate employment are not consistent (Pearson, this volume; Aston and Bekhradnia, 2003), but the claims of politicians about a graduate premium are. The latest statement (HoC, 21.12.2004), based on the Labour Force Survey data, suggests graduate earnings from age 21 to 59 are just over £1m gross, compared to an average across the population as a whole of £675,000, with non-graduates being, obviously, lower. Those figures are, of course, based on present reality and past achievements. There is no guarantee that they will be similar when graduates are a bigger proportion of the workforce (Pearson, this volume).

Education Maintenance Allowances now provide a carrot, in England, to encourage staying on in education after 16, contrasting with the stick of withdrawing benefits used previously. Student funding in higher education has changed and will change again. It was the issue raised most frequently on the doorstep in the 2001 election campaign, a consequence of the extension of participation, and the response to withdrawal of grants and introduction of fees by the New Labour government. This led to a fall in participation rates in England that has continued for men. By contrast, in Scotland, participation rates continued to increase after up-front fees were abolished by the devolved administration. Recent figures for admission rates show a fall across the UK, suggesting either a saturation of demand, or the impact of students re-calculating the rate of return on an investment in HE study, and the risk of long-term debt (Callender, 2003). 2005 did see a surge in applications ahead of the introduction of higher fees.

Funding of the supply side has also changed and will change further. My own view differs from that of Bekhradnia; I think that the funding regime *did* drive up the figures in the earlier period, through affecting student recruitment policies, and by institutions generating demand. The proportion of qualified 18–19-year-olds attending HE courses rose from 65 per cent in 1989 to 90 per cent in 1992 (Gorard, 2005). It has risen further, so the market is saturated. The introduction of higher fees in England will lead to competition through bursaries to attract students, though prestige universities in England are turning away from the home undergraduate market in favour of international students and postgraduates, where fees are unrestricted. The number of EU students declined by 20 per cent after fees were introduced until the new members gained accession (HoC, 3.11.2004). Their fees will remain capped. Recovery of grants/loans, to which they have an entitlement, poses problems in the new fees regime, and ways will continue to be sought to reduce the UK subsidy to students from elsewhere in the Community. The wider international market has been affected by the new global context of high suspicion and security, with some ministers promoting UK HE abroad, and others introducing or extending restrictions on entry to the UK by prospective students. The number of rejected visa applications has increased dramatically since 2001.

The different policies adopted within devolved administrations may have an impact on the pattern of access and provision within the UK. The Scottish Executive is concerned about competing when English institutions have the benefit of additional fee income. It has allocated general funding and resources for research at a higher level to provide some balance, but may not be able to maintain that. The Welsh Assembly has now ruled out higher fees, and there may be inward cross-border flows of students, at least in the short term. In Northern Ireland all political parties are against top-up fees, and the Northern Ireland Grand Committee rejected proposals in parliament. However, the Westminster government imposed the English policy, but with higher grants, through an Order in Council endorsed by MPs from outside Northern Ireland. That may lead to cross-border flows across the water and to the South, increasing the outflow of students that already exists (see Osborne, this volume).

I do not comment on the future of the economy, but other factors that led to the rise in participation in the late 1980s are present 20 years later. That may presage a further surge of increased participation, moving the system to what Trow labels 'universal' participation.

Mass HE – meaning and manifestation

When New Labour came to power, the concept of mass higher education was strongly linked to lifelong learning, with a flavour of personal development of the citizen and a social equity agenda, reflecting the background of the Secretary of State (Blunkett, 2000). This has continued in the devolved administrations (e.g. Scottish Executive, 2003). An anticipation of a bespoke education experience for individual learners disappeared between the draft and the final version of a HEFCE strategic plan (HEFCE, 2002). The targets for lifelong learning, which seem also to have disappeared, were all work-related, and participation rates all deal with young people, not the increasing group of older citizens. Even the *social equity* agenda on access is related to enhancing the skills base (Ryan, 2005). Research is about competitive *excellence* in a global economy or about *economic engagement* with local and regional communities. The *efficiency* agenda, monitoring value for money, continues within those narrow concepts of purpose and output, and with *electability* an ongoing political concern (*Research Fortnight*, 2005). The declared aims may not be as bald as the 1987 White Paper – 'to serve the economy more effectively' – but the underlying message is the same – 'the production of graduates as lumps of human capital' (Mayhew *et al.*, 2004).

In 1995, Scott anticipated a move to 'a more explicit division of institutional missions' within the UK's mass HE system. Newby (2002) noted the English (*sic*) genius for turning diversity into hierarchy. Scott saw stratification as the next evolutionary stage from a unified system. Gallacher's chapter gives evidence of this in Scotland. In Wales, Cardiff stands alone, with about 60 per cent of the HEFCW research allocation (Tysome, 2005), while the Assembly ministers try to drive through regional clusters and mergers in the rest of a small system. Funding-driven distinctions can be seen most starkly in England. Research funding has been concentrated in a small group of traditional, elite institutions (see Lucas, this volume). That is compounded by HEFCE withdrawing funding for PhD study from all but the higher graded units, with no assessment of the quality of supervision. Promising research active staff in units with lower grades in the research assessment exercise (RAE) are funded for secondment to higher graded units, from which they will not return (like postgraduate students sponsored by developing countries on courses in the USA and elsewhere). Research funding through research councils doubled between 1997 and 2005, whereas the unit of funding for teaching hardly changed. Even the new fees structure will benefit the institutions with, currently, more generous funding, with many fewer of their students qualifying for bursary support than in those committed to widening access. The proposed post qualification application process for young potential undergraduates is also designed to benefit the elite, 'selecting' institutions. As Neave (2005: 18) notes, 'stratification . . . now serves as an explicit instrument of public policy . . . (it) has become purposive rather than descriptive'.

There is, then, a hierarchy of privilege, with unequal funding, and with a stigma of blame attached to institutions lower in a pecking order determined by historical criteria, leading to tensions and fragmentations in the system. Universities UK is an uneasy coalition with warring factions – note the use of 'non-aligned' by one group, reminiscent of the cold war – unable to represent the essential diversity of provision even-handedly. Since the unification (*sic*) of the English HE system in 1992, Douglass (2005: 4) notes that this 'collection of fiefdoms' has meant that 'government has pursued HE policy virtually uncontested . . . the cultural gap between the higher education community (*sic*) and government priorities and power is substantial'.

Scott also recorded the tension between the public and private lives of institutions, with continuing commitment by academic staff to a liberal ideal, 'a personal engagement between teachers and students'. A survey in 2005 (McNay, 2005) showed the continuing tension between these values and the perceived operational norms of the system (Becher and Kogan, 1992), with the emphasis on economic instrumentality. Seventy-two per cent believed that 'higher education has lost its role as conscience and critic of society'. Seventy-seven per cent believed that 'the joy of learning has reduced with the focus on job preparation through skills development' (a sentiment expressed by the junior minister for HE at the time). Eighty-five per cent agreed (56 per cent strongly) that 'the emphasis within universities is now more on systems than on people and much of the humanity and excitement has been lost'. Scott's 'grand unifying theme' may, therefore be neither grand, nor unifying, but it is the dominant theme of mass HE in the UK.

The survey showed most academics striving to retain their personal values and a concept of higher education articulated by the Robbins Report. Most would not be aware of Trow's view (1989: 55) that 'The values and assumptions that define an English "idea of a university" . . . accepted by Robbins and the academic community as a whole, are incompatible with the provision of mass higher education.' He had seen the elite form as shaping the mind and character of a ruling class; a mass form was about transmission of skills and preparation for a broader range of technical and economic roles (Brennan, 2004). Most UK institutions align, therefore, with the 'professional' model rather than the 'personal' one in Gellert's (1993) classification, used by Scott, with a few in the 'knowledge' tradition of Johns Hopkins out of Humboldt. Scott notes that, despite a struggle to encompass a diversity of traditions, mass systems are likely to become more alike in their policy responses. This may help locate them in another demand on their identity – the European HE Area, developing as part of the Bologna process of harmonization of qualification structures. A European Research Area is also mooted. Such developments demand an assertion of a European model of 'mass' HE drawn from traditions other than those in the USA, from which the Trow model was drawn. It seems likely to have a stronger role for the state, or the European super state, in steering strategy towards 'nation-building' (Boyer, 1990) at several levels of subsidiarity. The rise of interest in citizenship is not, in my view, coincidental, and is part of a government agenda in a globalized society of defining the role of individuals in relation to the state, a new 'compact' as part of the post-welfare state.

Trow (2005), reviewing developments since his seminal paper, notes the loss of trust between governments and universities, the political weakness of the universities and their lack of 'friends' beyond their own borders. He outlines the balancing act between a market and a managed system, concluding that the rhetoric is market, but the reality is firm central government management. The single structures have led to loss of diversity, compounded by limitations on institutional autonomy through regulation, which reduces educational experimentation in response to diversified students, extended missions and specialization of knowledge.

The record of the state as manager is poor, evidenced by failures of manpower planning, e.g. for teacher supply, and of projects such as the eUniversity and the NHS 'University' (an illegal title under the government's own regulations). Government has moved from provision of funding and avoidance of planning, to promotion of initiatives, damned by Coffield (2002), to being a purchaser through agencies. Other agencies cover consumer protection in the evaluative state developing throughout Europe (Neave, 1998).

Moving to universal provision?

One of the predicted characteristics of *universal* provision is that 'decision-making flows into the hands of the political authority' (Brennan, 2004: 23) and government gets closer (Court, 2004). Other parts of the 'universal' conception echo the agendas in access and lifelong learning:

- a breakdown of distinctions between learning and life (informal and experiential learning);
- participation displacing formal attendance on campus;
- loss of common standards and a shift to value added for individuals;
- a less privileged and isolated academia;
- new managerial techniques.

(adapted from Brennan, 2004)

At present, the system is in transition, with some aspects seen as a dilution of provision as academic staff think it should be, and, as yet, no perceived balancing benefits. The survey referred to above (McNay, 2005) found that:

- 86 per cent agree that 'funding pressures have led to the admission of weaker students without resources being provided for extra support to them';
- 73 per cent agreed that 'there is a risk of supporting student so much that it becomes spoon-feeding, not encouraging them to find their own stance';
- 75 per cent agreed that 'pressures from performance indicators and formula funding have led to pass/fail decisions being pushed towards leniency'.

Two aims of mass provision are not seen as being achieved:

- only 27 per cent agreed (43 per cent disagreed) that 'graduates are now better prepared for work because of the emphasis on skills development';
- only 20 per cent believed (47 per cent disagreed) that 'courses now make students more aware of the wider world – Europe and beyond – preparing them for a globalized society'.

And, although 47 per cent agreed that 'universities are more open to their local communities' (only 37 per cent of those from pre-1992 universities), only 12 per cent agreed that 'with nearly half of all young people going in to higher education, the public perceptions of universities has improved'. Their overall judgement: only 27 per cent agreed (and 43 per cent disagreed) that 'despite all the talk of "dumbing down", the gains from growth of higher education have outweighed the losses'.

Conclusion

There are, then, issues to tackle in current mass provision before the next leap in participation rates to universal levels in Trow's categorization. The purpose of the ESRC seminar series was to identify and consider some of those. There are lessons to learn. The chapters that follow attempt to cover parts of that agenda. The next section starts with student issues – getting in and moving on. This is followed by a section on academic functions, not only teaching and research, but assessment – in urgent need of research based improvement – and knowledge transfer. The third main section deals with staff issues and what are labelled for alliterative reasons, system issues of internal organization of HEIs. The final chapter outlines an agenda for any incoming government looking to develop a 2020 vision.

Some messages emerge from this chapter.

First, it reinforces Court's (2004) view that the UK has become something of a 'policy laboratory' at national level since devolution. If, then, different solutions 'fit' better with different polities, the reasons for this should provide lessons for any administration claiming to be committed to evidence-based policy making.

Second, if the case for diversity is made at that level, the evidence is that the wider objective of diversity is not being achieved because of the lack of perceived equity across diverse activities on the policy agenda. Unless that equity of esteem can be evidenced, and equitably resourced, there will remain an abdication of institutional autonomy in striving to imitate, palely, the elite model, to the detriment of many citizens and electors. If the means to achievement of policy objectives are differentially funded, those policy ends will be seen to be rank-ordered in terms of esteem and priority. But there are many different kinds of excellence other than that of the elite; indeed, their 'excellence' may not fit the needs of many of the diverse student population and so has low quality in a marketized mass system.

Third, the models of Trow and Scott can be seen to have had some predictive value, so that some features of current mass provision should not surprise. That is particularly true both of the continuation of an elite system, which Trow did not see being displaced, but complemented by mass provision, and of the role of the state and its relations with institutions and individual citizens.

A new covenant needs to recover trust and restore mutual confidence from present conflict. It needs to rebalance management and market responsiveness, reducing regulatory accountability to allow autonomy in diversity of response to change. What is now needed is new work for the new context, and from a different experience base. This volume aims to provide some evidence of that experience to inform a strategic conversation about the future.

References

Aston, L. and Bekhradnia, B. (2003) *Demand for Graduates: A Review of the Economic Evidence.* Oxford: HEPI.

Becher, T. and Kogan, M. (1992) *Process and Structure in Higher Education.* London: Routledge.

Bekhradnia, B. (2004) 20 years of higher education policy in the United Kingdom: looking back 10 years and forward to the next decade, in CHERI *Ten Years On: Changing Higher Education in a Changing World.* London: Centre for Higher Education Research and Innovation at the Open University.

Blunkett, D. (2000) *Modernising higher education.* Speech given at the University of Greenwich, 15 February. London: DfEE.

Boyer, E. L. (1990) *Scholarship Reconsidered. Priorities of the Professoriate.* New York: Carnegie Foundation/Jossey Bass.

Brennan, J. (2004) The social role of the contemporary university: contradictions, boundaries and change, in CHERI *Ten Years On: Changing Higher Education in a Changing World.* London: Centre for Higher Education Research and Innovation at the Open University.

Callender, C. (2003) *Attitudes to Debt – School Leavers' and Further Education Students' Attitudes to Debt and their Impact on Participation in Higher Education.* London: UUK/HEFCE.

Coffield, F. (2002) 101 initiatives, but no strategy: policy on lifelong learning in England. Open lecture, Institute of Education, London, 8 January.

Court, S. (2004) Government getting closer: higher education and devolution in the UK, *Higher Education Quarterly*, 58 (2/3).

DfES (Department for Education and Skills) (2005) *14–19 Education and Skills*, Cm 6476. Norwich: The Stationery Office.

Douglass, J. A. (2005) Less than the sum? What is missing in UK mass HE? *Perspectives*, 9(1).

Gellert, C. (1993) Structural and functional differentiation: remarks on changing paradigms of tertiary education in Europe, in C. Gellert (ed.) *Higher Education in Europe.* London: Jessica Kingsley.

Gorard, S. (2005) Where shall we widen it? Higher education and the Age Participation Rate in Wales, *Higher Education Quarterly*, 59(1).

HEFCE (Higher Education Funding Council for England) (2002) *Strategic Plan, 2003–8.* Bristol: HEFCE.

HoC (House of Commons) (2004) Parliamentary replies, dates as given.

McNay, I. (2005) Shifting values and standards in academic life. Consultative conference on *Higher Education and Human Good*, Sarum College, March.

Mayhew, K., Deer, C. and Dua, M. (2004) The move to mass higher education in the UK: many questions and some answers, *Oxford Review of Education*, 30(1).

NCIHE (National Committee of Inquiry into Higher Education) (1997) *Higher Education in the Learning Society* (The Dearing Report). London: HMSO.

Neave, G. (1998) The evaluative state reconsidered, *European Journal of Education*, 33(3).

Neave, G. (2005) The supermarketed university: reform, vision and ambiguity in British higher education, *Perspectives*, 9(1).

Newby, H. (2002) Higher education: some thoughts on a future strategy. Lecture at City University, 15 May.

OECD (Organisation for Economic Co-operation and Development) (2004) *Education at a Glance*. Paris: OECD.

ONS (Office for National Statistics) (2004) *Population Trends*, 118, Winter.

Research Fortnight (2005) Labour looks for votes in research council budgets, 9 March.

Ryan, A. (2005) New Labour and higher education, *Oxford Review of Education*, 31(1).

Scott, P. (1995) *The Meaning of Mass Higher Education*. Buckingham: SRHE/Open University Press.

Scottish Executive (2003) *Life through Learning; Learning through Life*. Edinburgh: Scottish Executive.

SFCs (Scottish Funding Councils for Further and Higher Education) (2004) *Higher Education in Scotland: A Baseline Report*. Edinburgh: SFCs.

Trow, M. (1974) Problems in the Transition from Elite to Mass Higher Education, *General Report on the Conferences on Future Structures of Post-Secondary Education*. Paris: OECD.

Trow, M. (1989) The Robbins trap: British attitudes and the limits of expansion, *Higher Education Quarterly*, 43(1).

Trow, M. (2005) The decline of diversity, autonomy and trust in post-war British higher education: an American perspective, *Perspectives*, 9(1).

Tysome, T. (2005) Wary Welsh welcome 4.95% leap, *The Times Higher Education Supplement*, 25 March.

Weaver, T. (1982) Policy options for post-tertiary education, *Higher Education Review*, 14(2).

Working Group on 14–19 Reform (2004) *14–19 Curriculum and Qualifications Reform*. Annesley, DfES (The Tomlinson Report).

Part Two

Student issues

2

Accessing Higher Education: Policy, Practice and Equity in Widening Participation in England

Carole Leathwood

Introduction

Widening participation in England has a long history. As one university vice-chancellor explained:

> In looking back over the last thirty years, I realise how the whole relationship of the English universities to the English people has changed and broadened. Within that time we have seen one barrier after another crumbling, parting, and being swept away. Thirty years ago the universities of England were the universities of the few; today they are the universities of the many; tomorrow, I trust, they will be the universities of all. The barrier of creed has practically gone, the barrier of sex is going, and now the task before us is to see that the social barrier shall go as well – that the possession of money or the want of it shall no longer stand in the way of getting a sound, solid, and complete university education.
>
> (Dale 1905: 1)

This was the Vice-Chancellor of Liverpool University speaking 100 years ago. More recently, the government insisted that 'Education must be a force for opportunity and social justice, not for the entrenchment of privilege' (DfES, 2003), and has developed a range of policy initiatives with the aim of increasing the participation of previously under-represented groups in HE.

Such moves have not been universally welcomed (Leathwood and O'Connell, 2003) and progress for some sections of society has been particularly slow. The 'social barrier' identified as an issue a century ago remains one today, with the expansion of higher education providing for the dramatically increased participation of the middle classes, with comparatively little change for those from working-class groups. In 2001, over 60 per cent of accepted applicants to higher education institutions were from middle-class groups, compared to less than 25 per cent from working-class groups, with only 1.72 per cent from social class V (UCAS, 2004). More women than men now apply for, and are accepted on to, undergraduate courses in England, and minority ethnic people are more likely to study in higher education than their white counterparts. However, it is still predominantly middle-class women who are benefiting from HE expansion rather than their working-class peers, and participation of minority ethnic groups differs by ethnicity, gender and age (Bhattacharyya *et al.*, 2003; Connor and Tyers, 2002).

As will be seen, there are also differential patterns of participation for those who do go on to higher education, in terms of the institution attended, subject studied, student experiences on course, levels of achievement and post-graduation outcomes. Whilst the main emphasis of widening participation policy and initiatives has been on getting students into HE, the question 'access to what?' has increasingly been asked (Little, this volume). This chapter will, therefore, address two major themes in current research and debates about accessing higher education. The first will focus on non-participation, and discuss research that seeks to explain the continued under-representation of particular groups of students in HE. The second will address the question 'access to what?' for those who do participate, moving the focus from the student to higher education itself. The chapter ends with a consideration of implications for policy and practice.

Non-participation in higher education

How do we explain the on-going low levels of participation of those from working-class groups? The government identified lower attainment and lack of aspirations as the main reasons why working-class students do not progress to higher education (DfES, 2003) – hence a range of policy initiatives aimed at raising achievement in schools and persuading pupils/students to 'aim higher'. It is certainly the case that fewer students from working-class backgrounds attain the necessary HE entry qualifications than do those from the middle classes, and there is plenty of research which illustrates how poverty, disadvantage and discrimination are implicated in lower levels of achievement (see, e.g. Ennals, 2004). Yet it is not simply about achievement, but also that working-class and minority ethnic students who stay in education post-16 are far more likely to take vocational qualifications. Although advanced level vocational qualifications are designed to be equivalent to A levels, they lack the status and prestige of their academic counterparts and so impact on 'choice' of university in a context in which HEIs remain differentiated by entry qualifications (Connor *et al.*, 2003). There is also concern that some young people with the potential to go to university choose not to (Keys *et al.*, 2002). Whilst, therefore, levels of school achievement go some way towards explaining differential rates of participation in higher education, they do not tell the whole story. They do suggest, however, that tackling socio-economic and other inequalities within the school system as well as in society more generally is crucial in attempts to widen participation in higher education.

The other main factor identified by the government is that of low aspirations. This is an example of the way in which, within much government policy discourse, non-participation in higher education tends to be constructed in terms of a lack or deficit, a construction of the working classes that is all too common (see, e.g. Walkerdine, 1990). Within such a discursive framing, working-class young people and their families are assumed to lack the right kinds of aspirations and motivation, with non-participation seen as irrational and based on ignorance or uninformed decision-making. Indeed, how could it be anything else when the government exhorts young people to consider higher education by stating that:

> going into higher education (HE) to study will help make your dreams a reality. It will open up more possibilities than you imagined possible, and you'll have the time of your life into the bargain.
> Did you know . . . individuals with HE qualifications currently *earn* on average around *50% more* than those without?
> (Aim Higher website: www.aimhigher.ac.uk, original emphasis)

Yet research conducted by myself and colleagues with ethnically diverse working-class participants and non-participants in HE (Archer *et al.*, 2003) suggests that, for many, non-participation 'made sense' and was a rational response to an unfair and unequal system. Many working-class people do not participate because the economic, social and personal risks and costs of participation are higher for working-class students (Archer and Hutchings, 2000; Archer *et al.*, 2002). These risks and costs were not the same for all respondents, but were differently constructed through their negotiations of classed, 'raced' and gendered identities and inequalities. We identified three main areas of risk: financial risks, risk of failure and identity risks – all issues which were raised as reasons not to go to university by some non-participants in our study, and which remain areas of struggle for many participants (Leathwood and O'Connell, 2003).

The financial risks of study have been subject to considerable debate following the gradual reduction in state financial support for students and the introduction in England, as a result of the Higher Education Act 2004, of differential top-up fees to be paid after graduation. On the whole, financial considerations are not seen as a major deterrent by the government – after all, graduates will earn much more than non-graduates on average. So, their outlay will be repaid, and some financial support for poorer students will mean that many will be exempt from the costs of the top-up fees (though not the cost of living while a student). This ignores, however, the differential perceptions and experiences of debt, and the body of research which illustrates this (Van Dyke and Little, 2002; Archer *et al.*, 2003). Callender (2002) found that those most averse to debt were the lower social classes; Muslim, Black and other minority ethnic groups; those with family responsibilities; and single parents. Fear of debt is not irrational, with students from lower income families more likely to be in debt, and to have higher levels of debt, than students from the wealthiest backgrounds (Callender and Wilkinson, 2003).

A second major area of risk that we identified was risk of failure. This included the risk of not getting a good and/or well paid job after graduation, of failure in course assessments, or of non-completion for other reasons such as the need to earn money. Some in our sample recounted stories of graduates unable to gain graduate-level work, and so going straight into employment appeared to be a less risky option, especially given the costs of full-time study. Others felt that a degree from the kinds of universities that would be open to them was likely to be less highly valued by employers than one from a more prestigious institution, increasing the risks involved.

A risk of failure at university was articulated by many non-participants, as well as by some participants. The experience of educational failure and/or low levels of achievement whilst at school was not uncommon, and some respondents recounted how teachers and/or careers advisers had directed them into lower level exam routes and vocational courses. Black respondents frequently talked about being held back at school (Archer *et al.*, 2001a), whilst some women reported being directed towards stereotypically feminine employment, revealing classed, racialized and gendered assumptions about students' ability and appropriate future direction. Some also reported that they had been advised against aiming for higher education, a finding also noted by Pugsley (1998). Many feared that if they went to university they would be at greater risk of failure than more 'traditional' students as a result of their non-standard entry qualifications, of their need to undertake paid work during term-time, institutional racism or, for mature students, of the length of time they had been out of the education system. Underpinning many of these fears is a vision of higher education as an alien world, and fears of not fitting in and/or of being rejected run through many respondents' accounts.

This leads to the third major area of risk, that of identity risks. On the whole, universities and students were seen as middle class by respondents in the study. Dominant government discourses around widening participation have tended to present higher education as an opportunity for social mobility and a higher income, and although some respondents aspired to the material benefits of a middle-class lifestyle, many resisted higher education on the basis that they did not want to change or to become middle class, but to hold on to working-class values. In particular, some respondents argued that whilst they did not have a university education, they did possess 'common sense', something that was seen as distinctly lacking in some university students/graduates and preferable to the less useful knowledge likely to be acquired at university. Working-class resistance to the perceived values of higher education, and to the idea that going to university would necessitate changing their identity, is not something that is new. In 1909, the editorial of *Plebs*, the magazine of the National Council of Labour Colleges, stated:

> No working-class student can undergo a University education and come through it untainted . . . University life is the breeding ground of reaction. It incites by its very nature towards breaking away from working class aspirations . . . (Oxford University) is the place where men are

taught to govern, it is the governing class who control it, it is they who decide what shall be taught and how it shall be taught and as the interests of these people are in direct antagonism to the interests of the workers, it is sheer folly for the latter to think that any good can come of sending any of their number there.

(*Plebs* 1909: 44)

Similarly, in 1927, working-class resistance to the threat that higher education was thought to present to working-class identities was still evident on the front cover of the same magazine (see Figure 2.1).

Some things have, of course, changed. The resistance we found in our study was not articulated as an aspect of a collective identity or the collectively organized resistance suggested by the *Plebs* extracts, but it does bear some resemblance to that expressed in *Plebs*, with universities and university students repeatedly talked about as 'posh' and alien by respondents. Resistance to HE was constructed differently, however, by different groups of respondents. Many women talked positively about higher education as a way of 'bettering' oneself, whether or not they planned to participate, and although some were resistant to the idea of identity change, others actively sought it, wanting to become 'a different (better) person' (Archer *et al.*, 2003:126). Such a desire for betterment is not, however, unproblematic (see Lawler 1999; Walkerdine *et al.*, 2001), and many non-participants did not want to take the risks involved. However, it was financial considerations, family responsibilities, the lack of formal qualifications and a positive valuing of 'common sense' as opposed to university-gained knowledge that were the main reasons given by women for not participating, rather than the risks of identity change per se.

For non-participant men, higher education appeared to provide an unwelcome challenge to their masculine identities. These identities, although differently constructed across different racialized identities (Archer *et al.*, 2001b), tended to be rooted in the world of work. University students were seen as not sufficiently masculine and as socially inadequate. Studying was seen as incompatible with the demands of working-class masculinities, which required one to be working and earning, and to have sufficient money to provide for a family and/or to finance the material symbols of a successful masculine lifestyle. Whereas many of the women saw higher education as a potential route to personal development and fulfilment, none of the young men articulated it in these terms. In contrast, as Archer *et al.* (2001b) argue, HE participation, in its perceived threat to working-class masculine identities, could be seen as a challenge to the power these men are able to exercise over women and other working-class men.

Many of these respondents, in their construction of higher education as alien, were articulating an awareness of dominant academic culture – a culture which reflects the normative student as being white, male and middle class (Mirza, 1995; Grant, 1997), and which disadvantages others (Tett, 2000; Leathwood, 2001). Some participants attempted to mediate this by 'choosing'

Figure 2.1 Plebs magazine

universities or modes of study where they could 'belong', for example by choosing a local post-1992 institution. Many minority ethnic students were also keen to study at an ethnically diverse university, as others have noted (Ball *et al.*, 2002). Such choices can be seen as an attempt to hold on to one's identity and to resist identity change, although gaining a sense of belonging can remain elusive even in what appear to be more 'appropriate' institutions (Read *et al.*, 2003; see also Quinn, 2003). As Reay (1998: 523) noted, there remains 'a lack of fit between a habitus still powerfully influenced by a working-class past and the middle-class field of higher education'.

Access to what?

The second major concern in the field of access and widening participation is that of 'access to what?' Students from working-class backgrounds, minority ethnic students and, to a lesser extent women, are more likely to be studying in those higher education institutions with lower levels of prestige and resourcing (Morley, 1997; Bhattacharyya *et al.*, 2003; Quinn, 2003; Leathwood, 2004), a finding mirrored in Scotland (Forsyth and Furlong, 2000; Gallacher, this volume). The reasons for this are likely to be multiple, including the possession of 'suitable' entry qualifications, financial and/or family responsibilities which may necessitate studying at a local institution, and an attempt to minimize the identity risks discussed above. There is also some evidence that minority ethnic applicants are less likely to be offered places in some universities (Shiner and Modood, 2002).

It is not only a matter of the kind of higher education institution that different groups of students access, but also the subjects that they study. Women are still seriously under-represented in the higher status science, technology, engineering, maths and computing subjects, whilst working-class students are more are likely to be on vocational and sub-degree level courses.

The quality of a student's learning experience in higher education is also likely to be highly differentiated, with many 'non-traditional' students describing their time in HE as one of continual struggle (Leathwood and O'Connell, 2003). This relates not only to the difficulties of engaging with an alien and exclusive academic culture, but to the need to work an excessive number of hours during term-time whilst also coping with an under-funded mass HE system in institutions with poor staff–student ratios and fewer material resources. This inevitably impacts on levels of achievement and retention, and surely goes some way to explaining the higher non-completion rates at some post-1992 institutions, despite many of these institutions' commitments and efforts in relation to widening participation, or because this commitment to espoused government policy is not matched by necessary resource allocations.

'Access to what?' is, therefore, a central consideration in widening participation policy and practice. The kinds of institutions students go to, the subjects they study and the quality of their learning experience all have real consequences for their futures. For example, Oxbridge graduates earn between 11 and 16 per cent more than those from post-1992 universities (Conlon and Chevalier, 2002), and they continue to dominate the higher levels of government, the civil service and the judiciary (Ryle Ahmed *et al.*, 2000). Whilst attendance at a high status university does not wipe out the disadvantages of, for example, a working-class background, there are clear employment advantages for students who graduate from such institutions. In addition, opportunities in the graduate labour market remain structured by social class, gender and ethnicity (Bowlby *et al.*, 2000; Brennan and Shah, 2003; Conlon and Chevalier, 2002). The risks of higher education study already identified are, therefore, real risks, and in a context in which many students, and especially students from poorer backgrounds, emerge from universities with high levels of debt, the risks may not be worth taking, despite government pronouncements about graduate earnings.

The solution is not simply to encourage more working-class young people to apply to elite universities and/or such universities to consider these applicants. As Roger Brown (2004) has pointed out, this is not the most important issue. As I have argued elsewhere (Leathwood, 2004), a perfect meritocracy in which the hierarchy of HE institutions is preserved but where entry is based purely on merit, is also far from desirable. This would simply ensure that the most money and status went to the most 'able', with students who for whatever reason have not managed to achieve as much, relegated to institutions with lower funding, fewer staff, and consequently restricted opportunities. As Young (2001) argues, 'it is hard indeed in a society that makes so much of merit to be judged as having none'. Meritocracy can be seen to legitimate inequalities, but it does not make such inequalities fair or socially just.

Conclusions

Higher education has changed considerably since the Vice-Chancellor of Liverpool spoke about the need to remove the 'social barrier' one hundred years ago. Yet despite the long history of attempts to widen participation, and the commitment to this goal shown by many institutions and staff in HE, there is still a long way to go and further progress will require action on a number of levels. Differential levels of participation are rooted in long-standing and persistent social and economic inequalities, and challenging these must remain a central plank of widening participation policy. This includes not only the need to tackle economic injustices, but also to address the all too common assumptions that middle-class values and priorities are the right ones, and that it is the new (and potential) students to higher education that need to change, rather than the institutions themselves. With this in mind, I conclude with some key issues for policy-makers, senior managers and staff in higher education institutions:

Issues for policy-makers

- At present there are a number of contradictions in widening participation policy. If widening participation is to truly succeed, social justice needs to be foregrounded in all HE policy.
- The current hierarchy of higher education institutions reinforces inequalities. Policy designed to mitigate rather than exacerbate the stratification of HEIs is needed.
- The risk of student debt remains a key deterrent for many who might otherwise consider higher education. Whilst the impact of top-up fees has yet to be assessed, it is highly unlikely that the new student financial arrangements will encourage more working-class students to attend university, and may well deter them (MORI 2004). Policy in relation to fees, grants and loans therefore needs to be re-visited.

Issues for senior managers

- A socially diverse higher education institution brings tremendous benefits for all. Recognition of this needs to inform all institutional policy.
- This requires not simply addressing policies for students, but also working towards a greater diversity in staffing, and ensuring that women and minority ethnic staff are well-represented at all levels (see Saunderson, this volume).
- Exclusionary institutional and academic cultures remain a significant barrier to participation and exacerbate the difficulties of 'non-traditional' students who do participate. A key priority must be to encourage all sections of the university to work towards greater inclusivity.

Issues for staff in HEIs

- Staff can have a real impact on the development of curriculum and pedagogic practices that are inclusive rather than exclusionary.
- It is important to challenge academic and disciplinary cultures that privilege some groups of students and marginalize others.
- Are some groups of students doing less well, not participating to the same extent as others, or more likely to drop out of modules and courses? If so, why, and how might this be addressed?

Acknowledgements

Thanks to Chris Coates, the librarian at the TUC Library Collections at London Metropolitan University, for assistance in accessing the material from *Plebs*.

References

Archer, L. and Hutchings, M. (2000) 'Bettering yourself?' Discourses of risk, cost and benefit in ethnically diverse, young working-class non-participants' constructions of higher education, *British Journal of Sociology of Education*, 21(4): 555–74.

Archer, L., Hutchings, M. and Leathwood, C. (2002) Higher education: a risky business, in A. Hayton and A. Paczuska (eds) *Widening Participation and Higher Education: Policy and Practice*. London: Kogan Page.

Archer, L., Hutchings, M. and Ross, A. (2003) *Social Class and Higher Education: Issues of Exclusion and Inclusion*. London: Routledge Falmer.

Archer, L., Leathwood, C. and Hutchings, M. (2001a) Engaging with commonality and difference: theoretical tensions in the analysis of working class women's educational discourses, *International Studies in Sociology of Education*, 11(1): 51–71.

Archer, L., Pratt, S. and Phillips, D. (2001b) Working class men's constructions of masculinity and negotiations of (non)participation in higher education, *Gender and Education*, 13(4): 431–49.

Ball, S. J., Reay, D. and David, M. (2002) Ethnic choosing: minority ethnic students, social class and higher education choice, *Race, Ethnicity and Education*, 5(4): 333–57.

Bhattacharyya, G., Ison, L. and Blair, M. (2003) *Minority Ethnic Attainment and Participation in Education and Training: The Evidence*. London: Department for Education and Skills.

Bowlby, S., Evans, S. L. and Roche, C. (2000) *Racialised Gendering, Locality and Young People's Employment Opportunities: Final Report of ESRC project no. L130251008*. ESRC Regard database: www.regard.ac.uk

Brennan, J. and Shah, T. (2003) *Access to What? Converting Educational Opportunity into Employment Opportunity*. London: Centre for Higher Education Research and Information, The Open University.

Brown, R. (2004) Admitting the workforce into higher education at all levels. Speech at the UVAC Consultative Conference, London Metropolitan University, 26 March.

Callender, C. (2002) *Survey of School and FE Students' Attitudes to Debt and their Impact on Participation in Higher Education: Key Early Findings*. London: Universities UK Student Debt Project.

Callender, C. and Wilkinson, D. (2003) *2002/03 Student Income and Expenditure Survey: Students' Income, Expenditure and Debt in 2002/03 and Changes Since 1998/99*. London: Department for Education and Skills.

Conlon, G. and Chevalier, A. (2002) *Rates of Return to Qualifications: A Summary of Recent Evidence*. London: Council for Industry and Higher Education.

Connor, H. and Tyers, C. (2002) *Ethnic Minorities in Higher Education and Beyond: Exploring Diversity and Disadvantage*. London: DfES.

Connor, H., Tyers, C., Modood, T. and Hillage, J. (2003) *Minority Ethnic Students in Higher Education*. London: DfES.

Dale, J. A. (1905) *Some Functions of a University*. London: An Association to Promote the Higher Education of Working Men.

DfES (Department for Education and Skills) (2003) *The Future of Higher Education: White Paper*. London: The Stationery Office.

Ennals, P. (2004) *Child Poverty and Education*. London: National Children's Bureau.

Forsyth, A. and Furlong, A. (2000) *Socioeconomic Disadvantage and Access to Higher Education*. Bristol: Policy Press and Joseph Rowntree Foundation.

Grant, B. (1997) Disciplining students: the construction of student subjectivities, *British Journal of Sociology of Education*, 18: 101–14.

Keys, W., Mason, K. and Kendatt, L. (2002) *Supporting Students Applying to Higher Education*. London: The Sutton Trust.

Lawler, S. (1999) Getting out and getting away: women's narratives of class mobility, *Feminist Review*, Autumn (63): 3–23.

Leathwood, C. (2001) The Road to Independence? Policy, pedagogy and 'the independent learner' in higher education, in L. West, N. Miller, D. O'Reilly and D. Allen, *31st Annual SCUTREA Conference*, Nottingham: Pilgrim College, University of Nottingham. Available at www.leeds.ac.uk/educol

Leathwood, C. (2004) A critique of institutional inequalities in higher education (or an alternative to hypocrisy for higher educational policy), *Theory and Research in Education*, 2(1): 31–48.

Leathwood, C. and O'Connell, P. (2003) 'It's a struggle': the construction of the 'new student' in higher education, *Journal of Educational Policy*, 18(6): 597–615.

Mirza, H. S. (1995) Black women in higher education: defining a space/finding a place, in L. Morley and V. Walsh (eds) *Feminist Academics: Creative Agents for Change*. London: Taylor and Francis.

MORI (2004) *Schools Omnibus 2004 (Wave 10): A Research Study Among 11–16 Year Olds on Behalf of The Sutton Trust*. CHECK, The Sutton Trust. Accessed online at www.suttontrust.com

Morley, L. (1997) Change and equity in higher education, *British Journal of Sociology of Education*, 18(2): 231–42.

Plebs (1909) Editorial, *Plebs*, 1(3): 44.

Pugsley, L. (1998) Throwing your brains at it: higher education, markets and choice. Paper presented to the BERA conference, Belfast, 27–30 August.

Quinn, J. (2003) *Powerful Subjects: Are Women Really Taking Over the University?* Stoke on Trent: Trentham.

Read, B., Archer, L. and Leathwood, C. (2003) Challenging cultures? Student conceptions of 'belonging' and 'isolation' at a post-1992 university, *Studies in Higher Education*, 28(3): 261–77.

Reay, D. (1998) 'Always knowing' and 'never being sure': familial and institutional habituses and higher education choice, *Journal of Education Policy*, 13(4): 519–29.

Ryle, S., Ahmed, K. *et al.* (2000) The war of Laura's rejection, *The Observer*, 28 May.

Shiner, M. and Modood, T. (2002) Help or hindrance? Higher education and the route to ethnic equality, *British Journal of Sociology of Education*, 23(2): 209–32.

Tett, L. (2000) 'I'm working class and proud of it' – gendered experiences of non-traditional participants in higher education, *Gender and Education*, 12(2): 183–94.

UCAS (2004) *Social Class: Applicants and Accepted Applicants 1998–2001*, http://www.ucas.ac.uk/figures/ucasdata/socio/classp.html

Van Dyke, R. and Little, B. (2002) *Universities UK Student Debt Project: Key Early Findings*. London: Universities UK.

Walkerdine, V. (1990) *Schoolgirl Fictions*. London: Verso.

Walkerdine, V., Lucey, H. and Melody, J. (2001) *Growing Up Girl: Psychosocial Explorations of Gender and Class*. Basingstoke: Palgrave.

Young, M. (2001) Down with meritocracy, *Guardian*, 29 June.

3

Differentiation and Stratification in Scottish Higher Education

Jim Gallacher

Introduction

The theme that higher education is moving towards mass or even universal systems in many countries has now been well documented by a number or writers (Trow, 1974; Scott, 1995). The drivers behind this change are partly economic, associated with globalization, and partly social, associated with widening access and social inclusion. The relative weight given to these different drivers varies from society to society, depending on history and political context, but in all cases they have brought about important and far reaching changes in higher education. These include the creation of not just a much larger, but also a much more heterogeneous student groups. Many of these students are quite different in social and cultural background from the students who were the participants in the smaller elite higher education systems. This creates new challenges for higher education institutions and for the staff within them. Higher education has also become more diverse with a greater emphasis on part-time, open or distance learning, and work based learning. However, state funding for higher education has not increased in line with student numbers, and as a result the unit of resource has declined in many societies. The structure of higher education has also changed. Dual systems have become binary; binary have become unified; and within unified systems new forms of stratification have emerged.

The emergence of new forms of stratification has itself been driven by a number of factors:

- First, the increasingly important role of institutions which provide 'short cycle' higher education in mass systems. This includes further education colleges in the UK, community colleges in North America and technical and further education institutes (TAFEs) in Australia. Many of these institutions are quite different in their role, funding and governance from the traditional universities. As a result their status and prestige has often been lower, both within the educational system and within the wider society.

- Second, student demand within national, and increasingly international systems creates a 'market' which reinforces the relative prestige of certain institutions. Developments such as the Bologna process and the globalization of higher education are tending to contribute to the creation of international 'markets' (Bologna Working Group on Qualifications Frameworks, 2005).
- Third, the research-led elite universities perceive these changes as actual or potential threats to their ability to maintain their position within an increasingly competitive global market. Trow (2003) has described this a 'crisis' for these universities. They will, therefore, seek ways to maintain their relatively privileged positions within their national systems.

This chapter will seek to explore the implications of these changes for the higher education system that has been emerging in Scotland over the last twenty years. In terms of Trow's classic definition, Scotland, with an Age Participation Index (API) of 51.5 per cent for those aged under 21, can already be considered as having moved beyond a 'mass' system of higher education into a 'universal' system (Trow, 1974). This chapter will examine differentiation within this system. Scott (1995) has referred to the tendency for systems to evolve from 'unified' to 'stratified' systems, while making it clear that such an evolutionary process is not a necessary consequence of development. Tapper and Palfreyman (2004: 3) have argued that we are likely to see the emergence of a 'diverse, stratified, hierarchical (but possibly "joined-up") system of higher education' by 2010. This chapter will consider the evidence of differentiation which already exists in Scotland, and the extent to which this can be considered to indicate diversity or stratification. It builds on earlier work on the theme of diversity and inequality in higher education in Scotland (Murphy *et al.*, 2002; Morgan-Klein and Murphy, 2004). These issues are of particular interest in a policy context in which the promotion of social inclusion and widening access have continued to be emphasized as priorities in Scotland (Scottish Parliament, 2002; Scottish Executive, 2003a; Scottish Funding Councils, 2003). The chapter will also consider options for the development of this system to meet the needs of students, and of the wider Scottish society, in the most effective ways.

Scotland's four higher education sectors

Four distinct sectors can now be observed within higher education in Scotland. First there are the 'ancient' universities. These four date back to the fifteenth and sixteenth centuries. They were part of the old 'elite' system of higher education in Scotland, and continue to be the most prestigious universities, enjoying a high level of demand for their places. Second, there are the 1960s universities, established or designated at the time of expansion of the British university sector in the 1960s. Together these two groups are sometimes referred to as the 'old universities'. The third sector is made up of the post-1992 universities, the former polytechnic type institutions which provided more vocationally oriented higher education. They were designated as universities, under the terms of the 1992 Further and Higher Education Act, at the time of the abolition of the binary line in Britain. Fourth, there are the further education colleges. Many of these colleges originally provided vocational education and training at craft and technician level. As the traditional industries died away they have sought new markets, and many can now be considered to be community colleges which provide a wide range of educational opportunities for people in the areas they serve. Most now have a significant proportion of higher education level work within their portfolios. However, almost all of their courses are what can be described as 'short cycle' higher education, provided through higher national certificates (HNCs) or higher national diplomas (HNDs) (Gallacher, 2003). These colleges account for a much higher proportion of higher education level work than is found in the similar colleges in England, or in many other similar institutions in other countries throughout the world (Gallacher and Osborne, 2005). This helps to explain why Scotland has moved so rapidly to a universal system of higher education.

The profile of the work undertaken in these different sectors, and some of the key characteristics of each sector, can be seen in Table 3.1. Data for students attending the art, music and education colleges is also included, though these colleges account for only a small proportion of all higher education work. The data are included to complete the picture of

Table 3.1 Students in higher education in Scotland, 1999–2000, by mode of attendance and sector

	Postgraduate (excluding research)	Research students	Full-time undergraduate	Part-time undergraduate	Total undergraduate
Ancients	7654 (25%)	4533 (60%)	42640 (30%)	8113 (12%)	50753 (24%)
1960s	13315 (43%)	2143 (28%)	29662 (21%)	5785 (9%)	35447 (17%)
Post-1992	7145 (23%)	810 (11%)	36862 (26%)	10552 (16%)	47414 (23%)
FE colleges	562 (2%)	–	30659 (21%)	41673 (62%)	72332 (34%)
Art, Music and Education colleges	2551 (8%)	79 (1%)	4026 (3%)	587 (1%)	4613 (2%)
Total HE	38792	7565	143849	66710	210559

Source: SHEFC, 2002 and Scottish Executive, 2002

higher education provision in Scotland, but the place of these colleges within the system will not be analysed in this chapter.

Table 3.1, using the latest year for which data of this kind has been published, provides an indication of the differentiation which now exists between the main sectors of higher education in Scotland. It can be observed that while the 'ancient' universities are still the main providers of full-time undergraduate education with 30 per cent of all students, their share of part-time students is much lower. Furthermore, the 12 per cent of part-time undergraduates recorded here will include a significant number of students who are not part of part-time degree programmes, but will be part of the universities' continuing education provision. It is also very noticeable that research students are disproportionately represented in this sector (60 per cent). The extent to which these universities continue to dominate research provision can also be seen when the distribution of research income from the Scottish Higher Education Funding Council (SHEFC) is considered. The four 'ancient' universities received 65 per cent of this income in 2004–05 (SHEFC, 2004).

The 1960s universities have a rather different profile from the 'ancients'. While undergraduate, and particularly full-time undergraduate provision continues to be important within this sector, these universities have now become the major providers of taught postgraduate courses in Scotland. They have a significant number of research students, with 28 per cent, and receive 30 per cent of the main research funding allocated by SHEFC. However, these universities have not established themselves in a comparable role to the 'ancients' with respect to research.

The post-1992 universities have now established themselves as major providers of undergraduate education (23 per cent). In this respect it can also be noted that a higher percentage of undergraduate students in this sector are part-time students (22 per cent) when compared with the 'ancients' and 1960s universities (16 per cent). When their role in the provision of postgraduate education is considered it can be observed that, while they have a significant number of taught postgraduates (23 per cent), which is close to the figure to be found in the 'ancients' (25 per cent), their role in providing opportunities for research students remains limited (11 per cent). This is confirmed by the fact that they currently only receive 3 per cent of the main research funding allocated by SHEFC.

The fourth sector we will consider here is the one consisting of the further education colleges (FECs). These colleges are now major providers of higher education with 21 per cent of all full-time undergraduates, and they are the main providers of undergraduate level part-time higher education courses (62 per cent) in Scotland. While a significant number of these part-time students will be enrolled on courses leading to qualifications such as HNCs, a significant group will be taking only one or two Higher National units. As might be expected, these colleges have only limited postgraduate provision. However the UHI Millenium Institute, which is the university designate serving the Highlands and Islands, and is being built around the local FECs, is now receiving a research grant from SHEFC (£463,000 or 0.3 per cent of the total for Scotland). Overall then, these colleges mainly provide short cycle higher education (HNC/Ds), which leads on to further study, employment, or enhanced careers prospects for part-time students who are already in employment (Gallacher *et al.*, 2004).

This initial profile of these fours sectors gives an indication of the differentiation in function between the sectors. This initial impression is further reinforced when the social and educational characteristics of students in each sector are considered further.

Differentiation and age

There are important age differences in the profiles of students in the four sectors. Data on these differences is available from a number of sources. First, the Scottish Executive data enable us to make an overall comparison between undergraduate level students in FECs and those in the higher education institutions (which include universities and colleges of art, etc). In 2000–01, whereas 55 per cent of these students in the FECs were aged 25 or over, only 27 per cent of students in HEIs were in this age range. By contrast, while 32 per cent of undergraduate level students in FECs were aged 20 or under, 45 per cent of undergraduates in HEIs were within this age range. Data available from UCAS enables us to explore these age differences between university sectors for full-time students (see Table 3.2). From Table 3.2 it can be seen that older students are much more likely to be accepted for the post-1992 universities than for either of the pre-1992 sectors. Murphy *et al.* (2002), in their study of widening access to higher education in Scotland, showed that the gap between the pre- and post-1992 universities was widening in this respect during the 1990s (see Table 3.3). While the percentage of full-time students aged over 21 who were accepted by the post-1992 universities increased by 9 per cent between 1994 and 1999, the percentage of students in this age group accepted by the pre-1992 universities fell by 5 per cent over the same period.

Table 3.2 Age of degree applicants accepted: Scottish universities 2002

	20 and under	*25 and over*	*Total*
Ancients	79%	6%	12626
1960s	81%	8%	8685
Post-1992s	64%	22%	11625

Source: UCAS database, accessed February, 2003

Table 3.3 Age of degree applicants accepted: Scottish universities 1994 and 1999

	Pre-1992		Post-1992	
	1994	1999	1994	1999
21 and over	19%	14%	20%	29%

Source: UCAS, 2001 in Murphy *et al.*, 2002

Table 3.4 Degree applicants accepted: Scottish universities: main qualification

	Pre-1992		Post-1992	
	1994	1999	1994	1999
Non-traditional	13%	10%	15%	31%
None	1%	5%	2%	13%

Source: UCAS, 2001 in Murphy *et al.*, 2002

Differentiation and qualifications

A further indicator of differences between the sectors, which is also related to age differences, can be observed in the qualifications of applicants who are accepted for entry. Once again a very marked difference can be noted between the FE colleges and the universities. Data drawn from the Scottish Further Education Funding Council database indicates that for 2001 entrants to HE courses in FE colleges, only 18 per cent had three Scottish Highers or two A levels, while an even lower figure of 11 per cent of entrants to HNCs had achieved this level of qualification (SFEFC, 2001). Three Highers or two A levels would be the normal minimum qualification required for entry to a degree level programme, and most degrees would expect a higher level of achievement. This reflects the wide range of alternative entry qualifications accepted within FE colleges. Data on qualifications at point of entry to the universities is also available from the study by Murphy *et al.* (2002) (Table 3.4).

Once more, evidence of a growing differentiation between sectors in terms of the qualifications they accept for entry can be observed, with the post-1992 universities becoming increasingly flexible in their approach. These differences in entry qualifications between the university sectors are also found with the opportunities for students to progress into degree courses on the strength of the HNC/D qualifications, which they have obtained in the FE colleges. It has been noted above that most of the higher education students in FE colleges are taking Higher National courses rather than degrees franchised from universities. A significant number of the students use these HN qualifications to proceed to universities to complete degrees. This is similar to the progression of students with associate degrees from community colleges in America. However, as can be seen from Table 3.5, the

Table 3.5 Students entering HEIs in Scotland for whom HNC/D or similar was highest qualification on entry: 1999–2000

	Number of entrants with HNC/D as highest qualification	Percentage of all entrants
Ancient universities	303	3%
1960s universities	568	8%
Post-1992 universities	2665	25%
Art/music colleges	167	13%
Total	3703	13%

Source: SHEFC, 2002

opportunities for progression are not equally spread across the university sectors.

A number of factors can help explain these patterns. Studies have shown that articulation links established to facilitate transfer between FECs and HEIs in Scotland are much more likely to exist between the FE colleges and the post-1992 universities than the older universities (Alexander *et al.*, 1995; Maclennan *et al.*, 2000; Osborne *et al.*, 2000). The post-1992 universities have generally made widening access and developing links with the FE colleges a much more central part of their mission. However it must also be noted that this has been in a context in which the older universities, and particularly the 'ancients', are for the most part 'selecting' universities, while in many cases the post-1992 universities are 'recruiting' universities (Maclennan *et al.*, 2000). This distinction refers to the 'market' in which the older universities can, for the most part, select students from a pool of traditionally well qualified applicants. By contrast a number of departments within the post-1992 universities need to be more active in recruiting suitable students, and FE colleges can be a valuable source of recruits. In this context there has been greater interest in the post-1992 universities in establishing articulation agreements to facilitate transfer of students from HNC/Ds to degree programmes.

Socio-economic background and differentiation

These differences in the ages and qualifications of students between the university sectors are also related to important differences in the socio-economic background of students. The most comprehensive data on this is available from studies based on the postcodes of students undertaken by Gillian Raab and her colleagues over a number of years (Raab and Storkey, 2001; Raab and Small, 2003). The most recent data from these studies is summarized in Table 3.6. In this study all students' addresses were allocated to one of five equal sized groups. These groups were based on the Carstairs

Table 3.6 Undergraduate level students in Scotland by Carstairs deprivation category 2001 (percentages)

Deprivation group	Ancients	1960s	Post-1992	FECs
1 = least deprived	37.8	29.7	28.1	19.5
2	23.5	23.4	21.2	21.0
3	17.8	20.5	18.5	21.5
4	12.4	15.3	17.4	19.6
5 = most deprived	8.5	11.1	14.8	18.4

Source: Raab and Small, 2003

deprivation index, initially developed to study health differentials in relation to area of residence. It has now been used more widely, and in particular in these studies of educational participation. In Table 3.6 those in Group 1 live in the least deprived areas, while those in Group 5 are in the most deprived areas. If opportunities to access higher education were equally divided it could be expected that there would be approximately 20 per cent of students in each group. However, there is considerable differentiation between the sectors. Among the universities, the 'ancients' are the ones in which students from the most advantaged social groups are most over-represented while students from the most deprived areas are under-represented in these institutions. The post-1992 sector is the one in which there is strongest representation from students from the more deprived areas, with the 1960s universities coming between these two sectors. However, when participation within the FE sector is considered, it can be seen that there is far more equal participation from students from all areas.

These patterns of differential participation are also repeated in the data from UCAS reported by Murphy *et al.* (2002). These indicated that 30 per cent of accepted applicants in the post-1992 universities and 22 per cent in the pre-1992 universities were from social classes iii, iv and v in 1999, with little change since 1994. However Raab and Small (2003) report evidence that differentials had increased between 1996–97 and 2000–01. While the overall participation from disadvantaged groups had decreased for the 'ancient' universities from a level that was already low, participation in the post-1992 universities had increased. For other institutions the proportions from disadvantaged areas had remained fairly level.

Differentiation and stratification

On the basis of the evidence presented above it can be seen that the higher education system is not just differentiated, but also stratified.

- The 'ancient' universities continue to be the elite institutions with a high proportion of students who are young, middle class and relatively highly qualified. Opportunities for progression from HNC/D programmes in FE colleges to degree programmes are limited in these universities. A high proportion of the research activity also continues to be concentrated in these universities.

- The 1960s universities have a higher percentage of undergraduates from less advantaged areas, but their students are for the most part young and full time. While they have a significant research profile it is much more limited than the ancient universities. However this sector is the main provider of taught postgraduate programmes.

- The post-1992 universities have a much more heterogeneous student population. Much higher proportions of their undergraduates are older students who do not have traditional qualifications and who come from less advantaged areas than in the other two university sectors. There are far higher numbers of students who progress from HNC/D programmes in FE colleges to degrees in these universities, and a higher proportion of undergraduate students studies part time. Research activity in these universities is still relatively low, although there is a growing profile of taught postgraduate programmes.

- The FE colleges present a striking contrast with all three university sectors. High proportions of students are older, do not have traditional entry qualifications, come from socially and economically disadvantaged areas and are part time. While the exact proportion of these students who progress to degree level study is not known, evidence from first destination statistics indicates that 56 per cent of full-time students proceed to some form of further study or training (Scottish Executive, 2004). However, progression to degree level study is much more likely to lead to post-1992 universities than pre-1992 universities. This has led a number of writers to suggest that, while the there is evidence of considerable success in widening access to higher education in Scotland, there is also a danger of ghettoization, in which the most prestigious section of the higher education is not really open to non-traditional students, many of whom come from socially and economically disadvantaged areas. It is suggested that this can in turn lead to more limited labour market opportunities for these students (Field, 2004, and see Little, this volume).

It would appear that the system is one with very definite patterns of stratification, and that this stratification has been become more clearly defined since the 1990s. Yet these developments have been taking place within a context in which policy has been placing emphasis on widening access and social inclusion, with some success. In this respect some distinctive features of the Scottish system can be noted. After the devolved Scottish Parliament was established in 1999 the coalition Labour/Liberal Democrat Scottish Executive agreed to abolish tuition fees, following the recommendations of the Cubie Committee (Cubie, 1999) and rejecting the policy established by the Labour government in Westminster. This course has been maintained in the decision not to follow Westminster in the introduction of top-up or variable fees. The Scottish Parliament has also expressed a clear commitment to widening access to higher education, and outlined a number of measures designed to tackle the barriers to access in its Final Report from the Inquiry into Lifelong Learning (Scottish Parliament, 2002). A number of these suggestions have been taken up by the Scottish Executive in its Lifelong Learning Strategy (Scottish Executive, 2003a) and its Higher Education Review (Scottish Executive, 2003b). These have included support for the Scottish Higher Education Funding Council (SHEFC) and the Scottish Further Education Funding Council (SFEFC) in measures designed to widen access to higher education. However, despite these policy initiatives, stratification is still a feature of the Scottish system, and it would appear that it is becoming more firmly embedded. This then raises a major challenge for the higher education system in Scotland, a challenge which it shares with similar systems elsewhere in the world. The challenge is this: can a system be developed which is differentiated, but not stratified in ways disadvantageous to the students involved?

Can a differentiated system be an equitable one?

It seems likely that any system of mass or universal higher education will be a differentiated one rather than a superficially unified one. Some universities will strive to maintain their place among an international elite of research led universities, and will seek funding systems that enable them to pursue this goal. These institutions will also continue to be attractive to highly qualified, and often socially more privileged applicants. In this context widening access and providing support for non-traditional students is not likely to be a key priority for these institutions or the staff within them. The 'ancients' are clearly the universities most likely to exemplify these characteristics in Scotland. Other universities are likely to prioritize other roles within a diversified system. While the 1960s universities do have a significant research profile, a number of them have clearly placed an emphasis on developing taught postgraduate programmes, and this is a role which they may wish to develop. Similarly the post-1992 universities are seeking distinctive roles within the system. This may involve developing strengths in certain key areas of undergraduate provision which have not been traditional areas of strength in the older universities, such as professions allied to medicine. These universities may also actively recruit non-traditional students, and strengthen their links with the FE colleges as a means of tapping into more highly motivated student groups, and they may put in place special measures to enable them to provide appropriate support for these students. These universities are also developing a significant portfolio of taught postgraduate programmes, and are seeking to develop research capacity in defined areas of strength. The FE colleges are strengthening their roles as community colleges providing a range of learning opportunities for the local communities they serve, including providing access routes for adult return-ers. Within that context a number of them are pursuing measures to strengthen their roles as providers of higher education. These include mer-gers to create larger, stronger colleges, collaboration between colleges, and closer links with universities. The most striking example of this type of cooperation is the collaboration among FE colleges in the highland and islands areas to create the University of the Highlands and Islands (UHI), currently designated as the UHI Millennium Institute. This will have no central campus. Students will be based in the colleges, with degrees built on HNC/Ds.

Differentiation of this kind can be seen to be appropriate, and indeed helpful in meeting the needs of the varied student groups who participate in a mass or universal system of higher education. It can also be helpful in enabling higher education to make the contribution to the development of society and the economy which is expected of it. However if the most detri-mental aspects of stratification are to be avoided it is important that the more prestigious institutions do provide access routes for non-traditional students, including those who wish to transfer from FE colleges with HNC/D qualifica-tions. It is also important that appropriate support structures are put in place to enable these students to successfully complete their studies.

This, then, raises questions about how change can be introduced in a higher education system, such as the Scottish one, which will allow differen-tiation, but reduce the most harmful effects of stratification. A key issue here is clearly the funding system. Funding is a means of supporting various kinds of activity within the institutions. The research assessment exercise (RAE) in the UK is one of the important mechanisms through which dif-ferentiated funding is distributed to the universities. Universities demon-strating strength in research are allocated higher levels of funding, which enables them to build on and consolidate this strength. There is evidence that the Westminster government is interested in reinforcing these differen-tials to strengthen the position of the leading research universities (Lucas, this volume).

The introduction of variable fees can be seen as another measure to pro-vide additional income for the universities, and in particular the more elite research led institutions. However the Scottish Executive, as well as resisting variable fees, has shown a stronger commitment to supporting research across the university system in Scotland, while recognizing a need 'to nurture the leading edge research institutions so that they remain competitive' (Scottish Executive, 2003b: 42).

With regard to supporting initiatives which will strengthen provision which widens access to higher education, a number of special funding mechanisms are in place. Thus universities receive a widening access pre-mium which is based on the numbers of students who come from certain designated postcodes. There is also a premium for part-time students and for students who come from FE colleges. These are all to reward institutions which have shown strength in these areas, and to enable them to strengthen their provision, and provide further support for these students. These sources of funding are valuable, but limited. Thus the widening access premium stands at 10 per cent although the Scottish Parliament Report suggested an increase to 25 per cent (Scottish Parliament, 2002). Furthermore, the levels of funding distributed through these mechanisms are insignificant when compared with the funding which a strong research university can receive through its RAE ratings. Some indication of the scale of these differences can be given by the figures for 2004–05 which indicate that, while the 'ancient' universities are receiving £107,870,000, or 48 per cent of their total SHEFC income in grants for their research activities, they are only receiving £2,216,000, 1 per cent of their income, for widening access and part-time incentive grants. This compares with the post-1992 universities where research funding amounts to only £5,970,000, or 3 per cent of SHEFC income, while income from widening access and part-time incentive grants amounts to £5,340,000, also approximately 3 per cent (SHEFC, 2004).

The very limited contribution which these widening access and part-time incentive grants are making in both real and relative terms in the 'ancient' universities is clear. This raises questions about whether other means can help ensure that all universities make appropriate provision in these respects. One option is to increase the level and range of incentive grants. Increasing the widening access premium from 10 per cent to 25 per cent has been mentioned above. There are also proposals for other changes to the mechanisms through which widening access funding is distributed, for example, using first generation students as an indicator. Opportunities exist to introduce support for other areas of work, such as links between FE colleges and universities. Grants have been provided for this purpose in 2003–04 and 2004–05, but it is not clear if this system will be consolidated. The Scottish Funding Councils are currently undertaking a review of their widening participation policies and strategies, and this may be an opportunity to address these issues.

Increases in funding of this kind are unlikely to provide significantly greater incentives for research led universities to make widening access a priority. However, increased grants of this kind could be of considerable value to the universities and colleges with significant numbers of non-traditional students, in enabling them to improve the quality of their provision. They could also help ensure that more adequate support facilities are available for non-traditional students in the older universities, which would make these institutions more attractive to these students, and help ensure that they are successful if they do enter them. The Funding Council could also strengthen the conditions of grant to ensure that all universities have to have appropriate arrangements in place to ensure that some of the existing inequalities in access are more adequately dealt with. A bill was introduced to the Scottish Parliament in September 2004, which will result in the merging of SHEFC and SFEFC to create in 2005 a new Scottish Further and Higher Education Funding Council. It remains to be seen how the new funding council, which will steer all education after school, tackles these problems of funding for higher education, and the links between the FE colleges and universities. It will certainly create a context in which new initiatives can be taken within an integrated approach to strategy.

A number of other initiatives are also underway which are designed to encourage cooperation, widen opportunities for access and provide opportunities for credit transfer. Three of these will be briefly commented on here. The first is the establishment of regional wider access forums. These bring together representatives of the universities and FE colleges in four regions throughout Scotland. They are designed to encourage cooperation between universities and colleges, to widen access to higher education and facilitate transfer from FE colleges to universities. This has resulted in a number of projects focusing on particular issues or problems, for example, the transition from college to university. The second is a national initiative, the Mapping, Tracking and Bridging Project, which has also been established by the joint funding councils. This has been designed

- to provide more comprehensive information about the opportunities for students to progress from HNC/D programmes in FE colleges to degree programmes (mapping);
- to track the progress of students who make this transition (tracking); and
- to assist in preparing them for the transition from FE to university (bridging).

The third initiative is the Scottish Credit and Qualifications Framework (SCQF) which has been established as a national unified framework through which learning of all types can be recognized and the relationships between qualifications can be clarified. One of the aims is to build more credit links between the different types of qualifications and through this to enhance flexibility and enable the accumulation and transfer of credit from different routes (SCQF, 2003). This framework has been developed on a partnership basis between the main stakeholder groups. The higher education institutions have agreed to cooperate in the implementation of this framework, and it should enable students to bring credit from other qualifications into universities.

These three initiatives are all valuable in recognizing the need for cooperation between the FE colleges and the universities. They are also seeking to establish more effective ways of enabling students to move between institutions with credit. All of these initiatives depend on institutions agreeing to cooperate. This approach clearly has much to recommend it: seeking to *impose* change, particularly within higher education institutions can often be difficult and ineffective. However, if the problems of stratification within a differentiated higher education system are to be overcome, and if opportunities for participation for students with non-traditional qualifications are to be more equally distributed across all of the higher education sectors, it may be necessary to secure agreement from institutions that they will introduce changes, and to put in place forms of support which will ensure that these opportunities exist. Trow cited the California Master Plan as an example of a formal agreement which imposes requirements on the higher education institutions in California. This was a plan agreed by the institutions themselves, although in a context in which the requirement to reach an agreement had been made clear. Under this plan the relationships between institutions within the various sectors, including the opportunities for transfer with credit from community colleges to the campuses of the internationally recognized University of California are clearly specified. While there may be disadvantages with a relatively formal plan of this kind, it is cited as an example of how the issue of stratification and diversity can be addressed. The Schwartz Report, which has sought to explore the issues of the changes needed to move towards a system of 'fair admissions' in England, also recognizes the need to balance autonomy and the requirement for change in its recommendations (Schwartz, 2004).

Conclusion

It has been argued in this chapter that we now have not just a highly differentiated higher education system in Scotland, but also a highly stratified one. This is a pattern which will be found in many other societies throughout the world, although the structures and relationships will differ. What is of added interest in Scotland is that this stratified system has emerged in the context of a society in which there has been, and continues to be, an emphasis on social inclusion and widening access in national policy. Indeed, it is partly because of the success of these policies that Scotland now has a very high participation rate, with many non-traditional students returning to study 'short cycle' higher education in FE colleges before progressing to degree level study. Despite this level of success, there is concern about the degree of stratification, which is a persistent feature of the system. It has been suggested that differentiation is likely to be a feature of mass or universal systems of higher education, and indeed differentiation may be an appropriate and useful feature of these systems. However, if higher education systems are to reconcile the goals of differentiation and social justice and equity, appropriate mechanisms must be in place to counteract the negative effects of stratification. This is a challenge that the Scottish system of higher education must continue to tackle.

References

Alexander, H., Gallacher, J., Leahy, J. and Yule, W. (1995) Changing patterns of higher education in Scotland: a study of links between further education colleges and higher education institutions, *Scottish Journal of Adult and Continuing Education*, 2: 25–54.

Bologna Working Group on Qualifications Frameworks (2005) *A Framework for Qualifications of the Higher Education Area*. Copenhagen: Ministry for Science, Technology and Innovation.

Cubie, A. (1999) *Student Finance: Fairness for the Future.* Report of the Independent Committee of Inquiry into Student Finance. Edinburgh: HMSO.

Field, J. (2004) Articulation and credit transfer in Scotland: taking the academic highroad or sideways step into a ghetto, *Journal of Access Policy and Practice,* 1 (2): 85–99.

Gallacher, J. (2003) *Higher Education in Further Education Colleges: The Scottish Experience.* London: The Council for Industry and Higher Education.

Gallacher, J., Caldwell, J. and MacFarlane, K. (2004) *Progression of HN holders in Employment: A Scoping Study of Data Sources.* Glasgow: SQA.

Gallacher, J. and Osborne, M. (2005) *Diversity or Division? International Perspectives on the Contested Landscape of Mass Higher Education.* Leicester: National Institute for Adult and Continuing Education (NIACE).

Maclennan, A., Musselbrook, K. and Dundas, M. (2000) *Credit Transfer at the FE/HE Interface.* Edinburgh: Scottish Higher Education Funding Council/Scottish Further Education Funding Council.

Morgan-Klein, B. and Murphy, M. (2004) Looking through the kaleidoscope; diversification, accessibility and inequality in Scottish higher education, in M. Osborne, J. Gallacher and B. Crossan (eds) *Researching Widening Access to Lifelong Learning: Issues and Approaches in International Research.* London: Routledge Falmer.

Murphy, M., Morgan-Klein, B., Osborne, M. and Gallacher, J. (2002) *Widening Participation in Higher Education: Report to Scottish Executive.* Glasgow: Centre for Research in Lifelong Learning.

Osborne, M., Cloonan, M., Morgan-Klein, B. and Loots, C. (2000) Mix and match? Further and higher education links in Scotland, *International Journal of Lifelong Education,* 19 (3).

Raab, G. and Storkey, H. R. (2001) *Widening Access to Higher Education in Scotland: Evidence for Change from 1996–1997 to 1998–99.* Edinburgh: SHEFC.

Raab, G. and Small G. (2003) *Widening Access to Higher Education in Scotland: Evidence for Change from 1996–1997 to 2000–01.* Edinburgh: SHEFC.

Schwartz, S. (2004) *Fair Admission to Higher Education: Recommendations for Good Practice.* Admission to higher education review. Nottingham: DfES.

Scott, P. (1995) *The Meaning of Mass Higher Education.* Buckingham: SRHE/Open University Press.

Scottish Executive (2002) *Standard Tables on Higher and Further Education in Scotland 2001–2002.* Edinburgh, Scottish Executive.

Scottish Executive (2003a) *Life Through Learning Through Life: The Lifelong Learning Strategy for Scotland.* Edinburgh: Scottish Executive.

Scottish Executive (2003b) *A Framework for Higher Education in Scotland: Higher Education Review Phase 2.* Edinburgh: Scottish Executive

Scottish Executive (2004) *First Destinations of HNC & HND Holders in Scotland 2000–01,* data prepared for the Centre for Research in Lifelong Learning by the Scottish Executive.

Scottish Funding Councils (2003) *Aiming Further and Higher: Joint Corporate Plan 2003–06.* Edinburgh: Scottish Funding Councils.

SFEFC (Scottish Further Education Funding Council) (2002) *SFEFC Infact Database.* http://www.sfefc.ac.uk/infact/

SHEFC (Scottish Higher Education Funding Council) (2002) *Statistical Bulletin 2/2002 Higher Education Institutions: Students and Staff 1999–2000.* Edinburgh: SHEFC.

SHEFC (2004) Circular letter to institutions. Edinburgh: SHEFC.

Scottish Parliament (2002) *Enterprise and Lifelong Learning Committee: 9th Report. Final Report on Lifelong Learning.* SP Paper 679. Edinburgh: The Stationery Office.

SCQF (Scottish Credit and Qualifications Framework) (2003) *An Introduction to the Scottish Credit and Qualifications Framework,* 2nd edn. Scottish Credit and Qualifications Framework.

Tapper, T. and Palfreyman, D. (2004) *Convergence and Divergence in the Global Model of Mass Higher Education: Predictions for 2010.* Oxford: OxCHEPS Occasional Paper No. 14.

Trow, M. (1974) *Problems in the Transition from Elite to Mass Higher Education,* in Policies for Higher Education, General Report on the Conference on Future Structures of Post Secondary Education. Paris: OECD.

Trow, M. (2000) From mass higher education to universal access: the American advantage, *Minerva* 37 (Spring): 1–26.

Trow, M. (2003) *On Mass Higher Education and Institutional Diversity.* Haifa: Samuel Neaman Institute for Advanced Studies in Science and Technology, Technion-Israel institute of Technology.

UCAS (2002) UCAS Database (accessed February 2003).

4

Participation and Access in Higher Education in Northern Ireland

Bob Osborne

Introduction

This chapter examines some of the key issues in higher education participation in Northern Ireland. To do so it examines key statistical indicators and then examines some of the policy contexts in which participation and access issues are being and could be developed. The chapter updates material partially discussed in Osborne (2001) and Osborne and Gallagher (2003), which includes a summary of historical developments to higher education policy in Northern Ireland.

Participation

There are two main issues around higher education participation in Northern Ireland. The first of these relates both to the level of participation and who enters higher education and more especially who is not participating. The second issue, which is closely related to the first, concerns the destination of those entering higher education – the question of migration.

Who enters higher education?

As with the analysis of higher education participation, two traditional key variables are gender and social class/socio-economic group. In the rest of the UK ethnicity is also of considerable importance and is becoming more important in Northern Ireland. Additionally, disability is of increasing significance as access by students with disabilities has progressed following the establishment of the rights of those with disabilities to access education and other spheres of life. In Northern Ireland, the importance of religious affiliation as a marker for the key social division is also of critical importance. However, data on religion is only partially collected and this leads to major problems in assessing contemporary circumstances. This issue is outlined below.

Participation

Recent data for full-time entrants to higher education of Northern Ireland domiciled students by destination are shown in Tables 4.1 and 4.2. Table 4.1 shows full-time sub-degree entrants while Table 4.2 shows full-time degree entrants. Full-time degree entrants have increased by almost a quarter (23.6 per cent) while full-time sub-degree entrants have increased by approximately half that rate (12.9 per cent). Both tables suggest that more students are staying in Northern Ireland rather than leaving and that both those going to Britain and those entering institutions in the Republic of Ireland have declined. Migration is considered further below.

Tables 4.3 and 4.4 show data for part-time provision, with a substantial drop in those entering part-time degree programmes (−24.2 per cent) but a substantial increase in sub-degree numbers (+77.5 per cent). By 2001 part-time sub-degree entrants represented 85 per cent of those entering part-time

Table 4.1 Destinations of Northern Ireland full-time sub-degree entrants

Year	Entrants	NI	GB	RoI
1996/97	2842	2429	378	35
1997/98	3412	3005	397	10
1998/99	3173	2773	391	9
1999/00	3372	3084	279	9
2000/01	3388	3108	271	9
2001/02	3208	2943	255	10
% change 1996–2001	+12.9	+21.2	−67.5	−71.4

Source: Department of Education and Learning (DEL) statistics

Table 4.2 Destinations of Northern Ireland full-time degree entrants

Year	Entrants	NI	GB	RoI
1996/97	9428	5375	3804	249
1997/98	10405	6173	3944	288
1998/99	10258	6278	3743	237
1999/00	10464	6724	3502	238
2000/01	10855	7301	3316	238
2001/02	11654	8013	3384	257
% change 1996–2001	+23.6	+49.1	−12.4	+3.2

Source: DEL statistics

Table 4.3 Destinations of Northern Ireland part-time degree entrants

Year	Entrants	NI	GB	RoI
1996/97	2028	1328	700	0
1997/98	1619	1475	144	0
1998/99	1979	1910	69	0
1999/00	1511	1445	66	0
2000/01	1550	1494	56	0
2001/02	1633	1567	66	0
% change 1996–2001	−24.2			

Source: DEL statistics

Table 4.4 Destinations of Northern Ireland part-time sub-degree entrants

Year	Entrants	NI	GB	RoI
1996/97	5086	4725	361	0
1997/98	7815	6797	1018	0
1998/99	8494	7508	986	0
1999/00	8744	7579	1165	0
2000/01	10042	8578	1464	0
2001/02	9029	7687	1342	0
% change 1996–2001	+77.5			

Source: DEL statistics

courses (compare Scotland: Gallacher, this volume). Overall, therefore, there has been a substantial increase in participation but with a change in the pattern of mode of study with part-time study representing 41.1 per cent of entrants in 2001 compared with 36.7 per cent in 1996.

Socio-economic characteristics

Tables 4.1 and 4.3 rely on official statistics derived from HESA. For a consideration of social class, however, we need to access UCAS data for Northern Ireland domiciled entrants. The change in the official definition of social class to that of a socio-economic classification as used from the 2001 population census provides a temporal discontinuity in the analysis of social background. For this reason the data for the 2003 entry year is shown in Table 4.5. Some caution must be exercised in assessing this table since approximately 20 per cent of students gave no information on socio-economic status. In addition, different institutions use UCAS in the different countries of the UK (e.g. higher education courses in further education colleges in Northern Ireland do not use UCAS). Nevertheless, the differences between Northern

Table 4.5 Accepts into full-time higher education courses, 2003 entry

Socio-economic groups	Northern Ireland		England		Scotland		Wales	
Higher managerial and professional	1425	13.5	50614	22.9	5071	22.8	2362	18.4
Lower managerial and professional	3070	29.1	69251	31.3	6772	30.4	4020	31.4
Intermediate occupations	1839	17.4	33465	15.1	3285	14.8	1987	15.5
Small employers and own account	1475	14.0	15714	7.1	1744	7.8	1059	8.3
Lower supervisory and technical	656	6.2	10783	4.9	1262	5.7	756	5.9
Semi-routine occupations	1269	12.0	29279	13.2	2956	13.3	1750	13.7
Routine occupations	812	7.7	12308	5.6	1178	5.3	885	6.9
Total	10546	100	221414	100	22268	100	12819	100
Not known	1912	15.3	55516	20.0	6010	20.9	3457	21.2

Source: UCAS

Note: Figures may not total exactly 100 due to rounding.

Ireland and the other parts of the UK are relatively small. Notable is the lower representation of entrants from higher managerial and professional occupations in Northern Ireland and to a lesser extent those from intermediate occupations compared with elsewhere. Similarly, there is a much higher representation in Northern Ireland from those 'smaller employers and own account' workers. Thereafter, Wales and Northern Ireland record the highest proportions from the lowest three social groups. Many of these differences parallel differences in the social structures of the four UK countries (Osborne, 2000).

Religion

One of the huge gaps in the information base on higher education participation relates to religion. Despite the obvious significance of this variable for understanding participation and access, there are no data available for entry cohorts. In the mid-1990s attempts were made by the then Department of Education, the two universities and the main religious anti-discrimination regulatory body, the Fair Employment Commission, to persuade UCAS to include a religion question on application forms. This UCAS declined to do. As a result, while the two main Northern Ireland universities monitor for religion there is no contemporary information on those who leave to study (see below). Given that the Department for Employment and Learning (DEL) has responsibility under Northern Ireland's mainstreaming equality provisions (Section 75 of the Northern Ireland Act)[1] to ensure that religious equality of opportunity is promoted in higher and further education, this matter ought to be given some priority.

Tables 4.6 and 4.7 show the figures for the University of Ulster (UU) and Queen's University Belfast (QUB). As can be seen, over 60 per cent of UU entrants being Catholic and the QUB figures approaching 60 per cent, both universities have a majority of Catholics. These figures are consistent with survey findings for the early 1990s which noted that Protestants were far more likely to leave to study in Britain than Catholics (Cormack *et al.*, 1997), and that they were unlikely to return some years after graduation (Leith *et al.*, 2002). Census evidence suggests that the longevity of these trends has

Table 4.6 Religion figures at UU, full-time undergraduates, 2002/03

Full-time undergraduates University of Ulster 2002/03	Entrants	Population	Excluding unknowns	
			Entrants	*Population*
% Catholic	56.3	56.0	62.0	61.7
% Protestant	34.4	34.6	37.8	38.2
% other	0.2	0.1	0.2	0.1
% not known	9.1	9.3		

Table 4.7 Religion figures at QUB, full-time undergraduates, 2002/03

Full time undergraduates			Excluding unknowns	
Queen's University Belfast 2002/03	Entrants	Population	Entrants	Population
% Catholic	51.4	50.7	54.5	55.1
% Protestant	39.1	37.8	41.5	41.1
% other	3.8	3.5	4.1	3.8
% not known	5.7	8.0		

Source: Data supplied by the institutions

resulted in a higher proportion of Catholics in Northern Ireland having third level qualifications than Protestants – a complete reversal of the situation thirty years before (Osborne, 2004).

Migration

As has been referred to above, a key characteristic of higher education participation in Northern Ireland is that of migration. Figure 4.1 shows the long-term patterns of student movements. These data demonstrate that the number of entrants remaining in Northern Ireland has increased slightly in the most recent years as is shown in Tables 4.1 and 4.2. The deliberate expansion of places in Northern Ireland has helped to reduce slightly the

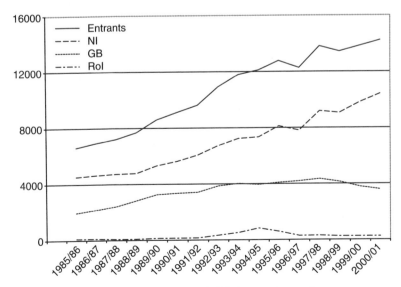

Figure 4.1 Destinations of Northern Ireland full-time undergraduate entrants

migration rate. As the data in Figure 4.1 also suggest, the Republic of Ireland is a statistically small destination, in spite of different fee regimes. Alongside the religious differences amongst those migrating for higher education, two other issues are worth considering. First is the fact that there are two groups amongst the migrants: those who have been described as 'determined' leavers and those who are defined as 'reluctant' leavers. Qualitative research suggests that 'determined' leavers are predominantly Protestant, from the large Protestant grammar schools, and are well qualified. As a result of the supply of places not matching the demand for places in Northern Ireland, the asking grades sought are higher, especially at UU, than with comparable universities in Britain. As a result many more modestly qualified entrants, who would prefer to stay, do not apply to the Northern Ireland universities in the belief that their grades will not be adequate. These 'reluctant leavers' are modestly qualified and are drawn more evenly from Protestants and Catholics. They tend to attend post-1992 universities. Analysis of 2003 UCAS data demonstrates that the 'migration rates' for different social groups continue. For example, while 46.4 per cent of those from higher managerial and professional backgrounds migrate, as do 35 per cent of lower managerial professional occupations, these contrast with 24.2 per cent of small employers and own account workers and 23.2 per cent of those from routine occupation backgrounds. As a result the two Northern Ireland universities have a high representation of those from the lower socio-economic groups – comfortably above any 'benchmarks' (HEFCE, 2003). These figures are not a function of a widening access strategy but are a function of these migratory patterns. Widening access is considered below.

In terms of the destinations for migrants there is a strong emphasis on Scotland and the more northerly parts of England. Universities in these areas have actively recruited in Northern Ireland. The 'Scottish raiding parties' have been particularly effective. These patterns may change after decisions on fee levels and student support in the different countries of the UK and in the Irish Republic (see McNay, Chapter 1, this volume).

In terms of the reason for migration by determined leavers the most common reasons given are: to get access to better universities, to widen horizons in general, to get away from home and to gain access to better job opportunities as graduates. In a minority of cases, negative views are expressed towards 'living in Northern Ireland', the quality of local universities and occasionally as expressed by some Protestants the 'republican ethos' at local institutions. Most students express the hope that they can return to live in Northern Ireland 'at some time'. Graduate surveys, however, continue to record a high desire to return home but many also recognize the difficulty of finding appropriate jobs if they try to return (Leith *et al.*, 2002).

Widening access

The election of the Labour government in 1997 produced a marked new policy focus on widening access or participation. Hitherto, widening participation was primarily concerned with increasing the participation of mature students and part-time provision. However, the Dearing Report of 1997 re-focused attention on the extent to which increased participation had only marginally changed the representation of those from socio-economically deprived backgrounds (NCIHE, 1997). Subsequently, alongside these concerns the massive under-representation of those with disabilities became a policy imperative. As widening access policies have developed, the policy focus has tended to be enlarged to include retention and completion through to access to the labour market. In Northern Ireland the intensity of the policy focus has been less. Under the general practice of policy 'parity' the same policies introduced in England have been largely followed in Northern Ireland.[2] In general terms 'policy parity' in higher education has not produced any significant policy innovations. Indeed, even with devolution, the DEL has preferred to follow developments in England rather than consider alternatives as is considered below in relation to student finance.

The main instruments of widening access policy are as follows:

- Funding of specific projects in the two universities designed to increase participation from the lower socio-economic groups: the Step-Up into Science programme at UU (operating in the north-west of Northern Ireland) which has received DEL funding of c. £356k from 2000–2004. The Discovering Queen's programme received £734k in the same period. The Step-Up programme received recognition in the Universities UK good practice study of widening access schemes (Universities UK, 2003). It involves around 50 to 60 students per annum with a very high progression into higher education. An assessment of both programmes suggested that they both were successful in their objectives (Storan, 2004) but ducked the issue of whether the objectives were the appropriate ones.

- The widening access premium, which has involved £3.8m in the period 2000–2004. Unlike the other parts of the UK which use a postcode mechanism for deciding institutional allocations under this mechanism, the DEL uses the numbers of full-time undergraduates who are exempt from paying fees. Major problems with the postcode mechanism have been identified by Osborne and Shuttleworth (2004) who argue that there is clear evidence that it is a very imprecise mechanism for such allocations. On the other hand, while the Northern Ireland approach avoids this 'ecological fallacy' issue, the awarding of the premium on the basis of non-payment of fees when the residual income for paying fees is £20k and with around 50 per cent of entrants not paying fees, this too seems to be a rather imprecise mechanism for the premium. Neither the postcode premium nor the 'exempt from fees' approach can point to any significant improvement in widening access statistics, nationally or regionally.

The approach to widening access was subjected to a review by an independent group which recommended, *inter alia*, that:

* improved statistical information was required, especially in relation to religion/community background;
* a regional strategy was required for widening access, including provision in further education and integrated with other DEL programmes;
* students from lower socio-economic groups, especially amongst the Protestant community, must be a priority for policy;
* DEL policies must be outcome oriented and in future payment of the premium should become outcome based; and
* any introduction of variable fees should involve the institutions having to enter access agreements which should sit within existing strategies. Northern Ireland should develop its own arrangements to validate access agreements.

(Expert Group Report, 2004)

Further education

The Dearing Report (NCIHE, 1997) suggested that one way of overcoming the under-supply of places in higher education was to provide more sub-degree places in the further education sector, through a variety of arrangements including franchising and other partnerships. The case was made on the basis, not of any demand for those with such qualifications in the employment market, but simply on the potential for transfer to universities to pursue degree level work. Some foundation degrees have been piloted, linking QUB and UU to seven colleges, and further places have been allocated to colleges as part of the general expansion of provision (Osborne, 2003). The proportion of HE students in FE colleges has slowly increased towards 13 per cent, balanced by a reduction in migration to sub-degree courses elsewhere, especially in the Irish Republic, where such numbers have reduced by 90 per cent, though this is from a base of only 213 in 1994–5 to around 20 six years later.

I have previously (Osborne, 2003) noted the tension in policy towards HE in FE with the Assembly Review Group (Northern Ireland Assembly, Committee for Employment and Learning, 2001) calling for concentration in a small number of colleges, and Assembly members defending 'localism'. In the event, 70 per cent of such students are in three colleges, and several of the other 14 units offering provision have fewer than 100 students.

Making higher education policy under devolution: student finance

The devolution *plus* settlement introduced by the Belfast Agreement of 1998 represented an imaginative, subtle and complex political attempt to resolve the political crisis and disturbances which had dominated the previous 30 years. Unlike the (asymmetrical) devolution arrangements for Wales and Scotland, the rhetoric of better government and the ability to make local policy decisions has been more muted in Northern Ireland. Moreover, there is no shared Northern Ireland national identity which also, arguably, underpins the other devolution settlements. Devolution in Northern Ireland (with all its structural complexities flowing from an enforced coalition) is more about the symbolism of reaching a political accommodation after the decades of terror and political stalemate rather than a mechanism for 'better' government. Although devolution existed in Northern Ireland from 1921–1972, policy was determined by a Unionist regime which wanted to demonstrate a continuing close association with the rest of the UK – meaning that there was little incentive for policy divergence. After 1972, under Direct Rule, the parity principle which in broad terms meant Northern Ireland following developments in England except for Northern Ireland specific issues (e.g. religious discrimination) was maintained, and this meant that by and large policy initiation rarely took place (Connolly and Erridge, 1990). The experience of current senior civil servants, therefore, has been more concerned with administration and implementation rather than policy initiation (Carmichael and Osborne, 2003).

These general issues help explain the way in which the review of student finance was undertaken in Northern Ireland. The issues and chronology have been outlined in detail in Osborne (2002). In essence, the review commenced prior to devolution going 'live' but was picked up by the relevant Assembly Committee after its first period of suspension in May 2000. Up to then the DEL had conducted a desultory consultation process which contrasted poorly with that achieved as part of the Scottish review of student finance by Cubie.[3] The message was clear: normal procedure would be followed – maintaining parity with England. The Assembly Committee, however, commissioned research and began to investigate the issue. Here it is worth recalling that the Committee consisted of four major parties (one of which was hostile to the Agreement), which had never sat down in the same room and tried to fashion an agreed policy on anything of any significance. Over the succeeding few months the Committee, guided by the Chair, Dr Esmond Birnie (Ulster Unionist), tortuously agreed a consensus report. The recommendation in the report was, by and large, to accept the model developed by Cubie of the abolition of up-front fees but with a Graduate Endowment. The DEL resisted these ideas both in presentations to the Committee and through off the record briefings. The devolution Minister, Sean Farren of the SDLP, made it clear that notwithstanding his own party's position which was to seek the abolition of fees, he intended to reject the Committee's proposals. The Committee's consensus broke over the ensuing months largely because of the complex power-sharing arrangements in the Assembly. The Minister then moved to raise the residual income level at which fees would be paid and introduced a means tested bursary of maximum value of £1500 per annum together with some fee exemptions in vocational courses. In this case the approach of 'parity' at the level of broad policy principle was maintained but could be 'sold' politically as having been finessed to suit Northern Ireland's circumstances. The Westminster government has now approved the adoption of a policy for fees and student support close to that for England (see McNay, Chapter 1, this volume).

Discussion

When devolution returns to Northern Ireland, higher education policy could be thought of as a test of the extent to which local political institutions are about managing the fractured society that is Northern Ireland. It will give the opportunity for local politicians to wean themselves from dependency thinking and fashion genuinely different policies. Civil servants too will be challenged by this prospect – no longer primarily taking their cue from England.[4] Not that the circumstances are entirely propitious. The higher education institutions will be wary of breaking with an all-UK environment. The realities of the budget constraints of the devolved administration through the Barnett formula have been demonstrated by Heald (2003).

However, issues which relate to the concerns of this chapter that ought to be top of the agenda are:

- What is the optimum level of participation in higher education for Northern Ireland?
- What proportion of entrants should be provided for with places in Northern Ireland?
- What are the targets for widening access in Northern Ireland?
- How can working-class Protestant under-representation in higher education be tackled through widening access policies?
- What structures are appropriate to allow Northern Ireland to also learn from experience in the Irish Republic in widening access and other matters?
- Should there be a policy response to the disproportionate migration of Protestant students from Northern Ireland?
- What should Access Agreements consist of and what powers should an access regulator have compared with the rest of the UK?

There is no doubt that there is scope for a dynamic policy approach to higher education for a devolved administration but it remains to be seen if there is any appetite for taking on the challenge.

Notes

1 Section 75 of the Northern Ireland Act of 1998 imposes a statutory requirement on all public sector bodies to ensure that all policy decisions consider equality issues in relation to religion and political opinion, race, disability, gender, age, sexual orientation and those with/without dependants. For a consideration of this policy in higher education see Osborne (2005).

2 The Department of Employment and Learning has a service agreement with the Higher Education Funding Council for England. In addition DEL takes particular advice on local circumstances from the Northern Ireland Higher Education Council (NIHEC).

3 The Cubie Report arose from the coalition negotiations between Labour and the Liberal Democrats after the first elections to the Scottish parliament.

4 The scale of the challenge is suggested by the fact that one senior civil servant in an off-the-record comment observed that he was impressed with the Luxembourg approach which largely consisted of tracking policy in the Netherlands. While dressed in international clothes this suggests the continuation of the parity principle.

References

Carmichael, P. and Osborne, R. D. (2003) The Northern Ireland Civil Service under Direct Rule and Devolution, *International Review of Administrative Sciences*, 69(2): 205–17.

Connolly, M. and Erridge, A. (eds) (1990) *Public Policy in Northern Ireland: Adoption or Adaption?* Belfast: Policy Research Institute.

Cormack, R., Gallagher, A. and Osborne, R. (1997) Higher education participation in Northern Ireland, *Higher Education Quarterly*, 51(1): 68–85.

Expert Group Report (2004) *Expert Group Review Report on DEL Strategy and Initiatives to Widening Participation in Higher Education.* Belfast: Northern Ireland Higher Education Council.

Heald, D. (2003) *Funding the Northern Ireland Assembly: Assessing the Options*, Research Monograph 10. Belfast: Northern Ireland Economic Council.

HEFCE (Higher Education Funding Council for England) (2003) *Performance Indicators in Higher Education 2000–2001 and 2001–2002*, HEFCE 2003/59. Bristol: HEFCE.

Leith, H., Osborne, R. D. and Gallagher, A. M. (2002) *Skill Development and Enhancement: A Study of Northern Ireland Graduates, Research Paper 7*. University of Ulster, Centre for Research on Higher Education.

NCIHE (National Committee of Inquiry into Higher Education) (1997) *Higher Education in the Learning Society* (The Dearing Report). London: HMSO.

Northern Ireland Assembly, Committee for Employment and Learning (2001) *Report on the Inquiry into Education and Training for Industry.* Belfast: The Stationery Office.

Osborne, R. D. (2000) *From Elitism to Inclusion – Good Practice in Widening Access – Statistical Supplement.* London: CVCP.

Osborne, R. D. (2001) Higher education, participation and devolution: the case of Northern Ireland, *Higher Education Policy*, 15: 45–60.

Osborne, R. D. (2002) Making a difference? The role of statutory committees in the Northern Ireland Assembly, *Public Administration*, 80(2): 283–99.

Osborne, R. D. (2003) Higher education in further education: Northern Ireland, *Higher Education Quarterly*, 57(4): 59–82.

Osborne, R. D. (2004) Education and the labour market, in R.D. Osborne and I. Shuttleworth (eds) *Fair Employment in Northern Ireland: A Generation On*. Belfast: Blackstaff Press.

Osborne, R. D. (2005) Equality in higher education in Northern Ireland, *Higher Education Quarterly*, 59(2): 138–52.

Osborne, R. D. and Gallagher, A. M. (2003) Higher education in a divided society: Northern Ireland, in M. Tight (ed.) *International Perspectives on Higher Education Research, Volume 2: Access and Exclusion*. London/New York: JAI Press.

Osborne, R. D. and Shuttleworth, I. (2004) Widening access to higher education in the UK: querying the geographic approach, *Higher Education Management and Policy*, 16(1): 101–18.

Storan, J. (2004) *Report on DEL Strategies to Widen Access in Higher Education*. Belfast: DEL.

Universities UK (2003) *Social Class and Participation – Good Practice in Widening Access to Higher Education*. London: UUK.

5

The Student Experience and the Impact of Social Capital

Brenda Little

Introduction

What does the student experience look like for the diversity of students following programmes in the UK's mass HE provision? Is the life of a 'full-time' student genuinely a full-time experience or are today's students caught up in a life of constantly struggling to meet different demands on their time: demands from study, from family commitments, from trying to make ends meet, from trying to have 'a life'? Are today's students so pressurized by competing demands on their time that they are unable to engage with the range of social activities that might traditionally have been seen as part and parcel of an undergraduate experience? What might such 'lack' of engagement mean for their immediate student experience and beyond?

Before going further we should try and unpack this phrase 'social capital'. The French sociologist, Pierre Bourdieu was one of the first to use the phrase 'social capital or capital of social relationships' when describing how lawyers, doctors and politicians invested in 'a capital of honourability and respect-ability which is often indispensable if one desires to attract clients in socially important positions' (Bourdieu, 1977: 503, quoted in Coffield, 2000). Bourdieu used the notion of different forms of capital, viz. economic, cul-tural and social to explain the reproduction of elites in France. Nowadays the phrase 'social capital' can be seen as taking on a slightly broader, and argu-ably looser, meaning. Field and Spence (2000) see the notion of social cap-ital as encompassing networks, norms and a shared sense of trust that are available to 'any group of actors, and not solely elite groupings'. Others see social capital in a more restricted sense of 'knowing the "right" people' (Brennan and Shah, 2003), the implication being that people might be 'right' for different groups of people, and for different purposes.

I shall be using the notion of social capital in a broad sense of higher education students networking with their fellow students and with staff, and interacting with others through 'university life' outside of those activities more directly focused on learning and teaching.

When considering the nature of the student experience in the early 1990s, McNay hypothesized that future scenarios for higher education could affect the student experience in a number of ways. For example, cost pressures on students might displace curiosity, and students would move to being more instrumental and less intellectual; changes in curriculum organization and methods of delivery would mean students became more isolated, but less insulated (McNay, 1994). But did this mean isolated in terms of intellectual enquiry and endeavour, or was there also a broader sense of isolation implied – with students less likely to be studying as a 'single cohort', less likely to be involved in aspects of university life outside of studying, having less time to 'be' a student, and arguably less time to develop their social networks?

Would increasing isolation matter anyway? What impact might this have on the student experience? I will draw on two studies recently undertaken by the Open University's Centre for Higher Education Research and Information to address these issues.

Accommodating term-time employment within the student experience

During 2002, we undertook a study investigating final year students' attitudes to debt and term-time working. The study was commissioned by Universities UK and the Higher Education Funding Council for England, and undertaken by a team of researchers from our Centre and London South Bank University. It focused deliberately on full-time, UK-domiciled (i.e. home) degree students in their final year of study. It was this cohort, graduating in 2002, that was the first to be liable to pay (up-front) tuition fees, and that had to rely exclusively on student loans throughout their time in higher education, whereas previously there had been maintenance grants and no tuition fees to pay (Van Dyke *et al.*, forthcoming). Overall, we found that just over half the students had worked during term-time at some point during their last two years in university. This is almost double the proportion reported from studies in 1991–92 (see for example, Pilkington, 1994). Since our study, national studies have quoted figures as high as 58 per cent of full-time young students working during term-time (Callender and Wilkinson, 2003). So term-time working is certainly a part of the student experience for a large number of undergraduates.

Our study covered a number of issues related to students' attitudes to debt, their levels of income from various sources, the nature and incidence of term-time work, students' perceptions of the effect of that work on their academic activities, and the relationship between term-time working and academic attainment. I want to concentrate on how students perceived their term-time work affected aspects of their lives as students, in terms of both academic and other activities. The activities most frequently 'squeezed' by working students' limited time – mentioned by at least three quarters of them – were studying independently, reading, and socializing and relaxing. Seven universities were involved in our study, and we found quite wide variations between these institutions in terms of students' responses. In one institution, almost two in five of working students felt they spent *a lot* less time on leisure and sports and seeing their family. At the same institution, almost half the working students said they spent *a lot* less time on socializing and relaxing, reading and studying independently. So although we did not ask students specific questions about their social networks, it seems that term-time work was getting in the way of activities that would give rise to developing such networks, for example socializing and relaxing and spending time on leisure and sports.

Overall, almost two thirds of working students felt they were constantly overloaded because of their job and the demands of their course, although a similar proportion also thought their job helped them develop useful skills. Although survey responses showed that students' prime reasons for undertaking paid employment during term-time were related to financial matters, viz. needing money for basic essentials, and the inability to manage on just a student loan, other reasons were also cited, albeit by a minority of students. These included wanting the experience, and thinking that the work would help in finding a job on graduation. In some of the student focus groups arranged as part of the study, some students indicated that having a job during term-time gave them a welcome break from studying.

Whatever the reasons for doing term-time work, such commitments meant that students had less time for other things: a significant minority were missing lectures and seminars and had difficulty accessing learning resources. Staff we spoke to clearly had a sense that the students were no longer engaging with the full range of academic and other activities that could be seen as enriching the student experience. They were regularly asked for multiple copies of lecture notes for students to pass on to their friends who (for whatever reason) had not attended the lecture. Some staff had even resorted to removing lecture notes from computer-based learning environments as a way of trying to remove the option of non-attendance. For those staff, the lecture notes in themselves were merely a map to the field of knowledge – the actual lectures were where students would be hearing all the discussions, engaging with the issues and debates. Academics at this same institution were very concerned that students' commitment to study was taking second place to their commitment to their jobs:

> We have students who have established patterns of term-time work to fit with the first semester timetable, but then find the 'fit' is no longer there when we move to the second semester with its different timetable . . . then it's a case of students saying 'this class clashes with my work . . . how important is it (the class)? . . . and that's strange because there's this philosophical flip because it's 'with my work' . . . this existence in academia isn't seen as their work, because we don't give them a pay-slip,

the person they're beholden to is their employer . . . they [the students] do have torn loyalties . . .

(Law lecturer at a new university)

The view expressed above indicates a sense of university study being just one of many commitments that students are aiming to fulfil whilst at university (and some of the other commitments may have very little to do with traditional notions of being a student). Does this matter? We found that students working term-time nevertheless managed to meet deadlines for coursework and assignments – 85 per cent indicated they never missed such deadlines. So although such students may consider that they have not spent enough time on their assignments (for example, through missing lectures and seminars, and not accessing additional learning resources) they have nevertheless tried to minimize the more obvious effects of term-time work on their marks, by avoiding being penalized for late submission of work. A small group of staff in another institution summed up such approaches to studying as follows:

Students adopt pragmatic learning strategies . . . whatever is necessary to 'pass' and this produces a broad cultural change that affects all students and teachers. Lecturers' expectations change, teaching styles change . . . a more instrumental and pragmatic higher education . . . and a vicious circle is established . . . lower expectations by staff make it easier (for students) to work during term . . . and less contact time – a result of other factors – also makes term-time work easier to fit in.

(Notes of focus group with staff at a new university)

At this point we should step back and consider what this more instrumental and pragmatic higher education really means for the student experience. From the foregoing I have given a sense of (some) undergraduates meeting the basic commitments to higher education studies, but not necessarily having the time (nor inclination?) to engage with other activities and processes, which staff at least do not see as 'optional extras', even though students may consider them as such. In trying to answer the question 'does this matter?' we can turn to some findings emerging from a comprehensive review of recent American research into how higher education affects students. Pascarella and Terenzini (2005) have reviewed the vast body of research published since 1990. They have identified some very clear messages relating to the wider aspects of student life: for example, student learning is shaped not only by formal learning and teaching processes but also

by the extent to which students take advantage of the range of learning opportunities provided by the institution both inside and outside the classroom . . . interactions with peers and faculty members appear to have the most consistent out-of-class impact on content acquisition and mastery, particularly when they extend and reinforce what happens in students' other, more formal academic experiences.

(Terenzini, 2004: 12)

In fact, Terenzini goes on to conclude that what matters most for students' intellectual development is the breadth of student involvement in the 'intellectual *and* social experiences of college, rather than any particular type of involvement' (p. 18, original emphasis).

Thus it seems clear that the more instrumental approaches to studying that we found in our study – doing 'just' what is necessary to pass – do indeed matter, since student learning is impoverished as a result.

But we should also recognize that the existence of term-time working as part and parcel of the undergraduate student experience is not the only reason why students may seem less engaged in the academic enterprise. The student population no longer consists mainly of young people studying away from home, with very few commitments other than 'being a student'. The more diverse student population is characterized by students of different ages, from a variety of ethnic groups having different social backgrounds, having different living arrangements, and experiencing different lives 'outside' of being a student. In this current climate of up-front tuition fees and reliance on student loans rather than widely available maintenance grants, we should also note that some students could not even 'afford' to be a student if it were not for the additional source of income that regular paid employment during term-time provides. In our study on debt and term-time working, we found it was low income students, minority ethnic students, older students and those living at home who were more likely to work term-time (or work longer hours) than their counterparts. Thus the adverse effects of term-time working on the 'whole' student experience are likely to impact upon different groups of students in different ways. The gap in accumulated social capital between those advantaged on entry and those less advantaged is likely to widen.

At this point I want to turn to another study recently completed by our Centre, which posed the question 'does extending opportunity to enter higher education necessarily extend opportunities in the labour market?' (Blasko, 2002; Brennan and Shah, 2003). In other words, to what extent is there social equity at the point of exit from higher education, and are there aspects of the higher education experience that serve as facilitators or barriers to the achievement of this equity? The study (the 'access to what?' study) can shed some further light on the issue of students' higher education experiences, and in particular their engagement with activities outside of the formal processes of teaching and learning which might add to their social capital.

Barriers to converting educational opportunity into employment opportunity

The study was undertaken in two phases: a re-analysis of a large data-set of a nationally representative sample of UK graduates collected in 1998/99, almost four years after their graduation in 1994/95; and interviews with staff and students in four universities plus more limited discussions in three other universities. The results of the data analysis supported those of other studies that indicate that graduate success in the labour market is to some extent associated with the social and educational characteristics of the graduates. The study found that social class, ethnicity and age, type of institution attended and subject studied, entry qualifications, and degree results all had an effect on employment success. Even when the type of institution attended and the subject studied, and factors such as entry qualifications and class of degree were taken into account, the study found that students' background characteristics still had an impact (albeit more limited) on employment (Blasko, 2002; Brennan and Shah, 2003). Moreover, these background factors (socio-economic background, ethnic background, age) interacted with educational factors (subject studied, institution attended) to create distinctive patterns of disadvantage. For example, going to a pre-1992 university gave labour market advantages to most types of graduates except for women from lower socio-economic backgrounds (Brennan and Shah, 2003).

The study then considered what the influence of other factors related to students' higher education experiences might be, in terms of subsequent success in the labour market. The original survey had collected data from students about their work experience during higher education, their participation in extra-curricular activities, any overseas experiences, their ways of looking for a job after graduation, and the characteristics of the employers they subsequently worked for. The picture that emerged from analysis of these various factors was not clear-cut, and while influences could be detected they were sometimes not very large (even though statistically significant). But many of these factors were found to be important in two different respects: they could assist in enhancing job prospects and they were not equally available to all types of students. We shall look at just one such factor – participation in extra-curricular activities.

In the study, we found that students who spent more than 10 hours a week on extra-curricular activities were particularly likely to be more successful in their subsequent employment. Such findings tend to confirm other studies which have shown that participation in certain extra-curricular activities (sports, clubs, societies) are likely to have positive impacts on employment prospects (Brown and Scase, 1994; Purcell *et al.*, 1999). We found that working-class students enjoyed similar employment benefits from extra-curricular activities. However, we also found that these students spent less time on such activities and were more likely than other students to spend no time at all on them. For working-class students, no time at all spent on such activities was particularly associated with less successful employment outcomes. Mature students did not seem to enjoy similar benefits. Moreover, they were far less likely to have spent a significant amount of time on extra-curricular activities: 62% of the 25+ age group had spent no time at all on such activities, compared with only 21% of the under 21-year-olds. So it seems that certain groups of students are less likely to engage in extra-curricular activities – long held as an important facet of the student experience – and their failure to participate seems to disadvantage them in the labour market.

Why are certain student groups less likely to take part in extra-curricular activities? One obvious reason might be that it is these same students who are more likely to be engaged in term-time work (as noted above) and so do not have the 'spare time' to do so. Older students are also more likely to have family/home commitments that will reduce their scope for participating. We should also note that students living at home or with their partner (rather than on their own or with other students) were also more likely to do term-time work. Other studies have also shown that students from working-class backgrounds often live at home whilst studying (NAO, 2002). But does 'living at home' whilst at university, rather than living on campus or near the campus with fellow students, mean that students will not engage in the wider social aspects of university life? As noted above, the student characteristic of 'living at home' is bound up with other characteristics (for example, being more likely to be from a working-class background; more likely to be working term-time) so it is difficult to isolate this one particular facet of a student's life. However, interviews held with some students as part of CHERI's 'access to what?' study can throw some light on students' views about living at home with their family. In the examples given below, both students were from working-class backgrounds, but neither student was mature, nor had their 'own' family:

> I wasn't staying there . . . I wouldn't see friends of mine at university as much as you would in the evening . . . 'cause I'd just go there for my lectures or whatever, and then I'd come straight home . . . more of a kind of job in many ways, just go for your lectures and assignments and then come back home . . .

When asked whether they had been involved in any extra curricular activities, the same student replied

> No, just played football . . . that's what I was into at the time . . . wasn't into anything like politics or anything like that . . . the debate clubs . . . looking back I suppose I could have done with mixing in a bit more . . . getting involved with clubs . . .

When pressed to explain 'what' might have come from such mixing, the student replied

> Sharing experiences really . . . mixing with other groups . . . about life or the world or whatever . . . different religions, different sets of people, from different parts of the UK . . . broaden your horizons really . . . make you more knowledgeable, less intolerant . . . when you're to-ing and fro-ing [to university] it makes it difficult . . . you've got no base to go to . . . whereas everyone else can go to their flat or wherever . . . 'cause if you did [stay around to go to clubs, to meet friends] by the time

you got home it would be late and obviously you've got things to do at home as well, just like anyone has things to do in their own home . . .

A second student indicated:

> I didn't really socialize that much . . . there were lots and lots of activities that you could get involved in . . . but I'm not really a sort of very active person into sports, socializing . . . my time was spent on my books really!

When asked if they regretted not socializing, the student replied:

> Don't regret that! . . . there were horror stories that you would hear on the Monday morning . . . people had been out raving all night, coming in not quite sure where they were . . . thought socializing all weekend just wasn't advisable!

As we see, for each student there did seem to be plenty of opportunities to engage in social networks: but whereas one student now regretted not having taken up those opportunities, the other student felt no such regrets.

We can contrast these experiences with another student from a working-class background who had moved away from home to study, and considered he had gained a lot from the social aspects of his university life:

> I picked up as much as a person growing up as I did educationally . . . friends that I made at university [are] better friends than friends I've known for 17/18 years back home . . . and I'm closer to them [from university] . . . got more in common with them even though we came from very different social backgrounds . . . so many different clashes of culture, classes . . . rather than say the friends I had back home . . . probably most of them working class with very little foresight or view of what happened outside that [home] area . . .

The experience of studying higher education courses in further education

So far in this chapter, we have tended to draw on empirical studies involving undergraduates studying in higher education institutions. However, we should not overlook the fact that, within mass provision, a significant minority of the undergraduate population studies in further education colleges. Traditionally such students have lived local to the college, and many will have moved into their higher education programme from another course in the college. Parry *et al.* (2004) considered the question: 'what, if anything, is different or distinctive about the higher education offered' in these colleges as compared to HE offered in higher education institutions? The study involved secondary analysis of existing data sets, a survey of higher education coordinators in further education colleges, and investigation of nine case studies involving matched 'pairs' of HE and FE institutions delivering the 'same' higher education programme. The case studies involved focus group discussions with students.

The study found that students shared similar perceptions of what was valued or problematic about their higher education experience, wherever they studied. For most students the most worthwhile features were career prospects and job opportunities, and this was underpinned by a strong appreciation of the wider personal, social and educational development associated with higher education study. However, it is interesting to note that, whereas younger students in universities welcomed the opportunities to have a social life and take part in a lively social scene, the younger college-based students felt that the absence of a social scene meant that 'it doesn't feel like being at university' (Parry *et al.*, 2004: 22). So in contrast to the situation noted above, whereby university students living at home may choose *not* to take part in the wider social life of the university, for these college students (who were also likely to be living at home) such a 'choice' did not present itself.

This rather specific example gives rise to further considerations about 'sites' of higher education learning, and aspects of social capital that might be accrued through student engagement within such sites. Take, for example, government's continuing commitment to expanding undergraduate higher education through foundation degrees, such that by 2010 there will be 100,000 (full-time equivalent) foundation degree students. These programmes, by their very design, are meant to be delivered through a combination of institution-based and work-based learning (and the institution-base may well be a further education college, rather than a higher education institution). It will be interesting to see to what extent foundation degree student experiences of engagement with social networks and development of social capital differ from those of other higher education students.

Conclusions

The term 'student diversity' is regularly used in UK higher education policy documents, and is used in a positive sense of providing evidence of greater social equity in access to higher education. But do we really know enough about the diversity of student experiences within higher education? Do we have a clear understanding of how different student experiences impact on students' general learning and development, over and above the more tangible outputs of grades and marks, and what consequences might flow for students' subsequent transitions out of higher education?

I have drawn on some empirical studies to show how the student experience is changing, and how diverse groups of students are now experiencing being 'a student'. What seems clear is that very many higher education students may now be 'missing out' (for whatever reason) on opportunities to develop and engage in social networks whilst at university, i.e. they may be failing to develop their social capital. For some students missing out may be a conscious decision to opt out, but for others they may have no option *but* to 'miss out' since they have other commitments (be it family responsibilities or doing their term-time job to finance their time at university). Yet it may be these same students who might derive most benefit from using their time at university to develop their social capital. Moreover, as noted above, the research evidence clearly suggests that students' intellectual development is weakened as a result of not having a broad involvement in *both* intellectual and social experiences. Furthermore, students' subsequent progress in the labour market might also be negatively affected by lack of engagement in extra-curricular, social activities.

What key messages can we draw?

First, policy-makers should not overlook the fact that a diverse student population also means a diversity of student experiences. The consequences of such diversity for the quality of student learning should not be neglected in modelling the consequences of policy decisions. More particularly the impact of policy interventions (be it changes in student finance or new forms of undergraduate programmes) on the student experience must be evaluated in a broad sense, as well as any narrow sense (say, size of student debt, employment success of foundation degree students).

Second, there is the question of what, if anything, higher education institutions might do to try and ensure that all their students have the opportunity to be able to benefit from a broad student experience, regardless of competing commitments. Our Centre's 'access to what?' report listed a number of suggestions, including a greater recognition of the diversity of sources of knowledge and learning, which the personal development planning element of the new student profiles might encourage (see http://www.qaa.ac.uk.crntwork.progfileHE7guidelines/policystatements for policy on progress files in HE), and a greater propensity to permit students to 'stretch' their course over a longer period of time, if needs be. Elsewhere, notions of rethinking the nature of the student experience as one of 'negotiated engagement' are being discussed (see, for example, McInnis, 2001; 2003) whereby universities are being encouraged to set some 'non-negotiables' for students. For McInnis, universities have 'a responsibility to assert their leadership in society and should therefore make demands on students in terms of their academic orientation and application, and *ensure that students reap the long-term benefits of a broader social experience of learning*' (McInnis, 2003: 17, emphasis added).

I suggest that before such negotiating positions are approached, let alone agreed, we need to have a much clearer understanding of what it currently means to be a higher education student, and to have a sense of what are the essential characteristics of the diverse higher education student experiences.

References

Blasko, Z. (2002) *Access to What? Analysis of Factors Determining Graduate Employability.* Bristol: Higher Education Funding Council for England.

Brennan, J. and Shah, T. (2003) *Access to What? Converting Educational Opportunity into Employment Opportunity.* London: Centre for Higher Education Research and Information, Open University.

Brown, P. and Scase, R. (1994) *Higher Education and Corporate Realities: Class, Culture, and the Decline of Graduate Careers.* London: UCL Press.

Callender, C. and Wilkinson, D. (2003) *2002/03 Student Income and Expenditure Survey: Students' Income, Expenditure and Debt in 2002/03 and Changes Since 1998/99.* Sheffield: Department for Education and Skills.

Coffield, F. (ed.) (2000) *The Necessity of Informal Learning.* Bristol: The Policy Press.

Field, J. and Spence, L. (2000) Informal learning and social capital, in F. Coffield (ed.) *The Necessity of Informal Learning.* Bristol: The Policy Press.

McInnis, C. (2001) Signs of disengagement? Responding to the changing work and study patterns of full-time undergraduates in Australian universities. Paper presented to the Consortium of HE Researchers annual conference, Dijon, France, 2–4 September.

McInnis, C. (2003) New realities of the student experience: how should universities respond? Paper presented at European Association for Institutional Research annual conference, Limerick, Ireland, 24–7 August.

McNay, I. (1994) The future student experience, in S. Haselgrove (ed.) *The Student Experience.* Buckingham: SRHE and OU Press.

NAO (National Audit Office) (2002) *Widening Participation in Higher Education.* Report by the Comptroller and Auditor General, HC 485.

Parry, G., Davies, P. and Williams, J. (2004) *Difference, Diversity and Distinctiveness – Higher Education in the Learning and Skills Sector.* London: Learning and Skills Development Agency.

Pascarella, E. and Terenzini, P. (2005) *How College Affects Students (Vol.2): A Third Decade of Research.* San Francisco, CA: Jossey-Bass.

Pilkington, P. (1994) Student financial support, in S. Haselgrove (ed.) *The Student Experience.* Buckingham: SRHE and OU Press.

Purcell, K., Hogarth, T., Pitcher, J. and Jacobs, C. (1999) *Graduate Opportunities, Social Class and Age: Employers' Recruitment Strategies in the New Graduate Labour Market.* London: Council for Industry and Higher Education/Institute for Employment Research.

Terenzini, P. (2004) How college affects students: a third decade of research. Plenary address to Academic Affairs Summer Conference of the American Association of State Colleges and Universities, Albuquerque, July.

Van Dyke, R., Little, B. and Callender, C. (forthcoming) *Impact of Debt and Term-time Working on Higher Education.* London: Universities UK.

6

The Demise of the Graduate Labour Market

Richard Pearson

Introduction

Students and society invest in higher education for a multitude of reasons. These include the advancement of knowledge, the education of students, generating skills and skilled people for the labour market and prosperity, and enhancing social mobility and equality.

The growth in higher education and associated participation rates in recent decades has been fuelled by demographics, exhortations for students to stay in education longer, rising levels of educational attainment, and the enhanced employment prospects for those with degrees. The need to finance this expansion of HE has led to the government transferring more of the cost to the student, initially reducing, then abolishing grants (although some have been subsequently re-introduced) and introducing fees for full-time undergraduates. The latter, which markedly increased the cost for many students in the late 1990s, barely made a dent in the rising demand for higher education. As a result, and with the effectiveness of UK degree pro-grammes, the UK continues to have one of the highest graduation rates (i.e. number of new graduates, as a percentage of the age group) in the developed world.

The government, with its 50 per cent participation target, argues that the expansion of higher education continues to be good economically, a view largely supported by the OECD (OECD, 2002). However, as the costs have risen for both the state and the students, there are sceptical voices who question the lack of economic evidence to support expansion. For example, while economic 'rate of return' analyses have shown a positive return to a degree holder in the past, they have inevitably related to very different numbers and types graduating, and to a different labour market context. Not all types of course and student have experienced such a good return. It is also unclear whether the returns are due to the innate abilities of the cohort, to their higher education, or to employer screening and credentials in the labour market. Looking ahead, while growth is expected to continue for managers and professionals, this is only part of the story, as much of the growth in employment is expected to be in low-level service jobs. A recent particular concern has been the lack of direct evidence to support expansion through the new foundation degrees (Keep, 2003). Here, history shows that many of those taking the equivalent, earlier qualifications such as HNCs and HNDs have found little demand for their skills in the labour market and have simply used them as a stepping stone to first degree programmes.

Concerns about graduate unemployment and the question as to whether the UK is 'producing too many graduates' have accompanied each modern growth phase in higher education. The question was being asked in the early 1970s, hot on the heels of the post-Robbins expansion, in the early 1980s, and then again in the 1990s when the growth agenda reappeared. Pearson *et al.* (2000) gives a historic perspective on trends in supply and demand. It has reappeared today as the system expands towards 50 per cent participation. What then have been the employment outcomes of successive generations of students? What might this tell us about the prospects for future generations of graduates? What are some of the messages for some of the key stakeholders: students, employers, HE and government?

The growth in higher education

While the last two decades have seen the numbers graduating double, this population of new graduates has also become far more diverse. Women are now the majority (over 55 per cent); one third are mature entrants; one in three enter with non A level qualifications; one in seven come from ethnic minority backgrounds; a growing proportion study while living at home; while more have studied for sub-degree, and for postgraduate qualifications. They now graduate from over 150 universities and colleges. The range of subjects studied has also grown dramatically with many more students graduating with degrees in the 'new' subjects such as media studies, than are graduating with traditional degrees in subjects such as history or chemistry. Indeed, there is now serious concern that the decline in student interest, and the number of new graduates, in chemistry and physics in particular, are likely to undermine the nation's scientific base, with departmental closures raising issues of where strategic decision-making should lie. Perhaps the one dimension to show the least change has been the proportion of students entering with backgrounds in the 'lower' social classes. While the proportions have shown a marked rise, albeit from a low base, HE is still dominated by students from middle-class backgrounds. Across all these groups, employment prospects associated with higher education are now a major consideration for most of those applying for places in HE, and especially those from 'non-traditional' backgrounds such as ethnic minority groups (Connor *et al.*, 1999).

The transition into initial employment

Looked at crudely, as HE in the UK has moved from an elite to a 'mass' system, the numbers of graduates gaining employment have continued to rise, paralleling the growth in HE. The proportion entering employment within six months of graduation rose from 40 per cent in the 1960s to a peak of over 60 per cent in the 1970s, fluctuating and falling to lows of 50 per cent in recessions, and returning to 60 per cent plus for the last decade. In addition a small minority, under 2 per cent, have gone into self-employment each year, a particularly important destination for those studying on art related courses. Here their careers resemble a patchwork of short-term contracts and projects, self-employment and freelance work, as well as work outside their profession with low monetary rewards. While initial unemployment rates have fluctuated with the economic cycle, reaching peaks of over 20 per cent, they have not risen with the long-term expansion of HE, and have fallen since the early 1990s to under 8 per cent. These low initial unemployment rates have been consistently below those experienced in many continental European countries. The numbers continuing immediately to further study have fluctuated over the years, but have formed a declining proportion of recent cohorts.

While increasing numbers have been moving into employment, many of the major recruiters have continued to complain about skill shortages and recruitment difficulties at almost every point in the economic cycle. On the face of it, this suggests a positive picture of graduates' employability and an encouragement for the system to expand. The truth is, of course, more complex.

Changing initial graduate employment

In the 1970s the majority of graduates entering employment did so via a small number of in-house management training schemes, and a growing number of professional and functional training schemes. In addition, a fluctuating but growing number were direct entrants into a widening range of jobs where they were often in direct competition with non-graduates. For example, the 1970s were the starting point for graduate recruitment into the retail sector. By the 1980s accountancy had moved to largely graduate intakes; employers in the sector are now some of the major recruiters of graduates. The legal profession followed seeking significant numbers, as have the armed forces, the police and nursing, while the IT and retailing sectors grew their graduate intakes dramatically in the 1980s and 1990s.

Interestingly, the major recruiters of graduates, as represented by the Association of Graduate Recruiters (AGR), have shown little change in their overall intakes over the last decade, the current numbers being similar to those recruited during the economic boom of the late 1980s. These (major) recruiters account for only about 15 per cent of more than 200,000 new graduates now entering employment each year. These totals are dominated by some major recruiters, each seeking 500 or more new graduates, with at least one accountancy firm recruiting over 1000 new graduates each year. In 2003, another 30,000 new graduates entered teaching, and a similar number entered health-related professions.

Of those going into employment in 2003, half went into what have traditionally been considered as graduate jobs, i.e. as managers, administrators, and in professional roles. One in six went into associate professional and technical occupations, which were not generally considered to be of graduate level a decade ago. One third went into lower level jobs. The numbers going into managerial and professional occupations has not, however, kept up with the expansion in supply, with the proportions entering such occupations having fallen in recent years despite the growth in the underlying economy. The percentage entering associate professional and technical level occupations has risen, with the proportion going into non-graduate jobs rising even faster (Figure 6.1). However, some of what have been traditionally 'non-graduate' jobs now require higher skill levels and recruiters are seeking graduates to fill them, as in laboratory work in the pharmaceutical industry. In other cases employers have been increasing the education requirements of jobs, in part because more graduates are available and apply, as has been the case with many retailers, although some appear to be reverting back to A level entry streams. Other employers recruit graduates because they apply, and regardless of their qualifications. In some but not all of these cases the graduates are adding value and 'growing' the job, transforming it for their successors (Mason, 1999).

Many graduates are now consciously postponing their move into employment by staying on for further study or research, or taking a belated gap year. In other cases they are taking on temporary, relatively low-skilled work while they consider career options, or to pay off the debts incurred while they were studying (Pollard *et al.*, 2004). Others wanting to enter sectors such as the media and advertising often have to take low-level jobs, sometimes without pay, to gain some work experience, which may then give them an opportunity to get a 'foot on the ladder' or as a stepping stone into a specific career. Overall, one in three graduates now enter jobs on fixed term or temporary contracts.

Within these averages, like all others, there are marked differences between different groups of graduates. Perhaps the most interesting are the marked differences in initial employment outcomes for graduates from different disciplines. Those in medicine, education, computer science and engineering have been the most likely to enter 'graduate jobs'. Not surprisingly, those from engineering and maths were more likely to go into professional roles, while those in business studies were more likely to go into management roles. In contrast, those graduating from the humanities, languages, biological sciences and mass communications were the least likely to enter 'graduate jobs,' i.e. as managers and administrators, professionals, and nowadays into associate professional and technical occupations (Figure 6.2).

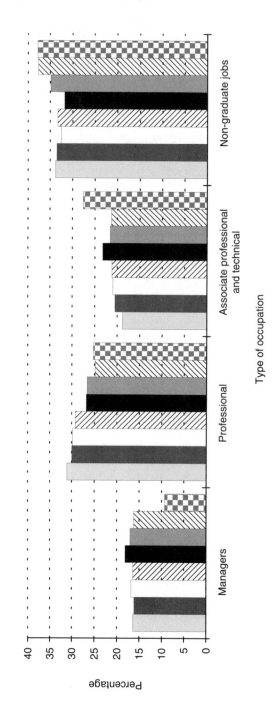

Figure 6.1 Changing first employment, 1996–2003

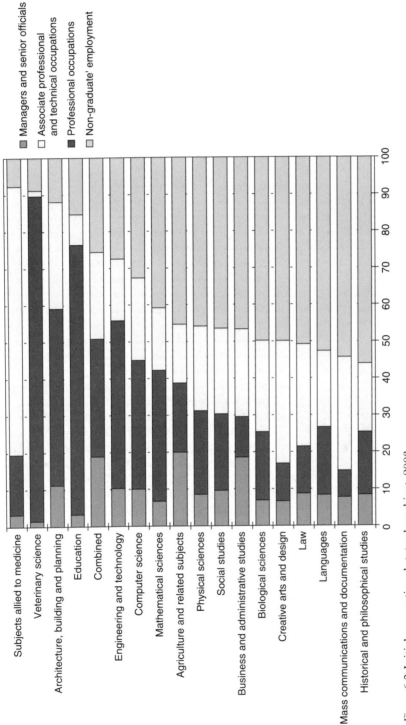

Managers and senior officials
Associate professional and technical occupations
Professional occupations
Non-graduate' employment

Subjects allied to medicine
Veterinary science
Architecture, building and planning
Education
Combined
Engineering and technology
Computer science
Mathematical sciences
Agriculture and related subjects
Physical sciences
Social studies
Business and administrative studies
Biological sciences
Creative arts and design
Law
Languages
Mass communications and documentation
Historical and philosophical studies

Figure 6.2 Initial occupational status by subject, 2003

They were also more likely to be unemployed six months after graduation. Similar patterns are to be found in other European countries and to some extent the United States (Pearson *et al.*, 2000).

Growth has not solved employers' recruitment difficulties

While the level of reported recruitment difficulties among the major recruiters has been strongly influenced by the economic cycle, the doubling of the numbers graduating in the 1990s only partially eased the incidence of recruitment difficulties among the major recruiters. However, recruitment problems relate more to issues of quality than quantity. They most frequently relate to the personal qualities of applicants and the need for recruits to have better 'personal' skills and competencies in areas such as business awareness and commercial skills, project management, team working and communication alongside any technical competence that is required. Indeed, in the UK about two thirds of jobs advertised for graduates are open to graduates from all disciplines, in contrast to many parts of Europe where there is a much closer alignment between degree subject and career. The main group where there have been serious numerical shortages has been in some public sector professions, such as teaching, especially in key subjects such as maths, physics and languages, although these concerns have eased considerably recently as teachers' pay has improved and special incentives have been offered. There are currently concerns about the small numbers wanting to enter social work and care roles, which may require similar government-funded incentives.

Despite these recruitment difficulties, the major recruiters have not responded by markedly raising starting salaries for graduates, suggesting that these problems are not seen as too severe. While the headline starting salaries for some graduates seem to rise ever higher, with a few recruiters now paying in excess of £50,000 in law and banking in central London, changes to the median starting salary for the major recruiters have largely tracked rises in median weekly earnings. Median figures can, of course, hide wide differences. While the median starting salaries among the major recruiters are now around £20,000 per year, as is also the case for teachers, the police and fast track civil servants, many jobs are advertised for graduates at salaries around or below £15,000, especially in the care and leisure sectors. Many other graduates are starting on salaries well below £13,000, especially outside London.

More graduates are settling in the longer term

The last decade has seen more graduates experiencing periods of uncertainty in the early years after graduation, as evidenced by the increasing incidence of employment on short-term contracts, and lower level jobs.

However, within seven years of graduation, many more had settled in to what they regarded as suitable, long-term employment. For example, seven years after graduation, half of those who started in 'non-graduate' jobs in the mid to late 1990s, had moved on into graduate level occupations: they painted a positive picture of their employment experiences. They said they were using their knowledge and skills, with even two thirds of those in non-graduate jobs saying they used skills they learned in HE in their jobs. Overall, the majority of graduates perceived themselves as being in appropriate jobs for people with their skills and qualifications (Elias and Purcell, 2003). The high initial rates of unemployment also fell quickly over time. Nevertheless, more than 10 per cent, a significant minority, appear to remain in non-graduate jobs seven years after graduation (Figure 6.3). These, and similar cohort studies have focused on those graduating in the early and mid-1990s, so some of this improvement in their prospects may be accounted for by the improvement in the wider economy in the 1990s. The marked subject differences in the early transitions, noted above, largely continued in the subsequent five to seven years of employment, with, for example, those from the humanities, arts and biological sciences, older graduates and women showing least satisfactory progression after graduation (Elias and Purcell, 2004; Connor *et al.*, 1997). However, what we do not know from these and other similar cohort studies, are the experiences of the third or more who did not reply, who may have had far less positive experiences, and lower satisfaction levels.

Finally, we do know from the national *Labour Force Survey* (ONS, 2004) that graduates across the generations earn higher salaries, have lower unemployment and have a higher investment in training than non-graduates. Whether this is attributable to innate abilities, the added value of higher education, or

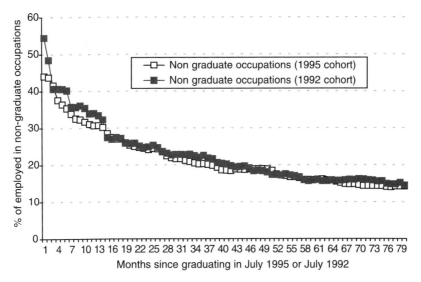

Figure 6.3 – see Elias and Purcell, 2004, and copy Chart 3

a form of credentialism that enables graduates to move to the head of the job queue remains unclear. Most importantly, all this data, by its nature, can only look backwards at the experiences of the past, and in the words of the financial regulator: 'past performance is not a guarantee for future performance'.

Conclusions

There have been massive changes in higher education since the 1970s in the characteristics of the population of new graduates, and in the labour market. At the start of the twenty-first century the labour market for graduates can be characterized by two words: 'diversity' and 'fragmentation'. Those terms appear in other chapters in this volume.

The increasingly diverse nature of the population graduating is clear, with women in the majority, and with significant numbers coming from the lower social classes, ethnic minority groupings, those aged over 25 at graduation, those who entered with vocational qualifications and those who stayed in their home area to study. The notion of the traditional 'new graduate' as being a young white middle-class male who had left home to study is a thing of the past.

Likewise the idea that all new graduates move effortlessly into 'graduate' jobs is a thing of the past, despite the attention given to this minority of jobs and their associated salaries in the media. For the majority, moving into employment is a slow transition with many experiencing several years of turbulence and having to compete for jobs with non-graduates and experienced candidates, before they settle into an increasingly fragmented labour market. A significant minority remains in low-level jobs five or more years after graduation. Personal backgrounds, motivations, and subject of study have a significant influence on their employment outcomes. Nevertheless, despite the growth in the numbers graduating, recruiters are still concerned that many candidates lack the necessary personal skills and competition for the best candidates remains intense.

As such, it is neither appropriate to think in terms of a 'typical' graduate, nor to think of a 'typical' graduate job or career or salary. To do so would mislead. A degree is not a guaranteed passport to a good job, although it should be beneficial when competing in the labour market.

The coming years are likely to see further fragmentation and segmentation in what has been thought of as the 'graduate labour market', with recruitment to many more 'graduate' jobs taking place in the operation of the wider recruitment market. The small graduate labour market that does exist will be focused on the activities of a minority of recruiters and professions, with structured recruitment schemes focused, by virtue of numbers and the qualities sought, on a small minority of graduates, perhaps echoing those of the 1960s and 1970s. For most graduates the transition from higher education into employment will take place within the context of broader labour market developments. As such we should no longer talk about the graduate labour market as a discrete entity, rather we are seeing its demise as most graduates enter work through the operation of the wider labour market.

The evidence as to whether the economy needs more graduates in the future, is ambiguous and growth raises many policy issues. I deal with three.

First, with the growing emphasis on the 'market' deciding student numbers, and undergraduates starting to pay more of the full economic cost of their study, a critical need is to ensure that they have realistic expectations and make as well-informed choices as is possible in an uncertain world. Students need to ensure that they develop their personal and employability skills, as well as the knowledge gained in HE. They need to be supported by up-to-date and accessible careers information and guidance well before, during and after they graduate if they are to make well-informed decisions about choices at these three stages. The provision of work experience can help students understand the work context, while helping recruiters by improving the supply of relevant graduates and acting as a filter or screen to help simplify the recruitment and selection process.

Second, the fact that many employers have not been able to get all the 'good' graduates they have sought in part reflects a growing emphasis on the need for recruits to both technical and more generalist roles to have the right personal qualities. That sends a message to students and HEIs. In other cases, however, it reflects an over-reliance on recruiting from certain universities or inadequately defined selection criteria. Recruiters need to consider carefully the diverse range of jobs and careers they need to fill, the competencies needed, and how they will identify them, as qualifications may provide little guidance as to capability. This problem may be exacerbated by the increased use of web-based filtering and screening of candidates now used by many recruiters. Overemphasis on targeting particular types of graduates or universities unnecessarily restricts the pool of talent seen and maximizes the competition for recruits (Barber and Hill, 2005).

Finally, the government's multiple objectives appear, on the face of it, difficult to reconcile. It wants to further widen participation, to ensure a suitable supply of graduates in key 'economic' disciplines such as maths and the physical sciences, where numbers of applicants have been falling for some years and to improve the financial position of HE so it remains internationally competitive, while keeping a lid on public expenditure. Moving more of the cost on to the students and encouraging the expansion of two-year (foundation) degrees has been a tentative first step to reconciling these goals.

A bolder policy would be for HE to restructure degrees into two-year basic degrees, followed by two years of specialization for a master's degree. The government could then focus public money on maximizing participation for the first two years, extending the educational maintenance allowances paid to 16–18-year-olds. It could also give focused bursaries and additional funding for HE for the second two years. This can underpin the advancement of knowledge in subjects such as history and philosophy, and underpin economic needs in more vocational areas, which range from languages to the physical sciences, by trying to stem the fall in applicants, though initiatives at secondary school level are also needed. Employers could then help to boost the supply in what they regard as key areas by sponsoring students in line with their economic needs, while as many students as wanted to could take out loans to fund their second two years if they think that beneficial. Thus the state ensures basic provision, and the market decides the balance.

References

Barber, L. and Hill, D. (2005) *Is Graduate Recruitment Meeting Business Needs?* Brighton: Institute for Employment Studies (IES) and Council for Industry and Higher Education (CIHE).

Connor, H., La Valle, I., Pollard, E. and Millmore, B. (1997) *What Did Graduates Do Next?* Brighton: Institute for Employment Studies

Connor, H., Burton, R., Pearson, R., Pollard, E. and Regan, J. (1999). *Making the Right Choice.* London: Universities UK.

Elias, P. and Purcell, K. (2004) *Is Mass Higher Education Working?* National Institute Economic Review. London: NIESR.

HESA (2003) Destinations of Leavers from Higher Education. Cheltenham: Higher Education Statistics Agency.

Keep, E. (2003) *HE Expansion and the Evidence on Economic Demand for Graduates – Another Failure of 'Evidence Based' Policy Making?* SRHE/ESRC seminar series.

Mason, G. (1999) *The Labour Market for Engineering, Science and IT Graduates,* DfEE Research Report RR112. London: DfEE.

OECD (Organization for Economic Co-operation and Development) (2002) *Education at a Glance.* Paris: OECD.

ONS (2004) *Labour Force Survey.* London: Office of National Statistics.

Pearson, R., Aston, J., Bates, P. and Jogger, N. (2000) *The IES Graduate Review 2000.* Brighton: Institute for Employment Studies.

Pollard, E., Pearson, R. and Willison, R. (2004) *Next Choices: Career Choices Beyond University.* Brighton: Institute for Employment Studies.

Part Three

Academic policies and processes

7

What Impact are Technologies Having and How are They Changing Practice?

Gráinne Conole

Introduction

The Internet and associated tools have now been used in education for more than a decade. This period coincides with a dramatic increase in participation in higher education (HE) which is likely to continue given the government's widening participation aim to increase participation in HE to 50 per cent by 2010 (DfES, 2003). Information and Communications Technology (ICT) is seen by many as one means of supporting this and as an essential element in delivering higher education efficiently and effectively to a diverse, mass audience. This chapter will reflect on the increasing impact of technologies on education and consider the ways in which tools are being used and how they are changing practice.

The best example of the increased use and importance of ICT is the now ubiquitous use of the computer as a work tool and the replacement of many traditional work modes of communication, such as memos, with email. The two main advances in terms of the use of tools has been their use for information handling and communication. Tools to provide different forms of visualization, to support collaboration or enable more complex cognitive functions are still in their infancy but are likely to form the next major shift in ICT as adaptive and intelligent technologies mature.

There are now a multitude of online learning environments and tools to support teaching and learning. These include communication (email, discussion boards, synchronous chat), authoring and assessment tools, integrated learning environments, information management tools and gateways and portals. The growth in the use of technology to support learning has been fuelled by a raft of national initiatives and strategies, including: the CTI initiative in the 1980s (which became the Learning and Teaching Support Network, now part of the HE Academy (http://www.heacademy.ac.uk/); the Teaching and Learning Technology Programme (http://www.ncteam. ac.uk/projects/tltp/); and a range of programmes from the Joint Information Systems Committee (JISC) – such as the e-Lib programme, X4L, the digital libraries programme and, most recently, the e-pedagogy programme (see http://www.jisc.ac.uk for more information). In terms of policy directives, Dearing made significant references to ICT, including the need for senior managers to be more e-literate (NCIHE, 1997). Building on this, both HEFCE and the DfES have developed e-learning strategies (HEFCE, 2004; DfES, 2004).

There have been a number of key catalysts influencing the uptake of ICT in education. In particular, Virtual Learning Environments (VLEs) quickly gained popularity because they offered easy to use, all in one environments to support learning and teaching. Practitioners found them accessible because they aligned with their existing practice in terms of preparation, delivery and assessment. There has also been a growth in tools for searching and retrieving information and software for managing and manipulating data. In recent years grid-enabled technologies have been applied to support globally distributed research in science (see for example http://www.nesc.ac.uk/.) and recently a national centre has been established to explore the use of these technologies to support social science research (http://www.ncess.org/). Technologies offer practitioners new ways of doing tasks (faster, easier, more comprehensively) but also can have associated drawbacks; for example although the Internet provides access to vast quantities of materials there are increasingly real issues about information overload, access and quality control/authenticity of materials (Conole and Dyke, 2004). Similarly, tools for communication offer opportunities for new forms of dialogue and collaboration but require new forms of literacy and skills.

There is much hype around the potential use of technologies to support learning and teaching: that their use will lead to new forms of learning; that they are adaptable, flexible and personalized; that mobile technologies mean learning can take place anywhere and that they offer the potential to provide students with new forms of representation. More specifically, technologies offer the promise of new opportunities to repurpose and share resources and in particular learning objects, defined by Wiley (2002) as 'digital entities deliverable over the Internet . . . that any number of people can access and use . . . simultaneously', are purported to offer the potential for reuse across a variety of contexts and uses (Littlejohn, 2003). Although there is a grain of truth in all of these, understanding the nature of technologies and their impact is much more complex and multifaceted than these simple headline statements might suggest. This chapter attempts to provide a critique of current tool use and considers how this use is changing practice.

Tools that have changed practice

This section categorizes and describes tools and their use, discussing the ways in which they have changed practice. The focus here is not to give a list of the most technically advanced and innovative tools but rather those that have had the most significant impact on practice. Tools can be classified in terms of their use:

- text and data manipulation;
- presentation and dissemination;
- data analysis;
- information seeking and handling;
- storing and managing information;
- personal management;
- project management;
- communication;
- visualization and brainstorming;
- guidance and support;
- evaluation and assessment;
- specialized, subject-specific use.

Tools are defined as 'software applications that can be used to undertake specific activities or sets of tasks'. They enable the user to undertake a task and are more generic in nature than resources which revolve around content. A more detailed account is available elsewhere (Conole, 2004a).

The following sections describe each category of tool type and their impact on practice.

Manipulating text and data

Word is used ubiquitously and has transformed practice radically since the early 1990s, to such an extent that roles have changed out of all recognition. The most obvious example of this is the demise of the traditional secretary, as there is now no longer a need for dictating, shorthand and typing. But Word has also changed the nature of practice. The ability to type thoughts straight into a document, and to cut and paste and move sections of text around a document, has changed the ways in which we create knowledge. Writing with pen and paper required the user to think linearly, writing only when the text was near completion; in contrast the use of a word processor allows you to think non-linearly and to adapt and develop ideas as they emerge.

Other features within Word are also important. In-built spelling and grammar checkers mean that it is no longer necessary to have an excellent command of English. Therefore, Word (as with many of the other tools discussed in this chapter) forms part of our distributed cognition (Salomon, 1993), or what Perkins refers to as the concept of 'Person-plus' – i.e. that our 'intelligence' is distributed between our minds and past experience and a range of mediated tools and resources (Perkins, 1993). These features mean that practitioners now routinely use Word to prepare for teaching and to create learning materials and assessments for students. Practitioners have become accustomed to building on and adapting previous material. This has enabled them to become more expert at reuse and repurposing and also offers opportunities for them to improve materials based on evaluation of and reflection on their use in practice.

However, the ability to build on previously created documents and to cut and paste chunks of other people's materials raises issues about authenticity in terms of who owns the knowledge created. As a result, academic and student plagiarism are now major concerns (Carroll and Appleton, 2001). It also raises questions about the value and worth of knowledge: if information is so freely and readily available what is its inherent worth? This has a major impact on curriculum development, suggesting the need for a shift away from content to process and the need for assessment strategies that go beyond knowledge recall.

Word and other presentation tools also mean that there is a general expectation that materials will be glossy and well presented. However, there are issues here in terms of a need for criticality – i.e. a well-presented document doesn't necessarily mean that the content is good.

It is worth noting that only a fraction of the features available within Word are used – users tend to use only those functions which are most relevant to their needs. This is a common feature of tool use in general, as there is a trade off between the amount of time needed to learn a package and the perceived benefits to the user. Furthermore, it is not always possible to predict in advance which features users will find most useful (Drori, 2004) and the way in which a tool is used often changes over time as users become more familiar with it and think of new uses; suggesting there is a complex relationship between tool use and changing practice.

A particularly valuable feature of Word, which is being used increasingly, is the ability to track changes and have multiple authors annotate documents and add comments. This collaborative working is becoming more common and is changing practice in terms of the way users are starting to develop and share ideas.

A significant barrier to the use of word processors when they first emerged was the problem of sharing documents across software versions or between different applications. This is no longer an issue but the level of interchange and the ability to manipulate and transform data is now much more sophisticated; material can be easily transferred between different types of application such as Word, Excel and PowerPoint, hence enabling data to be repurposed.

Tools for data manipulation, spreadsheets and databases have also transformed practice by providing mechanisms for dealing with routine calculations. In particular, spreadsheets are used extensively in teaching, particularly in the sciences. They are also used for administration, finance and for assessment purposes. This does raise issues about transfer of sensitive data about students (such as assessment marks) from local machines to the institution's student records system, in terms of maintaining the data integrity. Specialized subject-specific tools for data manipulation have also gained popularity. However, there are concerns that the use of these types of tools may result in students losing general mathematical manipulation skills.

Presentation and dissemination

Like Word, PowerPoint has transformed the way we create knowledge and in particular how we present information and findings to others. An important aspect of this is the ability to build on and adapt previous presentations. PowerPoint has in-built wizards that provide skeletons for different types of presentations, which is useful, but does influence the style and format of the presentation.

The Web is now used routinely in education to support learning and teaching activities for a range of purposes, from searching for information or resources, to booking events or travel. The core benefit of the Web is that it is easy to use and provides access to vast amounts of information. Fundamental to this is that there is now a critical mass of teaching materials available on the Web. This was achieved surprisingly quickly after the release of one of the earliest Web browsers, Mosaic. The key to achieving this was that creating and publishing materials was relatively easy and hence it was possible for practitioners to create websites themselves rather than having to go through an intermediary, such as a publisher or technical support contact. However, there are associated issues about the quality of materials produced and the lack of mechanisms for editing and document control.

An interesting development in presentation of material has been the emergence of prepackaged systems such as Adobe. PDF files produced by Adobe maintain the format and look and feel of the document, but also importantly offer a degree of security to the author as PDF files cannot be edited.

Analysing data

A wide range of software has emerged to facilitate research. Specialist statistical packages such as Statistical Package for the Social Sciences (SPSS, available from www.spss.com) can support quantitative data analyses, enabling researchers to focus less on routine calculation and more on the analysis of statistical outputs. Computer-assisted qualitative data analysis software (CAQDAS) facilitates management of data sets from large-scale projects, from coding through to sophisticated analysis and modelling. Tools for qualitative analysis such as NVivo (available from suppliers such as http://www.qsrinternational.com/) enable the user to manage large quantities of text, enabling them to code, sort and present text in a multitude of ways, allowing them to make richer interpretations of the data than might have been possible when sorting through piles of paper text.

However, there are concerns about the use of such tools; researchers may take the results presented by the packages as given and hence adopt a more superficial and less critical take on the data than they would have if they had manipulated and analysed the data by hand. In addition, these packages offer a sophisticated range of tools and complex operations, which are not always fully understood by users. Lack of understanding of the calculations behind the functions available within these tools means that results can be taken at face value and then presented, and accepted, as significant without the greater understanding that comes from fuller immersion in working directly with the data.

Information seeking and handling

Search engines and portals help to make sense of the vast amount of information available over the Internet by provided tailored views or access to sources of information. Search engines are perhaps one of the most significant of these, providing access to data via simple keywords. Google is now used routinely to support all aspects of practice, from finding a colleague's email address or website to locating resources or reference materials. Internet Google has also produced more specialised services, such as Google Scholar, which focuses on academic output available on the web (http://www.scholar.google.com) and a desktop version (http://www.desktop.-google.com) for managing files on individual machines. As a result we have shifted from a mentality of browsing for materials and use of indexes and tables of content predominant in searching paper-based information to use of metadata as a means of locating relevant information (Duval, 2004). Search tools are becoming more sophisticated, for example by incorporating advanced filtering facilities and using intelligent and adaptive approaches. However, a key criticism of these tools is that they are indiscriminate, returning a mix of unrelated items. Effective use requires criticality on the part of the user and understanding of the context within which the search is undertaken.

Portals provide customized views of a particular set of resources and are often associated with presenting information about an organization or service. For example, institutional portals provide a structured view of information held about the organization and the people who work there. Portals can provide different views for different users and act as a statement about the institution in terms of how it is presented to a wider audience. University portals offer a number of views of information; for example, a prospective student might be guided towards general marketing about the institution and information on courses and the enrolment process, whereas existing students and internal members of staff might be given a view which provided links to departments and their resources, university events and staff contact details.

Storing and managing information

Bibliographic software facilitates powerful online literature searches. Interactive e-journals are changing the nature of academic discourse and the relationship between authors and referees (Hey, 1997; Ingraham, 2000).

Free academically owned publishing mechanisms such as ePrints (Hey, 1997) are now becoming more respected and referenced within the research community, but how does this impact on the future of more traditional journals?

An example of a tool which illustrates the power of interactive journals is the Journal of Interactive Multimedia (JIME) which allows authors and referees to engage in a detailed debate on a submitted academic paper online (http://www-jime.open.ac.uk). The more interactive and detailed discussion possible with this type of system results in a much richer academic discourse and radically impacts on the shape and quality of the paper produced.

A range of tools have emerged for managing information and documents. Documents can be managed within the Windows environment into folders, whereas Endnote and Reference Manager are examples of document management tools specifically designed to help manage research papers and references. They consist of a database in which information about papers is stored, providing an easy way to search and retrieve references. A particularly important aspect of these tools is the way in which they can easily be integrated into Word.

Personal management

Email systems typically now come with a range of tools to support personal management. For example, Microsoft exchange includes a diary tool, a task manager and an address book. These integrated tools are fundamentally changing practice and the way practitioners manage their time and activities. Therefore, an activity in an email can be translated into an action point on the 'to do' list, contact details can be searched and used easily, appointments can be entered on the calendar. In addition these tools also have the potential to be shared, enabling group appointments. Again the value of these tools is dependent on a critical mass of users with a common understanding of how to use them and the perceived benefits. These applications are increasingly being synchronized with hand-held devices, such as mobile phones and Personal Digital Assistants (PDAs), extending the range of desktop function on the move.

Project management

The types of tools prevalent within a particular sector tend to be closely aligned with the types of activities undertaken by that sector. Tools for managing and presenting information and for providing different forms of communication are important within the education sector. In contrast, in the business world where there are often global teams working on joint projects, tools for collaboration and for document management are particularly important. One tool that has transcended the business domain is project management software. This is probably because project management has become increasingly important within education since the early 2000s, as institutions top up their income through externally funded projects and consultancy. The nature of this 'third stream' work is different from the core business of teaching [Wedgwood, this volume]. It focuses around specified projects with an associated set of milestones and deadlines.

Communication

As with the Web, the importance and wide-scale adoption of email as a tool for communication required a critical mass of users to make it useful. An important trigger arose when email was adopted at institutional level, where it quickly became routinely used for supporting all aspects of the business – teaching, learning, research and administration and effectively replaced the memo as the main communication tool. One of the benefits of the use of discussion forums is that they provide a means of extending face-to-face discussions and encourage reflective thinking, provide opportunities for small group work and collaboration. Chat fulfils a different function in terms of enabling real-time synchronous discussions. The length and detail of discussion within chat differs from the more reflective and in-depth discussions which can occur in a discussion forum, but can be valuable for supporting interaction across small groups.

Visualization and brainstorming

Digital cameras are rapidly replacing traditional cameras. Tools such as Adobe photoshop and PaintShopPro are packages that can be used to manipulate digital images and present different views and forms of visualization.

Another important category of visualization tools is the software now available to create electronic concept maps and mindmaps. These have become increasingly important in terms of practitioners using these to develop ideas and prepare materials, and also, directly with students, to take forward and discuss issues and ideas.

Support and guidance

Most commercial software now comes with some form of in-built help system and reference manual. Many also provide templates or 'how to' wizards to guide the user through a particular set of activities. A wizard is a software tool that makes decisions on behalf of the user, based on solicited information and drawing on pre-defined templates. In most cases, the way in which these outputs are generated is hidden from the user. As a result, it is easy to use, but is restrictive in terms of the type and variety of potential outputs or ways in which the user can interact with the tool. Word's paper clip and PowerPoint's template presentations are good examples.

As a consequence, practice has shifted from a culture of reading manuals to a just-in-time culture based on immediate need. This is echoed in research into children's use of gaming software which shows that children learn to use these applications through trial and error and by exploring the package rather than referring to the manual (Sutherland *et al.*, 1999). Another form of guidance is exemplified by a tool for guiding practitioners through the process of learning design called LAMS (Learning Activity Management System) (Dalziel, 2003). In this instance the tool is organized so that users can pick and mix different types of learning activities.

Another category of support tool is toolkits, decision-making systems based on expert models, positioned between wizards and generic conceptual frameworks. They can provide a theoretical overview of an area and hence be used as a point of reference for decision-making (Conole and Oliver, 2002; Oliver *et al.*, 2002). The DialogPlus project has developed a specification for a learning activity design toolkit which aims to guide practitioners through the process of developing pedagogically effective learning activities and appropriate use of relevant tools and resources (Conole and Fill, in press; Bailey *et al.*, 2006).

Evaluation and assessment

Monitoring users online and more specifically tracking and assessing student activities are important parts of the educational process. A number of tools have become popular in recent years for Computer-Assisted Assessment (CAA), including in-built assessment engines in Virtual Learning Environments (VLEs) like Blackboard and WebCT and more specific CAA tools such as Questionmark Perception (http://www.questionmark.com/) or TOIA (http://www.toia.ac.uk). There appears to be marked subject differences in terms of the uptake of CAA and the ways in which it is used. In languages, CAA is often used for diagnostic purposes, whereas in science and engineering CAA has been used for a range of summative and formative purposes. A number of these disciplines have also produced shareable national item-banks (Sclater, 2004). Amongst the perceived benefits of creating online assessments is the reduction in marking of assignments by tutors and the ability to reuse developed items. Interesting questions arise in terms of the difference between paper and computer-based tests. For example, what impact does it have on outcomes if a graph is sketched by hand or manipulated on screen? The differences between paper and computer-based testing have been explored in an extensive study, Pass-IT, across Scottish schools and FE (http://www.passit.ac.uk).

An additional important function available in many educational tools is the ability to monitor and track students online. Many VLEs have in-built tracking facilities which record which pages students have visited and for how long. Also the imprint left of discussions in different tools – such as discussion boards, mailing lists and archived records of chat sessions – can be used to analyse student interactions and track their learning and progress. However, there are some concerns in terms of the research issues of what information can be gleaned by analysis of the content alone (Conole, 2004b), and what meanings can be inferred.

There is increasing concern about potential infringements on individuals which the infiltration of technological applications make possible. Land and Bayne (2001), for example, have critiqued the default inclusion of monitoring tools within virtual learning environments that mean teachers have the power to monitor student activities more closely than ever before. McKenna (2002) critiques the use of the blind copying function in email being used as a potential power tool unknown to recipients of the main email. Similar concerns are being voiced about many of the new 'smart' devices and personal tags which are being included in commercial products that enable providers to target and personalize products more accurately. There are concerns about how these tracking devices might be used for other purposes (such as surveillance) or by other agents.

Specialized, subject-specific use

In addition to the generic tools discussed so far there are a range of more specialized subject-specific tools. Examples include:

- tools which enable students to manipulate data;
- tools for visualization that demonstrate a concept or allow students to see the impact of a change in variables;
- tools for analysis of a corpus of text;
- tools for manipulation and providing different forms of visual representation;
- tools for engineering and design;
- tools which provide virtual 3D presentations, such as the creation of virtual worlds to support authentic language learning;
- tools which enable modelling and simulation;
- tools for audio and video streaming to enable authentic online communication.

An important characteristic here is that they align with the particular culture and activities of the subject domain and to the conceptual approaches and epistemologies of each domain; for example, visual tools in subjects where visualization and manipulation of models are important, communication tools where discursive activities are central.

Factors influencing the uptake of tools

There are a number of common characteristics across these tools which give an indication of why they have had such a significant impact on practice (Table 7.1). Not all indicators need be present. In some cases it will be the perceived ease of use and the ready availability of a tool which have led to the uptake of a tool; in other cases it will be the fact that it has become a de facto standard and, therefore, adopted as a core institutional tool (as is evident with Microsoft office software and increasingly the use of commercial VLEs).

Table 7.1 Factors which influence the uptake of tools

Success factors	Barriers
<ul><li>Easy to use</li><li>Cheap</li><li>Recommended or used by peers</li><li>Support in the form of a workshop</li><li>Closely linked to user needs</li><li>Obvious benefits</li><li>Provides a solution to a problem</li><li>Integrates with existing tools and resources</li><li>Interesting or fun</li><li>Support by a vendor</li><li>Open source</li></ul>	<ul><li>Expensive</li><li>Difficult to obtain</li><li>Complicated to use</li><li>Doesn't link with existing systems</li><li>Too many functions or too much information</li><li>Risk of systems breaking down</li><li>Increased risk where the tools become mission critical</li><li>Functionality which does not obviously map to existing practice</li></ul>

Conclusions and recommendations for policy-makers

The rapidly changing nature of technologies is an inevitable characteristic which needs to be taken account of in decisions about the use of technologies by policy-makers and, in particular, the way in which the prevalence of abundant and rapidly changing information is mediated through communication technologies (Conole and Dyke, 2004). This has a significant impact on social behaviour and practice in that our world is increasingly constituted by information rather than pre-given modes of conduct. This requires practitioners to continuously reassess their needs and also the information which is part of these experiences, instead of relying on custom and tradition to guide action.

The immediacy of access to rapidly changing information is a core feature of new technologies, enabling unprecedented speed of access to materials and world events as they happen. However, this speed also raises issues about the quality of materials and the lack of authority of sources. For policy-makers this gives rise to a number of unintended consequences such as the rise of plagiarism and ownership questions – for example, if a lecturer puts their material on the Web do they own it or does the institution? The speed of change may also militate against reflective and critical thought, fostering surface approaches to learning, raising challenging questions about the very nature of teaching and assessment. How can ICT be used to enable practitioners and students to navigate their way through the maze of changing information and make more informed decisions? There is also a constant tension and mismatch in terms of the skills levels of students and tutors. Students at times may appear to have more sophisticated e-skills levels than their tutors. However, these are often skills of a particular kind (for example, for gaming), whereas the e-literacy skills necessary for academic work (such as critical evaluation of the value of online resources or experience of using office applications) may not be so well developed. Institutions need to be aware of this and put in place appropriate mechanisms to address skills gaps for both students and teachers.

The communication and collaborative abilities of technology offer the potential for learning enriched by enhanced student–student and student–tutor interaction. New technologies have opened up the possibility of new forms of dialogue and communication. ICT offers the potential to develop new forms of online communities and new means of communicating and sharing information. However, this can lead to issues in terms of individuals being 'spread too thinly' across communities, as well as issues of lack of identity and peripheral engagement. Practitioners need support in making effective use of the potential of technologies by providing them with guidance on how to create authentic and engaging learning environments.

Asynchronous communicative tools offer the potential for encouraging reflection and critique with users engaging in discussions over a longer time frame than is possible in face-to-face discussions. The use of CAA tools for formative assessment also has the potential to promote reflection by providing students with immediate feedback on their progress. Clearly, there is nothing inherent in ICT that nurtures reflection – the key is how it is used. ICT has the potential to enable reflection and criticality to be enhanced. But there is a risk that the speed and pace of information change outlined above militates against reflection. It leaves no space for contemplation and considered judgement, and promotes a more pragmatic, immediate response to new information.

Technologies offer the potential for multi-modal and non-linear modes of navigating through information. The non-linearity of the Web leads to the potential for different routes through, and forms of, learning. ICT enables the learner to move beyond linear pathways of learning. Yet much current computer-based training material still appears to follow a linear, assembly line, mode of learning. Many 'e-learning' packages are built on behaviourist principles of atomized experiences that need to be completed in a specified order before the individual is positively reinforced and permitted to move on – a form of electronic page-turning. More complex, multi-modal and non-linear approaches also create issues in terms of increased navigational skills and problems with student potentially getting lost or confused.

We need to find new means of capturing and harnessing user needs as they co-evolve with the use of technologies and, in particular, study and learn from user patterns of behaviour and interaction with the technology. However, how best to predict for the unknown and study changing needs is still a critical issue. We may need to develop innovative approaches to gathering data, for example by using ethnographic research as a means of understanding individuals and considering how technologies can be harnessed for their needs.

To conclude, it is clear that technologies are changing practice. Laurillard has stated that we need to encourage more reflective researchers/ practitioners, so that teachers can reflect and learn from their own interaction with technologies (Laurillard, 2004). Drori has described some of the changing roles which have arisen as a result of the use of technologies and predicts that there will be a shift from passive to more interactive engagement with technologies (Drori, 2004). We need to support the real needs of teachers and ensure that developments are driven by a user-centric rather than technological approach. It is, therefore, important for us to return to the fundamentals of learning in relation to appropriate use of technologies. New developments in learning design are a powerful mechanism for achieving this.

Laurillard also suggests that we need to harness technologies to develop new forms of communication and new models for society. She describes an adaptive model for governance that enables closer dialogue between researchers, practitioners and policy-makers.

It is clear that technologies will continue to have an increasing impact on our lives. There is a real need for research in this area to gain a better understanding of how they can be used to support learning and teaching and for this to be fed back into policy making and practice. What is important is the use of tools in specific contexts. For example, discussion forums do have the potential to move practice on by providing opportunities for sharing ideas and developing thoughts through a network of peers with similar interests. However, it is evident that success depends on a number of factors, e.g. the relevance and timeliness of the topics discussed, the support and guidance provided, and the ways in which the forum is structured and managed.

The next decade will be critical in terms of research into the use of ICT and its impact on practice finding a clear niche and position alongside more established research fields. Research can offer us a real insight into the ways in which technologies can effectively support learning and teaching, and an understanding of how they can be used to improve organizational processes. We should also begin to see the development of new underpinning theories and models of explanation to account for the use of learning technologies, and perhaps even the emergence of new learning paradigms and working practices. Only time will tell.

References

Bailey, C., Fill, K., Zalfan, M. T., Davis, H., Conole, G. and Olivier, B. (2006) Panning for gold: designing pedagogically-inspired learning nuggets, *Educational Technology & Society*, accepted.

Carroll, J. and Appleton, J. (2001), *Plagiarism: a Good Practice Guide*, a JISC commissioned report, available online at http://www.jisc.ac.uk/uploaded_documents/brookes.pdf

Conole, G. (2003) *Understanding your Organisation*, in the JISC Infonet 'Creating an MLE' infokit, http://www.jiscinfonet.ac.uk/InfoKits/creating-an-mle

Conole, G. (2004a) *Report on the Effectiveness of Tools for E-Learning*. Report for the JISC commissioned 'Research Study on the Effectiveness of Resources, Tools and Support Services used by Practitioners in Designing and Delivering E-Learning Activities'.

Conole, G. (2004b) Research questions and methodological issues, in J. Seale (ed.) *From Individual Enthusiasm to Institutional Implementation: A Review of Learning Technology in Post Compulsory Education*. Lisse, NL: Swets and Zeitlinger.

Conole, G. and Dyke, M. (2004) What are the affordances of Information and Communication Technologies?, *ALT-J*, 12(2): 113–24.

Conole, G. and Fill, K. (in press), 'A learning design toolkit to create pedagogically effective learning activities', *Journal of Interactive Multimedia Education*, Special Issue on Learning Design. C. Tattersall (ed), http://www-jime.open.ac.uk/

Conole, G. and Oliver, M. (2002), Embedding theory into learning technology practice with toolkits, *Journal of Interactive Media in Education*, special issue on learning technology theory, http://www-jime.open.ac.uk/

Dalziel, J. (2003) Implementing learning design: the Learning Activity Management System (LAMS), *Proceedings of the ASCILITE 2003 Conference*. Adelaide, 7–10 December.

DfES (Department for Education and Skills) (2003) *The Future of Higher Education*, Government White Paper, available online at http://www.dfes.gov.uk/hegateway/strategy/hestrategy/foreword.shtml

DfES (2004), *Towards a Unified E-Learning Strategy*, http://www.dfes.gov.uk/elearning-strategy/

Drori, J. (2004) Sex, drugs and new interactive services – creating new services for a networked work. Invited public lecture, Colston Symposium. Bristol, 22–23 March.

Duval, E. (2004) 'We're on the road to . . .' *World Conference on Educational Multimedia, Hypermedia and Telecommunications* 2004(1): 3–8 (online). Available at: http://dl.aace.org/15368

HEFCE (2004) Consultation on HEFCE e-learning strategy, available from http://www.hefce.ac.uk

Hey, J. (1997) E-journals for research: the user perspective, *Serials* 10(1): 65–8.

Ingraham, B. (2000) Scholarly rhetoric in digital media, *Journal of Interactive Multimedia Education*, http://www-jime.open.ac.uk

Jones, C. (1999) From the sage on the stage to what exactly? Description and the place of the moderator in co-operative and collaborative learning, *ALT-J*, 7(2): 27–36.

Land, R. and Bayne, S. (2001) 'Screen or monitor? Issues of surveillance and disciplinary power' in *online learning environments'*, *9th Improving Student Learning*

Symposium, *Improving Student Learning Using Learning Technologies*. Heriot Watt University, 9–11 September.

Laurillard, D. (2004) E-learning in the knowledge economy: the right context for innovation. Invited keynote, Colston Symposium. Bristol, 22–23 March.

Littlejohn, A. (2003) *Reusing Online Resources, A Sustainable Approach to E-learning*. London: Kogan Page.

McKenna, C. (2002) What do we mean by electronic literacy? in *Proceedings of the Improving Student Learning Using Learning Technology Conference*. Heriot Watt University.

NCIHE (National Committee of Inquiry into Higher Education (1997). *Higher Education in the Learning Society* (The Dearing Report). London: HMSO.

Oliver, M., McBean, J., Conole, G. and Harvey, J. (2002) Using a toolkit to support the evaluation of learning, *Journal of Computer Assisted Learning* 18(1): 199–208.

Perkins, D. N. (1993) Person-plus: a distributed view of thinking and learning, in G. Salomon (ed.) *Distributed Cognitions – Psychological and Educational Considerations*. Cambridge: Cambridge University Press.

Salomon, G. (ed.) (1993) *Distributed Cognitions – Psychological and Educational Considerations*. Cambridge: Cambridge University Press.

Sclater, N. (ed.) (2004) *Final report for the Item Banks Infrastructure Study* (*IBIS*). JISC commissioned review.

Sutherland, R., Keri, F., Furlong, R. and Furlong, J. (1999) A new environment for education? The computer in the home, CAL99, special issue of *Computers in Education* 34: 195–212.

Wiley, D. (ed.) (2002), *The Instructional Use of Learning Objects*, Agency for Instructional Technology and the Association for Educational Communications and Technology, available online at http://www.reusability.org/read/chapters/wiley.doc

8

Assessing Complex Achievements

Peter Knight

My argument is that as higher education comes closer to being a universal pastime, so British ways of assessing individual achievement become, literally, useless.

An assessment success story

In the UK more and more 18-year-olds are succeeding in the examinations that permit entry to higher education. On 21 August 2004 (p. 2) *The Times* stated:

> Just 25 years ago results day brought certainty of failure for a third of entrants. This week's claimed failure rate was 4 per cent and finding a student with no passes was infinitely harder than identifying teenagers clutching six A grades.

'Universal' success brought problems because there were so many good A level scores that it was becoming impossible for universities to discriminate amongst the growing number of well-qualified applicants. Some commentators called for the introduction of a new A* grade, others said that raw scores, not grades, should be reported and some universities considered introducing American style 'aptitude' tests. The first two suggestions make dubious sense in terms of assessment theory and the other has its own problems. As a result, although few A level students go directly into the labour market, employers and the public are no longer sure what A level scores *mean*.

The same problems are now evident in higher education where, in the UK, the modal degree class is an upper second and where, despite national subject benchmarks (QAA, 2001), there is considerable diversity in assessment practices, standards and rules (Sadler, 2005; Yorke *et al.*, 2000; Yorke 2002a, b). Worried by this collapse of meaning, the English government commissioned the Vice-Chancellor of the University of Leicester to investigate the problem. His report (Burgess, 2004) recognized the emptiness of the UK degree classification system but, following his terms of reference, his committee did not recommend an alternative.

Arguably, universal higher education will cause the whole system to collapse.

Of course, it has always been difficult to know what achievements were denoted by the award of a degree but, in an elite system, this was not a big problem and it could reasonably be assumed that entry into an elite signified worth, even if a student graduated with 'a gentleman's third'. In a mass system the problem is pressing simply because there are so many people with good degrees in a labour market that is increasingly a *graduate* labour market. The move to universal higher education can only fortify the forces for assessment change.

I will develop some of these ideas by concentrating on the quintessence of higher education's work, the formation of complex achievements. In doing so I shall make some remarks about the inadequacies of more traditional assessment practices. The argument is that traditional assessment is in disarray and that it is largely insensitive to the assessment of quintessential achievements. New thinking is needed now, otherwise the advance to universal higher education will collapse the whole system.

Higher education as the promotion of complex achievements

Higher education is certainly in the business of developing advanced understandings of demanding material. It does a lot more than that and it is expected to do more. Consider a summary of research into what employers say they look for in recruiting new graduates. It lists achievements such as:

- imagination/creativity;
- adaptability/flexibility;
- willingness to learn;
- independent working/autonomy;
- working in a team;
- managing others;
- working under pressure;
- good oral communication;
- communicating in writing for varied purposes/audiences;
- attention to detail;
- time management;
- taking responsibility and decisions;
- planning, coordinating and organizing.

Interestingly, when presented with this list, which is based on the work of Harvey *et al.* (1997) and Brennan *et al.* (2001), most teachers in higher education say that these achievements lie close to their own academic values and that they want degree programmes to promote them. They also lie close to the goals of those committed to 'citizenship education' (Colby *et al.*, 2003).

This involves discarding the naive notion that employability is about collecting a fistful of 'key skills'. One reason for objecting to the employability = skills formula is that the notion of skills, let alone of general, transferable skills, flies in the face of much work in psychology, philosophy and sociology (for a swift summary of objections, see Bailey *et al.*, 2004, Chapters 5 and 6). The second is that, as the list above shows, employers do not just value *skills*. They value a much wider range of achievements, assets or attainments – imagination, flexibility and willingness to learn are not skills. It is important to insist on this point because routines for promoting and assessing skills are not the same as routines for promoting and assessing attitudes, dispositions and qualities. Imagining otherwise leads to misconceived curricula, mismatched pedagogies and mistaken assessment practices.

Nor are these straightforward achievements. They are advanced, by virtue of being associated with degree-level work; they tend to lie in the field of 'practical intelligence' (Sternberg *et al.*, 2000), rather than being outgrowths of 'fixed' intelligence, such as IQ; they are the outcomes of 'slow learning', rather than being mastered in a few weeks (Claxton, 1998); and they are not determinate, in the sense that we cannot specify in some general and content-free way what graduate-level 'adaptability/flexibility' looks like. For these reasons I describe them as complex achievements, which adds overtones of unpredictability, in that a developmental trajectory cannot be predicted with confidence and the relationship between a curriculum and outcomes is uncertain.

Higher education does promote more determinate achievements – understandings of subject matter, fluency in applying formulae and heuristics to – often – relatively well-defined problems, and mastery of procedures in subject areas. However, a consistent message from employers, from those who see education as a route to better citizenship and from many teachers in higher education, is that complex achievements are also prized.

If higher education really is to take seriously the promotion of such outcomes, what arrangements should be made for doing so and how is assessment to be associated with them? I want to approach the assessment question by first considering the woeful state of present practices.

Assessment practices

'Assessment' is one of those words that everybody knows but which is often misunderstood. It is often taken as a synonym for 'measurement'. It is broader than that; it is about judgement. Measurement is a specialized process of judgement that is entirely unsuited for judging *many* aspects of thought, feeling and behaviour. Some (for example, Cliff, 1996; Mitchell, 1997) go further and argue that measurement is inappropriate to *most*.

Turning to higher education, we find serious difficulties, which I have elaborated elsewhere (Knight, 2002) with the belief that we do measure student learning. We certainly do a lot of quasi-measurement but the data that we create fail to meet the standards of measurement theory and tend to have local, often temporary meanings. There are particular problems when the stakes are high, as with awarding course grades that will go on a transcript or count in degree classification. Not only must the marks be as reliable as possible (because the stakes *are* high), but there is a tendency to make fine-grained judgements, most commonly seen in the use of a 101 point marking scale. The problem is that the more decision points there are (101 in this case), the harder and costlier it is to be confident that the marking is reliable.

Even where people do not say that assessment = measurement, they will often act as if it were – for example, by arguing over whether a mark is really 63 per cent or 65 per cent, or by saying that a student is 'a 2:1 student', or by claiming that a student 'has' the skill of communication. If it is difficult to measure, with any degree of validity and reliability, fairly determinate achievements (understandings of subject matter, fluency in applying formulae and heuristics to relatively well-defined problems, and mastery of procedures in subject areas), then we might wonder in what sense it would be possible to 'measure' complex achievements. Some will point to content-free tests, used in some places to 'measure' critical thinking, for instance. Whatever they might be doing, it is questionable whether 'critical thinking' is really being 'measured' here (Moore, 2004) – there is an acute validity problem. Others will claim that assessment centres are reliable *and* valid. Both claims may be challenged (Sternberg 1997; Brown and Hesketh, 2004), while the cost of assessment centres excludes them from normal university practice.

Apart from these limitations of high-stakes assessment practices, they are open to objection on the grounds that 'you can't fatten a pig by weighing it'. Well, you can if you use information about weight to plan the pig's diet and medical regime. As it is, though, high-stakes assessments seldom create timely information to help students to do better on their next assignment. *Low-stakes* assessment, designed to create feedback as well as feed-forward for improvement, can have a powerful effect on learning, *when done well* (see Gibbs and Simpson, 2004 and Yorke's chapter in this volume). However, it is common for high-stakes assessment to elbow out the low-stakes practices that can make such a difference to learning.

Assessing complex achievements

The implication of this Jeremiad on high-stakes assessment is that more systemic and subtle ways of thinking are needed if assessment is to foster complex achievements. Anyone hoping to assess such achievements for high-stakes purposes deserves sympathy because complex achievements will resist reliable, fine-grained, valid and affordable judgements.

However, low-stakes approaches can reach complex learning, especially if:

1   We provide sufficient interactive task sequences that engage the complex achievements we want to develop. This shifts attention from assessment to the creation of sequences of tasks that evoke support, advice and practice. Interactive computer programmes, group activities, mentoring and coaching, and peer-assisted reflection are examples of such tasks.
2   Students know the 'rules of the game', specifically that:

- These complex achievements are important;
- Feedback on achievement can fuel later success;
- Feedback can come from other students, computer systems, online conferencing and from tutors;
- Feedback is created in genuine conversations;
- Feedback only works if it is acted upon.

3   Students have a grasp of the 'fuzzy' criteria that will inform feedback on their complex achievements, and understand that 'final language' (Boud, 1995) is not appropriate to them.
4   Students realize that they will need to make and defend claims to these achievements because universities and colleges will not be able to warrant them.

On the basis of the analysis so far, I propose a threefold approach to assessing learning.

1   Some learning can be relatively directly assessed by conventional high-stakes methods.
2   Some learning resists *measurement* and is best handled by low-stakes, conversational approaches whose aim is to create feed-forward for further learning and claimsmaking.
3   In between lies learning that can be tolerably-reliably assessed at a price. Programme teams have to decide which outcomes deserve sufficient investment to allow achievement to be certified reliably and validly.

Implicit in this is the idea that assessment is best planned at the level of the programme, not of the single course. Although this presents challenges, it is possible, even in high-choice modular schemes (Knight and Yorke, 2003). Without it, assessment generates shreds of information with essentially module-level meanings.

Assessment problems

This resolution leaves two outstanding problems – communication and trust. With the modal student in England getting a 2:1, how can achievement be communicated and why should employers trust anything a mass, let alone a universal, higher education system says?

Communication

If we want others to understand the meanings of our judgements we need to say in good, clear language what the numbers and letters symbolize. Nor will it do to say that they mean someone has demonstrated skill at oral communication, or in numeracy. When addressing mass audiences like this, unless the subject is one where meanings are generally shared, it is necessary to build in redundancy, which means spelling out what these terms mean. The implication is that summative judgements need to be in the form of transcripts that considerately say what judgements are intended to mean.

Current reporting practices in higher education fall short of this requirement.

Yet, useful though this transmission theory of communication is, it is not enough (Fiske, 1990). People do not simply receive messages; they make individual sense of what is communicated to them. Part of this sense-making is filling in the gaps or implicatures – the unsaids. In Williams' words (2002: 100), 'Speakers have countless beliefs and many different ways of expressing them. They could always have said something else, mentioned a different matter, made their statement more or less determinate.'

Agreed, the understandings that people construct relate to the communications they receive, but they are not completely constrained or determined by the message. In the case of warrants to achievement, the data and transcripts are symbols of achievement. Where symbols and contexts are familiar and carry simple messages – road signs, for example – people interpret them in very similar ways. Where there is less familiarity and less certainty, interpretations will differ, perhaps enormously. In times when educational qualifications and programmes are proliferating, conventions once used to interpret them have been disrupted. Some symbols, awards, are not recognized (Graduate Apprenticeships, for instance) or not understood (foundation degrees, perhaps). Others may be recognized but the official reading may be distrusted (the vocational GNVQ awards were often seen as second rate 'A' levels, despite official claims of parity). The disruption of conventions that has been caused by the expansion and diversification of higher education is associated with uncertainty about how to interpret warrants, transcripts and other symbols of achievement.

Trust

Questions about why we should trust assessment warrants raise philosophical problems. True claims are to be trusted. If a warrant to achievement is true, we should trust it. This is no solution, though, given different accounts of what is to count as truth. Williams (2002) says that truth may be elusive but argues that truthfulness – a truth-seeking bent – is possible. Both rest on two virtues, accuracy and sincerity.

If others are to rely on what you tell them, you need, as well as not
misleading them about what you believe (sincerity), to take trouble to
make sure that your belief is true (accuracy). This may affect the investigative investment you think appropriate. To the degree that you owe
them the truth . . . to that degree you owe them an appropriate effort to
get hold of the truth.

(Williams, 2002: 148–9)

Sincerity may be free but, except with 'low-level' knowledge, accuracy is not.
It is secured by 'investigative investment' – investment in establishing criteria, creating shared understandings of them amongst students and
teachers, double and triple marking and formal review and appeals procedures. Moreover, I have been claiming that there are severe problems in
accurately – or reliably – judging achievement. In Williams' words,

Inquiries in the real world about questions do not typically yield certainty, and the pursuit of certainty would either be impossible or
absurdly expensive in terms of effort and time. So, very often we leave
certain avenues unexplored; and this means, also very often, that we do
not know exactly what avenues have been left unexplored.

(Williams, 2002: 134)

Grade inflation, the proliferation of different degree programmes and a
growing diversity of expectations have disrupted communication about
achievement. We do not know what an award means. What basis is there for
trusting any particular interpretation of these half-empty signifiers?

Universal assessment

If the experience of higher education becomes almost universally available,
it is not likely to take the form of more people thronging to lectures.
Work-based learning (WBL) is an obvious line of development. It is unlikely
that WBL will concentrate on mastery of propositional knowledge. It is more
likely to address procedural and affective areas, to emphasize the importance
of the sorts of qualities, dispositions and other achievements listed early in
this chapter.

While there are questions about making sure that WBL is good quality
WBL, there are deeper questions about assessing the complex outcomes
associated with WBL and higher education in general. Current practices are,
generally, not fit for purpose. Better practices depend, amongst other things,
on academic staff thinking in terms of *programme* assessment schemes.

Yet even the best schemes will not produce warrants to many complex
achievements. Instead, it will fall to students to develop claims to achievement, supporting the claims with evidence generated by low-stakes assessment, co-curricular activity, work and other out-of-class experience. English
higher education now has a system to support this claims-making in the form

of personal development planning. But what of the receivers, especially employers? How well equipped are they to move from selection driven by warrants to selection based upon documented claims to achievement? And how is this to be done in a mass, let alone a universal higher education system?

I have taken two themes – the growing disruption of the meanings of higher education awards and the failure of existing assessment practice to reach the complex achievements that are quintessential to higher education's role. I have argued that only systemic – programme-level – responses will be acceptable and that they will fuel a move from warranting (by institutions) to claims-making (by students). The concern is that the receivers of assessment information, notably employers, will not be in a position to handle these claims.

This leaves us with a quandary. One response would be to develop national, content-free examinations of so-called 'key skills'. One of the many objections to this is that whatever was being judged, it would not be students' learning in higher education. Another response would be to try and improve our national understanding of higher education and our national ability to judge claims to complex achievement. This is probably utopian. Where, then, does this leave the assessment of students' learning?

Perhaps in such a mess that we should consider investing less in assessing individual achievements and more in the design of programmes that are rich in the affordances that favour the development of complex achievements: rather than a fruitless search for powerful assessment methods, we might do better to invest and then trust in powerful learning environments (Merriënboer and Paas, 2003); rather than investing so heavily in differentiating amongst the achievements of individuals, the British might follow other countries' lead and grade only on a pass-fail basis. Were we to adopt pass-fail assessment, employers might then prefer to recruit graduates of departments known for their powerful learning environments.

We can go further and envisage a national body that would judge and, when appropriate, warrant departmental claims to operate powerful learning environments. (This would not be the UK Quality Assurance Agency by another name.) The upshot would be that as less emphasis was put on fine-grained assessments of individual achievements, more would be put on appraising the quality of learning environments.

The argument, then, is that as higher education comes closer to being a universal pastime, so British ways of assessing individual achievement become, literally, useless. An alternative is to concentrate our powers of judgement on the quality of programme design, pedagogic practices and the student experience as a whole.

References

Bailey, T. R., Hughes, K. L. and Moore, D. T. (2004) *Working Knowledge: Work-based Learning and Education Reform.* London: Routledge/Falmer.

Boud, D. (1995) Assessment and learning: contradictory or complementary? in P. T. Knight (ed.) *Assessment for Learning in Higher Education*. London: Kogan Page.

Brennan, J., Johnstone, B., Little, B., Shah, T. and Woodley, A. (2001) *The Employment of UK Graduates: Comparisons with Europe and Japan*. London: The Higher Education Funding Council for England.

Brown, P. and Hesketh, A. (2004) *The Mismanagement of Talent*. Oxford: Oxford University Press.

Burgess, R. (2004) *Measuring and Recording Student Achievement*. London: Universities UK and Standing Conference of Principals.

Claxton, G. (1998) *Hare Brain, Tortoise Mind*. London: Fourth Estate.

Cliff, N. (1996) *Ordinal Methods for Behavioral Data Analysis*. Mahwah, NJ: Lawrence Erlbaum Associates.

Colby, A., Ehrlich, T., Beaumont, E. and Stephens, J. (2003) *Educating Citizens. Preparing America's Undergraduates for Lives of Moral and Civic Responsibility*. San Francisco, CA: Jossey-Bass.

Fiske, J. (1990) *Introduction to Communication Studies*, 2nd edn. London: Routledge.

Gibbs, G. and Simpson, C. (2004) Conditions under which assessment supports students' learning, *Learning and Teaching in Higher Education*, 1: 3–31.

Harvey, L., Moon, S. and Geall, V. with Bower, R. (1997) *Graduates' Work: Organisation Change and Students' Attributes*. Birmingham: Centre for Research into Quality (CRQ) and Association of Graduate Recruiters (AGR).

Knight, P. T. (2002) Summative assessment in higher education: practices in disarray, *Studies in Higher Education*, 27(3): 275–86.

Knight, P. T. and Yorke, M. (2003) *Assessment, Learning and Employability*. Maidenhead: Society for Research in Higher Education and the Open University Press.

Merriënboer, J. and Paas, F. (2003) Powerful learning and the many faces of instructional design, in J. Merriënboer and F. Paas (eds) *Learning Environments: Unravelling Basic Components and Dimensions*. Dordrecht: Elsevier Science.

Mitchell, J. (1997) Quantitative science and the definition of measurement in psychology, *British Journal of Psychology*, 88: 355–83.

Moore, T. (2004) The critical thinking debate: how general are general thinking skills? *Higher Education Research and Development*, 23(1): 3–18.

QAA (Quality Assurance Agency for Higher Education) (2001) Benchmarking Academic Standards. Gloucester: Quality Assurance Agency for Higher Education.

Sadler, R. (2005) Interpretations of criteria-based assessment and grading in higher education, *Assessment and Evaluation in Higher Education*, 30(2): 175–94.

Sternberg, R. J. (1997) *Successful Intelligence*. New York: Plume.

Sternberg, R., Forsythe, G., Hedlund, J. *et al.* (2000) *Practical Intelligence in Everyday Life*. Cambridge: Cambridge University Press.

Williams, B. (2002) *Truth and Truthfulness*. Woodstock, Oxfordshire: Princetown University Press.

Yorke, M. (2002a) Subject benchmarking and the assessment of student learning, *Quality Assurance in Education*, 10(3), 155–17.

Yorke, M. *et al.* (2002b) Does grading method influence Honours degree classification? *Assessment and Evaluation in Higher Education*, 27(3): 269–79.

Yorke, M., Bridges, P. and Woolf, H. (2000) Mark distributions and marking practices in UK higher education, *Active Learning in Higher Education*, 1(1): 7–27.

9

Formative Assessment and Employability: Some Implications for Higher Education Practices

Mantz Yorke

Introduction

In the UK, the development of mass higher education has involved:

- widening access to a more diverse, and differently prepared range of students;
- an emphasis on higher education as preparation for employment in a modern economy; and
- organization of curriculum provision on a modular basis to emphasize student choice and promote more efficient use of resources.

All of these have implications for the way learning is encouraged, enhanced and evaluated. Formative assessment has a significant contribution to make to all three elements.

Formative assessment works

Formative assessment's primary purpose is to assist students to develop as learners. It informs students about their performances and should also give them pointers as to how they might 'do better next time', whether 'next time' refers to a further attempt at the same task or to new tasks. After all, many students will not be required to undertake the same task for a second time unless it is necessary for a 'pass' in the unit of study. It is important to note that formative assessment can be either formal or informal, and can be provided from sources other than teachers. Table 9.1 summarizes the complexity inherent in formative assessment.

Formative assessment from teachers has been the subject of a number of experimental studies, the majority of which have been undertaken in school settings, though some have involved higher education. Black and Wiliam (1998) undertook an extensive meta-analysis of these studies,[1] which found that that the statistical size effect of interventions using formative assessment

Table 9.1 A typology of formative assessment

Feedback . . .	Formal	Informal
from teachers	Probably the main approach in HE; feedback from computerized packages might be included here.	Where circumstances permit, such as in a studio or laboratory; or during fieldwork.
from peers	For example, via peer assessment activities.	Perhaps over coffee or a stronger beverage.
from others	This can be problematic if the 'other' is also a mentor or supervisor, as might be the case during work experience.	Probably the main approach in work-based learning contexts.
from self	Only if it is an assessment requirement – in some assessment regimes it is.	Where the student is acting self-critically.

Source: Based on Yorke, 2004b

was 0.7. They point out that this size effect is 'amongst the largest ever recorded for educational interventions' (Black and Wiliam 1998: 61). In other words, formative assessment can make an important contribution to student learning. The issue to be addressed in this paper is the extent to which the potential of formative assessment is fulfilled in higher education.

The UK context for formative assessment

Background

During the 1990s, curricula underwent a shift towards modular structures. There were two overriding arguments for this shift. First, it was seen as increasing student choice in respect of both the flexibility with which students could combine modules from different institutions and also the character of students' study programmes. Second, it held out the possibility of greater efficiency in the use of resources. Neither argument has been justified to the extent that had been anticipated.

Since the 1990s higher education institutions have been exhorted to widen participation in order to include considerably more students from disadvantaged backgrounds. Data presented in the UK government's White Paper of January 2003 (DfES, 2003, para 1.28) show that, whilst participation of those from lower socio-economic groups (SEGs) has increased steadily since 1960, the participation 'gap' between them and those from the higher SEGs has remained roughly the same size. In England, the policy aim under the New Labour government has been to engage 50 per cent of people aged between 18 and 30 in higher education by the year 2010. The data available to the DfES in 2003 showed that the most recent enrolment rate of such entrants was 43 per cent (DfES, 2003, para 5.7). In Scotland, where the education system is differently structured, a rate of 50 per cent has already been reached for those under 21 who enter full-time higher education (see Gallacher's chapter, this volume).

Since 1999 data have been published on institutional performance across the whole of the UK, covering retention, completion, the widening of participation, employment outcomes and some aspects of research performance.[2] These data have attracted attention in the press, with some institutions being shamed or praised for their performances regarding completion or widened participation. Press interest has shifted according to prevailing political concerns (Yorke, 2003).

The tendency for students (in the UK as in other countries) to engage in part-time employment in order to fund their passage through higher education is also relevant, not least because those from less advantaged backgrounds are more likely to do this, and to do it to a greater extent. Comparing the US, Australia and England, the extent of working is highest in the US, with the figures for England and Australia roughly two-thirds of the average US level.[3] Students who work have to strike a balance between study and employment, sometimes to the detriment of the former: McInnis and Hartley (2002) found that the academic performance of young entrants (but not older entrants) was weakened when the students perceived a conflict between study and employment. Weko (2004) observed that students who work above the average weekly rate (22 hours in the US in mainstream 2- and 4-year institutions, according to Choy and Carroll, 2003 – rather higher than the figures for Australia and the UK) were 'at a measurably increased risk of being unable to continue with their studies'.

Consequences

The publication of institutional performance data has focused attention on retention and completion, and on the participation of students from disadvantaged backgrounds. The improvement of retention and the widening of participation have become priorities for those institutions appearing to 'underperform' in one or other of these respects.

The shift to modularity typically meant that courses which had hitherto run over a whole academic year (and whose summative assessments took place at the end of the academic year) were reshaped to fit, typically, a two-semester structure, with summative assessment points at the end of each semester. The pressure on students to prepare for summative assessments, and that on academics to grade these assessments, had the effect of reducing the amount of formative assessment taking place. Further, feedback – such as it was – from summative assessments often arrived too late to be useful to students in choosing subsequent modules of study.

First-year full-time students were typically faced with summative assessments two to three months after arrival in higher education. The transition to higher education is difficult for many students, and is particularly difficult for those who lack 'cultural capital' (Bourdieu and Passeron, 1977), perhaps because they have little or no familial background exposure to higher education. In the UK system, the first year of full-time study on a degree-level programme is typically a qualifying year for honours-level study, and the requirement on the student is – at root – merely to satisfy the assessors that he or she should progress to that level. Provided that the minimum pass level is achieved, the level of the grades earned is irrelevant since grades do not carry forward to honours level.

Summative assessments at around Christmas time may have little value for learning and could deter some students from progressing when, given time and encouragement, they could do so. With retention and completion being used to index institutional performance, it is not surprising that some institutions are discarding early summative assessments and seeing the whole first year in more formative terms – in effect, as an extended induction into higher education. At least one has taken the step of allocating resources disproportionately in favour of first-year students,[4] on the grounds that an investment in developing students' ability to learn then can pay off later on, when they can work more autonomously.

'Employability' and formative assessment

The expectations, now common around the world, that graduating students should contribute to nations' economic good (e.g. Haug and Tauch, 2001) make particular demands on curricula, and by extension on teaching, learning and assessment. The USEM account of employability (Knight and Yorke, 2002; 2004) was developed to address these issues, and is consistent with the approach to formative assessment taken in this chapter.

Employability has been defined as

> a set of achievements – skills, understandings and personal attributes – that make graduates more likely to gain employment and be successful in their chosen occupations, which benefits themselves, the workforce, the community and the economy.
>
> (Yorke 2004a: 7)

The definition is related to the USEM account which stresses that a curriculum that exploits the inter-relatedness of four broad constructs (**U**nderstanding, **S**kilful practices in context, **E**fficacy beliefs and **M**etacognition) increases the chances that students will develop their employability. Exactly how this development takes place in an individual depends on the characteristics of the student (for example, the developmental needs of a school leaver will clearly differ from those of an older person entering higher education who has held down a full-time job).

A key point to be made is that employability and good learning are strongly correlated. If students develop their capabilities across a range of kinds of engagement, then the chances are that they will develop their employability to a comparable extent. The virtue of the correlation for the academic community is that its traditional commitment to student development is not undermined by a narrow conception of skills. The challenge, for many in higher education, is to respond to the implicit expectations of the USEM account as regards pedagogy.

Understanding of, and skilful practices in, the subject discipline are unproblematic for most academics, who have been socialized into its norms and expectations. For academics teaching on non-vocational programmes, understanding and skilful practices in employment situations present more of a challenge, since these require the application of the 'practical intelligence' that Sternberg (1997) sees as being critical to the success of most graduates in employment. The emphasis on work-based learning (especially strong in the foundation degrees[5] recently introduced into the UK, apart from Scotland), offers the prospect of formative feedback from colleagues in workplaces, whether formal or informal (Table 9.1), regarding the exhibition of skilful practices in work environments. A challenging issue, however, is the extent to which mentors in workplaces have developed expertise in formative assessment, since it is often unclear whether they have been fully trained for their role.

There is a considerable amount of evidence bearing on the importance placed by employers on the personal qualities and attributes possessed by graduates (e.g. Harvey *et al.*, 1997; Blackwell *et al.*, 2001; Brennan *et al.*, 2001; Knight and Yorke, 2004, Chapter 4). Theoretical backing for the aggregation of constructs making up the 'efficacy beliefs' of the USEM account can be found in the following:

- Dweck (1999) – the value of having a theoretical position regarding the 'self' that admits the possibility of development (say, as regards intelligence);
- Dweck (1999) – the importance of students focusing on learning-related goals rather than performance-related goals (the latter refer to 'looking good' or 'not looking bad' in relation to peers, though Pintrich, 2000, subsequently showed that the desire to 'look good' was not necessarily deleterious);
- Sternberg (1997) – the importance of practical, as well as academic, intelligence;
- Boekaerts (2003) – the connection between emotional state and cognitive functioning;
- Rotter (1966) – the importance of an internal, as opposed to an external, locus of control;
- Bandura (1997) – self-efficacy (the belief that one can, probabilistically, 'make a difference' to the situations in which one finds oneself);
- Seligman (1998) – 'learned optimism', as opposed to learned dependence or learned helplessness;

- Salovey and Mayer (1990) – emotional intelligence, subsequently rendered more popular by Goleman (1996).

The notion of metacognition, proposed by Flavell (1979), and the more work-related writing of Schön (1983) (despite criticisms such as those levelled by Eraut, 1994), have influenced higher education towards the adoption of 'reflective practice' in curricula. Pintrich (2002:220–1) saw metacognition as consisting of three broad areas of knowledge (understanding might be a better word here, with its stronger connotation of depth):

- general strategies for learning, thinking and problem-solving;
- differentiation in task difficulty which can require different cognitive strategies; and
- awareness of how one tackles tasks and learns.

The curricular emphasis on metacognition acknowledges (sometimes explicitly, sometimes implicitly) the desire of many employers to recruit people who are able to reflect critically on practice and to act in a self-regulated manner.

The research on student learning, stimulated by Marton and Säljö's (1976) seminal article, has also had a powerful effect on curriculum design and implementation, not least because it has led many students to become more aware about the way in which they learn and to develop their capacity for self-regulation. However, Pintrich indicated that there was some way yet to go in this direction, expressing surprise at 'the number of students who come to college having very little metacognitive knowledge' and saying that metacognition needed to be taught explicitly (Pintrich, 2002: 223).

A validation of the importance of working on the development of students' self-systems and metacognitive ability has been provided by Marzano (1998). In extensive meta-analyses, he found from experimental investigations that the statistical size effect on learning was 0.74 in 147 studies involving the self-system, and 0.72 in 556 studies involving metacognition. As with the meta-analysis conducted by Black and Wiliam (1998), these size effects are large. Paralleling Black and Wiliam's work, most of the studies were undertaken in school settings, with some in higher education. It seems not unreasonable to see the findings as having a broad transfer value into higher education.

A complex signalling system

An analysis of formal formative assessment by the teacher shows that it is a complex system of signalling between academics and students, in which there are plenty of opportunities for misinterpretation (Knight and Yorke, 2003). The implicit demands on the academic are more extensive than many probably appreciate, involving an understanding of

- subject structure
- curriculum specification

- pedagogy
- theories of student development
- the psychology of student agency
- communication.

For all but the first, there is a substantial body of theory that can be called upon in order to support professional understanding and practice. This does not imply that academics need to develop personal expertise in these areas, but it does imply that they need to have some appreciation of the main ideas and how they might be applied in practice. This gives a key role to educational development staff.

The signalling system can be summarized as follows.

1 The teacher specifies the assessment task and assessment criteria, bearing in mind the structure of the subject discipline, the programme specification, and the point at which the students are expected to have reached.
2 The student interprets the task in the light of the assessment criteria, and is influenced by their general intellectual development and also the beliefs (or implicit theories, Dweck, 1999) that they hold about their capacity to achieve.
3 The student undertakes the task.
4 The teacher grades the student's performance against the stated criteria and ideally accompanies the grade with comments on the performance and on how improvements might be made.
5 The student (again, ideally) interprets the feedback received, learns from it, and hence develops.

There is an additional feedback loop for the teacher/assessor, in that they may learn, from the way that students tackle the assigned task, about the way that students have perceived both the task and also, indirectly, the teaching they have received. The outcome could be a revision of the assessment task and possibly of the teaching of the topic concerned.

Where can the signalling system break down?

- There may be a disjunction between the student's current state of development and the expectations relating to the discipline. One particularly prominent disjunction is the weakness in mathematics of students studying engineering and cognate subjects, which can be tracked back to a widening gap between school curricula and expectations of higher education programmes (Kahn and Hoyles, 1997; Baty, 2004).
- Assessment criteria are inadequate by themselves to convey what the assessment task really expects. Wolf (1995:123–5) showed that teachers did not necessarily mark reliably (implying that they did not have a common interpretation of what was expected), nor did they necessarily follow the assessment rubric in the manner intended by the designer of the assessment when it was not themselves (p. 67ff). Exemplars were necessary to make clear what was expected.

- The assessor may believe that a grade is a sufficient signal of the level of performance, and not provide the amplification that enables the student to appreciate where the submitted work might have been improved, or how future work might better be approached. Where amplification is provided, this may be too cryptic for the student to decipher – question marks in the margin, and phrases such as 'This is a weak argument' do not, by themselves, help the student to move forward.
- The student may treat the feedback superficially. Anecdotal evidence suggests that for some students all that matters is the grade, with formative comments being ignored. In such cases, the student is treating formative assessment as summative. It is critical for learning that the student reflects on feedback and acts upon it.

A further issue is that of time. For feedback to be effective, it needs to be rapid. The technical requirements of summative assessment (that it be valid, reliable, and so on) can be relaxed for formative assessment which is better viewed as a conversation (Laurillard, 2001) between teacher and student that addresses the latter's development. Rapid feedback that is relatively rough and ready is more useful in practice than highly crafted feedback that arrives long after the completion of the assessment task – the student's mind will have move elsewhere by then. Imaginative teachers might also discern that their role can include the creation of conditions under which students can receive appropriate formative feedback, rather than the supply of all the feedback themselves. Gibbs (1999) provides an interesting case study of feedback developed through classroom activity that led to marked improvements in student performance.

The way in which formative assessment is handled is important, since there is a risk that some students will interpret criticism of their work as being criticism of them as persons. In their study of student learning at Alverno College in the US, Mentkowski and Associates (2000: 82) show that the College's approach to formative assessment supports students not only psychologically, but also in respect of their development of the metacognitive capacity for self-regulation:

> Students observed that feedback was given in such a way that they did not feel it was rejecting or discouraging or placing an unbalanced focus on negative aspects of performance. Instead, they experienced it as supportive criticism . . . [and] as an important support for learning and motivation. [. . .]
>
> Students observed that feedback procedures assisted them in forming accurate perceptions of their abilities and establishing internal standards with which to evaluate their own work. For some students, positive interactions with faculty or peers appeared to have been an important factor motivating achievement in the absence of grades. Students responded . . . to their teachers' expectations and personal recognition.

Implications of emphasizing formative assessment

The analysis contained in this chapter points towards the importance of formative assessment to student achievement, and to implications for pedagogic practice. The importance is strengthened where the purpose of higher education is taken as explicitly supportive of employability. The development of formative assessment can be envisaged at three levels – that of the individual academic or team of academics responsible for a particular study unit (or module); the department or programme team as a collectivity; and the institution.

Irrespective of the level of engagement with the issue, there are implications for the role of the academic. If employability is construed in the manner suggested earlier in this paper, then it follows that academics' engagement with students needs to be wide-ranging. For some in the UK, this will be a considerable challenge. For those in other systems, for example, the Humboldtian and Napoleonic systems of continental Europe, the challenge could be equally demanding.

Institutions

Institutions are in a position to take strategic initiatives to enhance the provision of formative assessment. They can, for example, review their curricular structures in order to test whether they are facilitating to the optimum the development of their students, in relation to the full spectrum of expectations that bear on the higher education system. The requirement that institutions in the UK produce learning and teaching strategies and update them at intervals has given a stimulus to the process of curricular review, but in many cases, this has not been linked to strategy on widening participation (HEFCE, 2001).

An institution-wide commitment to formative assessment (and, more widely, to student learning), requires vision and leadership, together with the managerial capability to ensure that the commitment is more than a rhetorical flourish. Fullan (2001) stresses that, whilst it is relatively easy to devise policies and practices, it is much more challenging to implement these in the socially complex environment that is typical of a higher education institution. Giving greater emphasis to formative assessment would, in many institutions, involve a considerable cultural shift regarding pedagogy. 'Quick fixes' are highly unlikely to be successful. The key to succeeding is sustained leadership and engagement. Exemplary in this respect is the level of institutional commitment that has characterized Alverno College in the US for more than a quarter of a century.[6] Important, but not quite so embracing as the Alverno example, is the encouragement of pedagogy in general through institutional systems for recognition and reward as demonstrated, for example, at the University of Sydney and as increasingly being adopted in the UK.

Two studies undertaken by members of the 'Action on Access' team sponsored by the HEFCE suggest that a systematic approach by institutions to the first-year experience is reaping the benefit in terms of student success. Thomas *et al.* (2001) conducted interviews with senior managers in six institutions that had bettered the 'benchmark' for retention and completion that had been calculated for them by the HEFCE statisticians, despite having intakes that were potentially likely to lead to non-completion. These institutions were likely to have emphasized formative assessment early in their programmes, and had made an explicit commitment to being supportive to students and 'friendly'. One of the institutions had acknowledged that the social dimension was important in learning activities, in part because learning in a social setting could mitigate the loss of the social aspect of higher education in clubs and societies due to students' need to undertake part-time employment in their spare time. Many full-time students, as well as part-timers, now study from a home base and have relatively limited opportunity to engage in campus-based social activities. Similar findings emerged from a subsequent study of a further nine institutions with high proportions of students from disadvantaged backgrounds, even though the published retention statistics had yet to provide evidence of the policy changes that had been implemented (Layer *et al.*, 2002).

These two studies focused primarily on the first-year experience in which both academic and social induction are important, with formative assessment playing a key role. However, formative assessment is important across the whole curriculum. The benefits to students of formative assessment throughout their time in higher education will probably change in character as they develop.

Institutions are, however, constrained in what they do as regards assessment since the national system for recording student achievements exerts its own pressures, which are accentuated if student achievements are included in 'league tables' of institutional performance. A greater emphasis on formative assessment is justified, not least because the summative assessments made in higher education are insufficiently robust to bear the weight that is placed upon them by external stakeholders.[7] A corollary of giving formative assessment a greater emphasis is that more weight could then be given to student claims to achievement (supported by evidence) than to numerical gradings such as the honours degree classification in the UK and the grade-point average in the US. The appropriateness of the honours degree classification in the UK is currently being reviewed, in part because there is a widespread feeling that it does not adequately reflect student achievement in contemporary higher education (UUK and SCOP, 2004).

Departments and programme teams

Whilst a real (as opposed to rhetorical) institutional commitment to student learning is helpful to groups of academics (often departments or programme teams) who devise whole curricula, it is not a necessary condition. It is open to groups to develop curricula in the light of the theoretical and empirical evidence regarding the ways in which student learning is most likely to be supported, whilst recognizing that there may be practical constraints on their freedom.[8]

Curriculum design involves both broad principles and their application to learning situations. The department or programme team (ideally) determines the principles underpinning the curriculum (in the context of this paper, the general approach through which formative assessment is to be built into the various curricular components). The detailed application is more a matter for the academics responsible for study units and particular learning situations.

Where a curriculum is already running, the department or programme team has opportunities to adjust the curricular approach to formative assessment. Programmes in the UK are typically subject to review at regular intervals (five years is common), enabling their various aspects to be reconsidered in some depth: of particular importance here are teaching methods and assessment. At a more day-to-day level, they can 'tune' their offerings by making appropriate adjustments to practices within the currently approved curriculum (Knight and Yorke, 2004). This possibility exists at both the programme team level and the level of the individual academic or sub-group of academics responsible for particular curricular units.

Academics

There would probably be broad agreement amongst academics that one of their key roles is to facilitate the development in students of the capacity to act autonomously. Put another way, it is to avoid inculcating or reinforcing the kind of dependency noted by Boud:

> Too often staff-driven assessment encourages students to be dependent on the teacher or the examiners to make decisions about what they know and they do not effectively learn to be able to do this for themselves.
>
> (Boud, 1995: 39)

This means shifting the emphasis in Table 9.1 from the top left cell to the bottom right cell. Formative assessment is critically important to such a shift.

If, as Black and Wiliam's (1998) work shows, formative assessment can be powerful, then learning situations that both engage students actively[9] in learning and also academics actively in supporting that learning are most likely to exploit that power. Well-designed 'low stakes' tasks can lead to considerable formative feedback (and not only from academics). Formative assessment is part of pedagogy: it has to be 'designed in' to learning situations, and not be treated as an add-on. The Oxford and Cambridge approach, involving feedback on weekly essays, is a version of designed-in formative assessment that is too demanding of resources for most institutions. The constraints on resourcing typical of higher education, and specifically for teaching in the UK's mass provision, accentuate the pedagogic challenge to teachers to be imaginative in the way that they construct learning opportunities and distribute their (very valuable) time. For example, the increasing availability of material on the Web enables relatively routine information transmission via lectures to be displaced, and offers the possibility of redeploying the contact time to activities with greater potential for student learning.[10] If change is needed to accentuate the use of formative assessment in teaching approaches, it is unlikely to be trivial.

Notes

1 Statistical meta-analyses are unable to incorporate non-experimental, typically qualitative, studies.
2 From 1999 to 2003 these were published by the Higher Education Funding Council for England (see, for example, HEFCE, 2003). From 2004 the data are published by the Higher Education Statistics Agency (HESA), and can be accessed via the HESA website (www.hesa.ac.uk).
3 See, for example, Callender and Wilkinson (2003: 15ff); Choy and Carroll (2003: 47ff); McInnis and Hartley (2002: 15ff). McInnis (2003) notes that part-time employment is undertaken by some students in order to sustain a particular lifestyle, and not merely to pay for basics. In making comparisons, there is a need to bear in mind differences in approach to calculating the number of hours worked per week.
4 This runs counter to the tradition of giving final year students the most favourable student/staff ratio.
5 These are two-year full-time equivalent programmes of a level broadly similar to the two-year diploma programmes typical of continental Europe and the Associate Degree in the US. The foundation degree is distinguished by its emphasis on work-based learning.
6 See Mentkowski and Associates (2000) for an account.
7 See Knight and Yorke (2003) for an extended justification of the point.
8 Examples include the requirements of professional bodies; the institution's framework for curricula; and the institutional regulations regarding assessment.
9 The word 'actively' is used in a relativistic sense here, in order to signal a level of engagement that is higher than, say, that of sitting through a comparatively uninspiring lecture which, nevertheless, might lead to some learning. Relatively little learning can be described as 'passive'.
10 For example, Bligh (1998) demonstrates, on the basis of considerable engagement with the research literature, that lectures are generally inferior to other teaching approaches where complex learning is desired.

References

Bandura, A. (1997) *Self-efficacy: The Exercise of Control.* New York: Freeman.

Baty, P. (2004) Students 'lack basics', *The Times Higher Education Supplement,* 16 July.

Black, P. and Wiliam, D. (1998) Assessment and classroom learning, *Assessment in Education* 5(1): 7–74.

Blackwell, A., Bowes, L. Harvey, L. Hesketh, A. and Knight, P.T. (2001) Transforming work experience in higher education, *British Educational Research Journal,* 26(3): 269–86.

Bligh, D. (1998) *What's the Use of Lectures?,* 5th edn. Exeter: Intellect.

Boekaerts, M. (2003) Towards a model that integrates motivation, affect and learning, in L. Smith, C. Rogers and P. Tomlinson (eds) *Development and Motivation: Joint Perspectives.* Leicester: British Psychological Society.

Boud, D. (1995) Assessment and learning: contradictory or complementary? in P. Knight (ed.) *Assessment for Learning in Higher Education.* London: Kogan Page.

Bourdieu, P. and Passeron, J. C. (1977) *Reproduction in Education, Society and Culture.* London: Sage.

Brennan, J., Johnston, B., Little, B., Shah, T. and Woodley, A. (2001) *The Employment of UK Graduates: Comparisons with Europe and Japan.* Bristol: The Higher Education Funding Council for England.

Callender, C. and Wilkinson, D. (2003) *2002/03 Student Income and Expenditure Survey: Students' Income, Expenditure and Debt in 2002/03 and Changes Since 1998/99* (Research Report RR487). London: Department for Education and Skills.

Choy, S. P. and Carroll, C.D. (2003) *How Families of Low- and Middle-income Undergraduates Pay for College: Full-time Dependent Students in 1999–2000* (Report 2003–162). Washington, DC: National Center for Educational Statistics.

DfES (Department for Education and Skills) (2003) *The Future of Higher Education.* Norwich: The Stationery Office, Cm. 5753.

Dweck, C. S. (1999) *Self-theories: Their Role in Motivation, Personality and Development.* Philadelphia, PA: Psychology Press.

Eraut, M. (1994) *Developing Professional Knowledge and Competence.* London: Falmer.

Flavell, J. H. (1979) Metacognition and cognitive monitoring: a new area of cognitive-developmental inquiry, *American Psychologist,* 34: 906–11.

Fullan, M. (2001) *The New Meaning of Educational Change,* 3rd edn. London: RoutledgeFalmer.

Gibbs. G. (1999) Using assessment strategically to change the way students learn, in S. Brown and A. Glasner (eds) *Assessment Matters in Higher Education: Choosing and Using Diverse Approaches.* Buckingham: SRHE and Open University Press.

Goleman, D. (1996) *Emotional Intelligence.* London: Bloomsbury.

Harvey, L., Moon, S. and Geall, V. with Bower, R. (1997) *Graduates' Work: Organisation Change and Students' Attributes.* Birmingham: Centre for Research into Quality (CRQ) and Association of Graduate Recruiters (AGR).

Haug, G. and Tauch, C. (2001) *Trends in Learning Structures in Higher Education (II)* [Follow-up Report prepared for the Salamanca and Prague Conferences of March/May 2001]. Available at http://www.oph.fi/publications/trends2/trends2.html (accessed 27 July 2004).

HEFCE (2001) *Review of Strategic Plans and Financial Forecasts,* Bristol, HEFCE

HEFCE (2003) *Performance Indicators in Higher Education 2000–01 and 2001–02.* Available at www.hefce.ac.uk/learning/perfind/2003/ (accessed 27 July 2004).

Kahn, P. E. and Hoyles, C. (1997) The changing undergraduate experience: a case study of single honours mathematics in England and Wales, *Studies in Higher Education*, 22(3): 349–62.

Knight, P. T. and Yorke, M. (2002) Employability through the curriculum, *Tertiary Education and Management*, 8(4): 261–76.

Knight, P. T. and Yorke, M. (2003) *Assessment, Learning and Employability*. Maidenhead: SRHE and Open University Press.

Knight, P. T. and Yorke, M. (2004) *Learning, Curriculum and Employability in Higher Education*. London: RoutledgeFalmer.

Laurillard, D. (2001) *Rethinking University Teaching: A Conversational Framework for the Effective Use of Learning Technologies*, 2nd edn. London: RoutledgeFalmer.

Layer, G., Srivastava, A., Thomas, L. and Yorke, M. (2002) Student success: building for change, in Action on Access (2003) *Student Success in Higher Education*. Bradford: Action on Access.

McInnis, C. (2003) New realities of the student experience: how should universities respond? Keynote address to the 25th Forum of the European Association of Institutional Research, Limerick. Available at http://www.cshe.unimelb.edu.au/pdfs/EAIRKeynote03McInnis.pdf (accessed 20 July 2004).

McInnis, C. and Hartley, R. (2002) *Managing Study and Work: The Impact of Full-time Study and Paid Work on the Undergraduate Experience in Australian Universities* (EIP Report 02/6). Canberra: Department of Education, Science and Training.

Marton, F. and Säljö, R. (1976) On qualitative differences in learning. I – Outcome and process, *British Journal of Educational Psychology*, 46(1): 4–11.

Marzano, R. J. (1998) *A Theory-based Meta-analysis of Research on Instruction*. Aurora, CO: Mid-continent Regional Educational Laboratory.

Mentkowski, M. and Associates (2000) *Learning that Lasts: Integrating Learning Development and Performance in College and Beyond*. San Francisco, CA: Jossey-Bass.

Pintrich, P. R. (2000) The role of goal orientation in self-regulated learning, in M. Boekaerts, P. Pintrich and M. Zeidner (eds) *Handbook of Self-regulation*. New York: Academic Press.

Pintrich, P. R. (2002) The role of metacognitive knowledge in learning, teaching and assessing, *Theory into Practice*, 41(4): 219–25.

Rotter, J.B. (1966) Generalized expectancies for internal versus external control of reinforcement, *Psychological Monographs*, 80: 1–28.

Salovey, P. and Mayer, J.D. (1990) Emotional intelligence, *Imagination, Cognition, and Personality*, 9: 185–211.

Schön, D. A. (1983) *The Reflective Practitioner: How Professionals Think in Action*. New York: Basic Books.

Seligman, M. (1998) *Learned Optimism*. New York: Pocket Books.

Sternberg, R. J. (1997) *Successful Intelligence: How Practical and Creative Intelligence Determine Success in Life*. New York: Plume.

Thomas, L., Woodrow, M. and Yorke, M. (2001) Access and retention, in Action on Access (2003) *Student Success in Higher Education*. Bradford: Action on Access.

UUK and SCOP (2004) *Measuring and recording student achievement* (Report of the Scoping Group chaired by Professor Robert Burgess). London: Universities UK and the Standing Conference of Principals.

Weko, T. (2004) *New Dogs and Old Tricks: What Can the UK Teach the US About University Education?* Paper written during an Atlantic Fellowship in Public Policy and presented at the British Council, London, 30 March.

Wolf, A. (1995) *Competence-based Assessment*. Buckingham: Open University Press.

Yorke, M. (2003) The prejudicial papers? Press treatment of UK higher education performance indicators, 1999–2001, in M. Tight (ed.) *Access and Exclusion (International Perspectives on Higher Education Research, Volume 2)*. Oxford: Elsevier Science.

Yorke, M. (2004a) *Employability in Higher Education: What it is, What it is not.* York: Learning and Teaching Support Network.

Yorke, M. (2004b) Formative assessment and student success. Paper presented at the Quality Assurance Agency seminar on assessment, University of Glasgow, 4 June. Now published in Quality Assurance Agency for HE (2005) *Reflections on Assessment*, Vol 2, Glasgow, QAA.

10

'To Them that Have Shall be Given, but . . .': The Future of Funding and Evaluating Research in UK Universities

Lisa Lucas

Introduction

The move to a mass system of higher education in the UK, aiming at 50 per cent of the age participation rate by 2010 (Department for Education and Skills, 2003), has been one of the main reasons for the increased levels of quality assurance in higher education. As the system grows and becomes more costly, there is a greater demand for assuring the quality of the outcomes of university work. Moreover, the expense of the research role within a university can be questioned by governments keen to cut costs. The use of performance indicators and systems of evaluation of teaching and research activities within universities across the globe is near universal. The extent to which evaluation of performance links to funding levels is not. There is substantial variation across national systems from, on the one hand, examples such as the German and Dutch systems maintaining historical funding based models, to the United Kingdom (UK) with a completely evaluation based funding model (Jongbloed and Vossensteyn 2001). Orr (2004) compares four European governments and their approach to research assessment as an instrument of policy steering, with the UK having the strongest linkage through funding decisions. The development of a European Research Area may create a context for convergence of policy.

It is because the UK lies to the farthest extreme of this continuum that the system of evaluating and, therefore, funding research, the Research Assessment Exercise (RAE), has become so important and significant to the identity, purpose and development of UK universities. In an effort to rationalize the process of funding university research, the UK RAE has served to increase the selectivity of institutions funded for research, thus resulting in greater differentiation and division between institutions. The significance of the RAE goes far beyond the possible funding and symbolic value rewards that can be attained by institutions; it challenges the identity and character of universities and what it means to be an academic within a UK university in the twenty-first century (Henkel, 2000). It is for this reason that the RAE has inspired such intense passion and debate within the higher education community since its inception. This contrasts with the second element of research funding by competitive bidding to research councils, funded, significantly, through the Department of Trade and Industry, which has a lower profile in policy debates by not having a national, publicized, large-scale exercise every four or five years. There is a more frequent cycle, split across 6 councils, without a major announcement of prize-winners. Third stream funding (see Wedgwood, this volume) has an even lower profile, being local and particular, and with much lower funding support from government agencies.

The 2008 UK RAE has been developed in light of a major review of the exercise (Roberts, 2003). This follows the pattern of continual revision, which has characterized each successive RAE. The intention of this chapter is to provide a reflection on these proposed changes and assess to what extent they address and respond to the critiques made of the RAE as a process and the claims for the negative impacts the RAE has had both on the development of research work within universities and on the non-research (mainly teaching) work done by the communities of academics. This chapter will focus in particular on the dilemmas posed by the ever increasing concentration of research funds to a smaller number of universities; and on the potential benefits and possible negative effects on the continued development of diverse and innovative research across different disciplines and across all UK universities. The differences across the devolved UK administrations in terms of research funding policies and procedures in Wales and particularly in Scotland are also explored and questions are raised as to the efficacy of further concentration and selectivity of research resources at the expense of possibilities for integration and collaboration. To date the need for UK research to be internationally competitive has driven the research funding agenda to universities. Perhaps this aim could be better served, however, by strengthening collaborative efforts across universities. Furthermore, research collaboration across universities may serve to protect and enhance staff involvement in research rather than furthering the possibility of creating 'teaching only' institutions. A mass system of higher education does not necessarily lead to an increasingly hierarchized and polarized university system but should provide opportunities for the majority to contribute to the best of their abilities in both teaching and research, working to unite the two where possible.

The UK Research Assessment Exercise – a phenomenal success story?

For non-UK readers I first give a brief account of the RAE's purpose and the basic procedures (see www.hero.ac.uk and www.hefce.ac.uk for fuller details). There is a dual support funding system within the UK and research monies can be gained via competitive funding of research proposals from the Research Councils, and Quality Research (QR) funding given by the

Higher Education Funding Councils across the UK, based on performance as measured by the RAE. It is this latter form of funding that is being discussed here. There have been five RAEs in the UK in 1986, 1989, 1992, 1996 and 2001 and the intention is to have the next exercise in 2008. Its purpose is to assess the quality of university research based on the judgement of academic peers. This then informs the levels of funding for research to be distributed to each university as part of its QR budget. The quality of research is assessed within subject units of assessment (UOAs). In 2001 there were 68 subject areas. Subject panels are made up of experts in the field of study and, in 2001, a number of research users and international experts were included by some panels to oversee and advise on procedure and ratings. The measure of quality is related to the demonstration of international and national excellence of the research work being done within UOAs in each university, ranging from international excellence to below national levels of excellence hitherto. The 2008 exercise introduces the concept of 'world-leading' as the pinnacle of quality. Universities provide a submission for each UOA to the RAE, including details of staff output (mainly publications), research funding and studentships and details of achievements and awards for all of the staff submitted. It has not been a requirement of universities to submit all academic staff, so they are free to choose who to classify and submit as being 'research active'. To date, each UOA from each university has been awarded a grading (1 to 5* and post-2001, a 6) and mention is made of the percentage of 'research active' staff submitted by awarding a further grade of A–F, with A representing the highest submission of 95–100 per cent of staff.

The critiques and questions raised by the RAE are numerous both in terms of the process itself and in terms of the detrimental impact it is perceived to have had on the development of research and academic work within universities. But many commentators would point to the achievements of the RAE in raising the research activity within UK universities and in providing the impetus for university leaders to better organize and manage that research activity. It also established a funding mechanism that is emulated by other national systems, most notably Hong Kong.[1] It has informed the development of new systems such as the 'Performance Based Research Funding' scheme in the case of New Zealand.[2] It should be emphasized that in both of these cases, significant differences exist in their funding system compared to the UK. The Hong Kong RAE has a different definition of research to include the Boyer (1990) categories of different scholarships of discovery, integration, application and teaching, and it is necessary for all academic staff to be included in the exercise. The New Zealand 'Performance Based Research Funding' includes a research quality evaluation like the UK RAE, but relies more on bibliometric data such as numbers of research students and research income, following the model of the Australian system.

The evidence, say the proponents, speaks for itself, as with each successive RAE gradings continue to rise: in 2001 almost 40 per cent of all submissions were awarded the top grades of 5 or 5* and 55 per cent of all research active staff were working in these top-rated departments (McNay, 2003). Research studies have given evidence of the power of the RAE to effect substantial changes to the organization of research activities within institutions (McNay, 1997; Lucas, 2001; Harley, 2002; Hare, 2003), and the imperative public demonstration of research activity has succeeded in ensuring that academics are keen to have the results of their research efforts in the public domain through publication in research journals, books and other outlets. Evidence from citation indexes and bibliometric data shows that research in the UK in many science subject areas is second only to the United States, in no small measure, it could be argued, due to the influence of the RAE (House of Commons Science and Technology Committee, 2004). Evidence from Universities UK indicates that the UK 'has continued to perform comparatively strongly among the G8 nations, where the greatest concentration of research funding and output is found' (Universities UK, 2003). The report emphasizes that indexes of research performance for the humanities and social sciences are more complex to compile but, in the sciences where it is accepted that such indexes are more reliable, there is substantial evidence that, taking some inconsistencies into account, the UK tends to 'perform above world average and has shown substantial improvement since 1992' (Universities UK, 2003). From the UK government perspective, therefore, the RAE may be achieving the desired goals of improving the international standing of UK science. Critics of the RAE may use other evaluative criteria in measuring its success.

The critiques of the RAE have been perhaps more voluminous and have resulted in the funding councils making moderations to each successive RAE. These critiques can be separated into those that are more concerned with the difficulties of ensuring reliability and equity in the process of the RAE and those more concerned with the negative impacts the RAE has had on the development and functioning of university life. Critics point to the increasing hierarchy and differentiation between universities, divisions created within university departments, steering and directing research efforts resulting in a homogenizing of research areas towards the mainstream, short termism and lack of innovation. They claim that research has become the prime motivator and mover within university departments detracting attention, resources and energy away from non-research activities, primarily teaching, and in the undervaluing of applied and interdisciplinary research (Brown, 2000; Henkel, 2000; Harley, 2002; Lucas, 2003; McNay, 2003). The head of the agency assuring quality in teaching is reported as warning that 'if care is not taken, some universities may be diverted from their teaching mission in their chase for better RAE grades' (Baty, 2005). The differential valuing of different components of academic work, although perhaps always a feature of university life, has intensified and left many feeling demoralized and undervalued (Lucas, 2003). Critics are also sceptical about the renewed vigour and increased achievement demonstrated by universities as the percentage of top rated 5 and 5* departments rise, pointing instead to the pernicious game-playing that can perhaps explain much of the improvement rather than the quality of the research (House of Commons Science and Technology Committee, 2004).

The concept of the 'research game' is taken up in my own study on the impacts of the RAE on universities and academic staff working within them (Lucas, forthcoming). Using the concepts of 'research capital' and 'academic capital' (Bourdieu, 1988), I analyse the changing rules of the 'research game' and attempts by universities, departments and individual academics to maximize their 'research capital' and thus reap the rewards of status and positioning afforded by success in the 'game'. The implication of this work, however, is not simply that greater strategying and game playing has been encouraged for RAE purposes, but that it has served to infiltrate the cultures and values of academic life such that these ends and means become the raison d'etre, or the 'symbolic capital' in Bourdieu's terms, which govern the meaning and value of research work and activities within universities more generally.

Critics of the process of the RAE have been making their views known since the beginning. Many of the voices of discontent have come from within the universities and not just those that have not performed well in the RAE. Many from the elite universities, the 'Russell group', have expressed dissatisfaction with the time and effort taken up by the RAE (Fazackerley, 2004; Thomson, 2004) and the *Times Higher Education Supplement* and other education press contain almost weekly references to and debates about the RAE (Barnard, 2004; MacLeod, 2004). Some critics focus on the difficulties of having a comparable and standard procedure across all the different panels (Sharp, 2004), of defining what it means to be international (McNay, 2003) and of the potential for bias of panels. The potential difficulty of ensuring robust criteria was illustrated well by the confusion caused by the involvement of an international expert in the social work panel during the 2001 RAE (Gambrill, 2002). She claimed that, despite constantly asking for the 'criteria' being used to make judgements, she was continually frustrated and concluded that judgements appeared to be being made based more on the prestige of a journal rather than the quality of the research work contained within them, although this was strongly denied in a reply to her article by the Chair of the social work panel (MacGregor, 2003). The research 'user' representative on the panel, though, agreed with Gambrill (Lewis, 2002).

Further difficulties recognized are the time taken up by institutions for preparation of submissions and for panels and their deliberations. This enormous investment in time is particularly problematic for those institutions who in the end do not score highly enough on some UOAs to be awarded funding. It has also been claimed that the current process does not adequately assess applied work (Fisher and Marsh, 2003; McNay, 2003; McNay, forthcoming) and is too concerned with traditional disciplinary criteria and therefore unable to deal with interdisciplinary work (House of Commons Science and Technology Committee, 2004).

Many of the issues and problems surrounding the process of the RAE are acknowledged by the HEFCE. The chief executive, Sir Howard Newby, identified stress of academic staff, distortions to the nature of research and decisions about staffing in institutions as well as the damage to non-research activities (Newby, 2001). In recognition of the major criticisms both of the process of the RAE and the negative impacts it may have on the development of research and non-research activities within universities, a review was commissioned to look into these issues and suggest possible changes. The Roberts Review (2003) produced some fundamental ideas for change, which will now be explored and the extent to which these have been adopted for RAE 2008 examined.

Roberts, review and revision of the RAE 2008 – more of the same or something completely different?

There have been a number of reviews and projects commissioned by the HEFCE to look into the ways of modifying and improving the RAE but perhaps the Roberts Report (2003) has been most influential in effecting substantial change to the structure and process of the RAE. The key ideas put forward by Roberts can be summarized as follows:

- separate funding streams to take into account the likelihood of success in the RAE (UOAs destined not to do well could opt out and enter another funding stream);
- a different panel structure with super-panels to allow more comparability across panels;
- a measure of institutional competences to be evaluated in terms of their research strategy, development of research, equal opportunities and dissemination of research; and finally
- replacing a final summative grade to submissions with a 'quality profile' of all the individual researchers submitted to the exercise.

The final construction of the 2008 RAE has incorporated only some of Robert's key suggestions, primarily the introduction of 'main' panels that would be able to oversee procedures across a number of units of assessment and the replacement of summative grades by a 'quality profile', which shows the range of staff outputs within a department in terms of their allocation to a 1* to 4* status, evaluated once again along the range of national and international excellence. The change to the panel structure signals a move towards greater comparability across UOAs in terms of the standards of research excellence and the use of criteria. It may also improve the possibilities for easier evaluation of inter-disciplinary research, though some of the groupings raise issues of knowledge boundaries. Education is grouped with psychology and sports related studies, implying support for *mens sana in corpore sano* as a defining principle (McNay, forthcoming). The new panel structure provokes wider scepticism about its ability to allow better evaluation of inter-disciplinary research and greater comparability across panels

(House of Commons Science and Technology Committee, 2004). In terms of the quality profiles, it is argued that changing the single seven-point scale to a profile based on a four-point scale will improve 'the degree of discrimination needed for a continuing policy of selective funding' (HEFCE, 2004: 1) and it will help to 'reduce the tactical element in preparing submissions' by encouraging 'institutions to include all their good researchers rather than aiming for a particular grade' (HEFCE, 2004: 1). The Roberts Review recommended 'moderators' to work across panels and this idea has been further supported as a means to ensure greater consistency of practice (House of Commons Science and Technology Committee, 2004). The move towards a 'quality profile' rather than a final grade could be perceived as a positive move to end the 'game playing' (Lucas, 2003) of institutions in terms of their submissions; however, in practice this hope may not be fulfilled since institutions will still want to avoid the presentation of a 'long tail' of non active or low rated researchers even if this makes no difference to the funding awarded. Similarly, the current 'interest' shown in the hierarchical positioning of universities and departments in league tables will ensure that the media amongst others will be keen to average more detailed 'quality profiles' into a single, simple grade (House of Commons Science and Technology Committee, 2004).

The well intentioned modifications for the 2008 RAE, therefore, may change to some extent the structure and process of the exercise. However, the impacts may be minimal. Moreover, the proposed changes deal only with some tweaking of the structure and process of the RAE and the opportunity was missed to engage with more fundamental questions, which recognize that the RAE has never been and never will be simply a means of identifying and rewarding excellent research. The research evidence shows clearly the important role the RAE plays in dominating the direction of activities within universities and creating competition and divisions between institutions, between departments and between individuals. The chance was perhaps missed to engage with a more radical repositioning of the exercise to better encourage constructive and collaborative support across and within institutions.

The House of Commons Select Committee on Science and Technology engaged further with more radical ideas for changing the RAE structure and process, primarily the possibility of relying more on a metric formula for funding in science subjects, where such quantitative indicators are meaningful, and for those high performing departments where information on funding and citation counts may be good indicators of quality. They argue that,

> . . . a range of measures could be used to replace the peer review process in some subject areas such as the physical sciences. There are strong reasons to believe that they could be as reliable as the current system while being more cost effective and imposing less of a burden on institutions and panel members.
>
> (House of Commons Science and Technology Committee, 2004: 31)

This raises the question of whether all subject areas need to be treated in the same way and also whether more fundamental changes need to be made to the RAE process than have been considered so far.

These ideas to some extent provide more of a radical questioning of the process of funding and evaluating research than simply the operation of the RAE but the fundamental principles of competitive evaluation and funding remain. Perhaps we need to re-vision and position the UK research funding system, relying not only on ideas for possible changes to the RAE but the research funding system as a whole to better respond and be more constructive in achieving different priorities and commitments. Priorities could include the possibilities for: encouraging collaboration between and within institutions; seeing research work as important to the identity and successful operation of universities and so supporting and encouraging research activity, where possible, inclusively across the sector; and expanding the definition of research to better incorporate excellent applied and interdisciplinary work. The current moves to require full economic costing and pricing of research projects for government and its agencies, including the research councils, will shift the balance of funding, so that infrastructure funding through the funding councils, based on RAE ratings, will reduce in size and significance.

It can be argued that the concentration of research funding to an increasingly smaller number of institutions in the UK has gone far enough and is detrimental to the development of universities and university research work (Universities UK, 2003). The point may be accepted that the funding pot is too small to fund research across all universities in the UK but it may be more constructive to search for ways to ensure that there can be further collaboration across institutions to allow for involvement in research to be spread more widely. This is a stated aim in the recent White Paper on Higher Education but it is perhaps less clear how this is to be achieved (Department for Education and Skills, 2003). The new funding for promising researchers in low rated units to be seconded to those gaining 5 and 5* ratings will simply lead to them not returning to their previous base, akin to third world students having doctoral scholarships to study in developed countries. Variation across the devolved systems in the UK to establish commonalities and difference may lead to sharing new ideas and even to questioning the core assumptions of the process and structure of the RAE, the means by which research in UK universities is evaluated and funded and to looking for ways to encourage, support and revitalize research activity across the sector.

A national system of research funding and evaluation? – comparison and difference across the UK

The report by the Universities UK on 'Funding Research Diversity' included a comparison of regional differences across England, Wales, Scotland and

Northern Ireland. Relying on RAE results and citation indexes, publication rates and rates of staffing, the report was able to demonstrate the disparities across the regions in England and also Scotland, Wales and Northern Ireland and to investigate how further concentration of research resources might affect levels of research achievement. The report found overwhelmingly that the three regions in the South-east of England, including London, had the highest density of departments rated 5/5* in the RAE. If further concentration of research resources from the RAE continues, then universities in these areas will be set to gain more funding, whereas places such as Wales and the East Midlands would be set to lose dramatically. The West Midlands and the North East would suffer less harsh losses (Universities UK, 2003). The substantial losses in some regions would result, they argue, in 'reduced regional research capacity [that] will have knock-on effects for regional economic performance and the capacity for technology innovation' (Universities UK, 2003: 31). The negative consequences of further concentration of research resources cannot be over-stated in this regard (AUT, 2003; Adams and Smith, 2004)

As countries within the UK both Wales and Scotland have devolved administrations, The Welsh Assembly and The Scottish Parliament. As a result they have control over particular areas such as education. The RAE operates as a quality measure of research activity across all the countries in the UK but there are differences in the model of funding in each and how research money is distributed as well as specific initiatives and focus for research priorities. The levels of funding attached to particular RAE grades, therefore, were not the same across the different UK countries from 2002, with Scotland and Wales awarding less stark differentials in funding than in England. In Scotland and Wales, therefore, there was less concentration of funding to the top rated UOAs (McNay, 2003).

In Wales, the results of the RAE have been disappointing across the exercises although improvement did occur, especially in Cardiff, which, after merger with the Welsh School of Medicine, now attracts 60 per cent of QR funding from HEFCW. The other Welsh institutions receive comparatively little money from the research councils and charitable bodies and there are concerns about the lack of strength and size in the research base. As a result of this a number of additional research initiatives were introduced, including the 'Research Volume Initiative' which was intended to increase the numbers of research active staff across Welsh universities and drive up the number of 4, 5 and 5* units of assessment as measured by the RAE. In terms of future development of the higher education base in Wales, a number of scenarios have been discussed. Scenario 1 involved maintaining the status quo, which was not widely supported. Scenarios 2 and 3 involved promoting closer collaboration between institutions and promoting institutional mergers. It is anticipated that some mix of the latter two scenarios will be implemented. In terms of developing research capacity, research partnerships have already been established and these could be further encouraged perhaps forming centres of research excellence as part of scenario 2. Scenario 3 would involve mergers rather than increased collaboration but with the same aim: ultimately to increase the critical mass of research in particular subject areas (HEFCW, 2002).

The picture for research capacity in Scotland shows areas of recognized strengths but there are still challenges to be faced. According to a recent report on achievement for research, Scotland appears to have been successful in RAE ratings in a number of areas, scoring top grades in biological sciences, veterinary science, computer science, history, applied mathematics and Middle Eastern and African studies, although in some cases 5 and 5* grades are achieved with very small submissions (Scottish Higher Education Funding Council, 2004). Compared to Wales and different regions in England, Scotland does comparably well again in certain areas, coming first in biology, second in mathematics and statistics and third in clinical sciences and engineering and related technology. Furthermore, Scotland has been successful in gaining more research council funding per capita than England and Wales and also in non-government research funding (Scottish Higher Education Funding Council, 2004). Despite some apparent success and of course possible scepticism over the validity of the RAE results and bibliometric data, Scotland, like other countries within the UK, is concerned with the difficulties of retaining international competitiveness in research. In response to this, however, the intention is to counter-balance the effects of increasing competition and concentration of research resources, caused in part by the RAE, to shift towards greater 'collaboration and pooling resources' across Scottish universities and within the next few years 'to see this process to have advanced and for sustainable collaborative arrangements to be in place' (SHEFC, 2004: 112). There have also been increases in general levels of institutional funding for research, in part to compensate for the different arrangements for tuition fees. Partly for pragmatic reasons, in order to compensate for the small system of higher education which Scotland has, and perhaps also influenced by more ideological, egalitarian and communitarian beliefs, there is evidence that Scottish research policy is becoming more distinctive in the same way as their policy in relation to student fees. This feature of Scottish academic life was referred to in the Garrick Report (1998) where it is suggested that

> commentators may disagree about the extent [but] there is also a spirit of co-operation for students and resources. We accept that this is possibly as much a function of the size of the higher education sector in Scotland as an innate collaborative willingness.
>
> (Garrick, 1997: 12, para. 2.6)

What is the evidence of this; will it work? These ideas are in part still embryonic and time will yet tell whether increased collaboration can become a reality. However, there is some evidence of significant changes in that direction. Universities are making collaborative ventures in physics and chemistry. The Scottish Universities Physics Alliance (SUPA) involves Edinburgh, Glasgow, Heriot Watt, Paisley, St Andrews and Strathclyde. For chemistry, regional universities have joined together to form WestChem (Glasgow and Strathclyde) and EastChem (Edinburgh and St Andrews) (Wojtas, 2004). These initiatives have been supported by the Scottish Higher Education Funding Council. Similarly the recent invitation for bids to the Applied Educational Research Scheme (AERS), an initiative intended to raise the profile of educational research in Scotland resulted in a successful consortium bid from the universities of Strathclyde, Stirling and Edinburgh. The stated aim of the consortium was to involve staff from across all education departments in Scotland and research users in the professional/practice communities (Ozga, 2005). This move towards increased collaboration, therefore, seems significant but the extent of this and its possible success are yet to be determined.

A competitive or collaborative future for research funding and development in the UK?

A number of issues have been raised in this chapter in relation to the negative and problematic influences of the RAE as a system of funding and evaluating research in the UK. The changes being implemented for RAE 2008 have been explored and the extent to which they can help to mitigate problems discussed. Despite the changes, most of the difficulties both with the process of the RAE and the negative impacts it has will continue. The different emphases of research policy in both Scotland and Wales have been identified: in these smaller higher education systems there seems to be a much greater degree of change towards increased collaborative efforts across universities. In the recent White Paper on the Future of Higher Education, there is a similar concern in the English context to encourage institutions to work more in partnership. For example, the White Rose Consortium is given as an illustration of three northern universities, Sheffield, York and Leeds, working to create a collaborative critical mass of 'research, teaching and enterprise facilities' (Department for Education and Skills, 2003). The importance of such developments is recognized in this policy document.

However, the continuation of the RAE and other significant policy decisions are critical to the possible success of such collaborative ventures and the continuation of a healthy research sector within universities across the UK. The RAE is driven as a means primarily to maintain and increase UK competitiveness in research globally and, as a result of this, policy has been mainly to increase competitiveness between institutions and concentrate resources. Universities may find it more difficult to collaborate as a result of this. Furthermore, the drive for further concentration of resources, as identified by the Universities UK report, shows that whole regions could suffer huge losses of research income and not just some universities within regions. Given the importance of regional economic and cultural development, further concentration of resources could result in deep impoverishment of universities in some areas of the UK. There has to be a balance struck between ensuring the possibility of international competitiveness with the development of regional communities of higher education institutions. Otherwise collaboration of universities in particular regions will be difficult if not impossible.

Another significant feature of the White Paper (Department for Education and Skills, 2003) is the recognition that teaching activities have been undervalued due to the increased emphasis on research and success in the RAE. The solution is to argue for the creation of teaching only institutions (most telling is the removal of the necessity of research degree awarding powers for university status). Evidence is cited from only one research study of the relationship between teaching and research within university departments, which shows that there is no *necessary* correlation between the two (Hattie and Marsh, 1996). It does not refer to any more of the vast amount of research in this area, demonstrated most effectively by a recent International Conference looking at this issue and the evidence from the Higher Education Forum (Jenkins, 2004; Zaman, 2004). The Higher Education Forum argues that 'it is becoming clearer that those students who are not learning in an HE environment that is informed by research, and in which it is not possible to access research-related resources, are at a disadvantage compared to those who are' (Department For Education and Skills, 2004). Successful teaching-only institutions in the United States are given as possible models. However, this fails to recognize the historic specificity and cultural differences between UK and US higher education systems and the differences in funding mechanisms whereby the more endowment rich US institutions are more able to fund their academic staff in teaching-only institutions to continue research and scholarship work, although not at the same level as the research-intensive universities. No one would doubt that quality teaching can be done at such institutions but would anyone equally deny the benefits of a rich research and scholarship based university environment for staff and students? Cannot collaborative efforts ensure that no university need be cut off from these benefits and should not our funding mechanisms encourage and reflect this intention? There are, of course, different models across Europe, where research and teaching are funded in separate structures.

Priorities for research funding need to be determined not just by pragmatics (how best to distribute scarce resources, how to evaluate quality research), important though this may be. They must also be informed by priorities and commitments to a university system that is not hierarchical and exclusive in its outlook but provides a stimulating and exciting learning environment for students and a stimulating working environment for staff across all universities, and reaches out to the potential changes and impacts research can have in the local, national and international arena.

Notes

1   Information on the Hong Kong RAE can be obtained from the University Grants Committee (UGC) at http://www.ugc.edu.hk

2   Information on the 'Performance Based Research Funding' scheme can be
    obtained from the New Zealand Tertiary Education Commission found at http://
    www.tec.govt.nz/funding/research/pbrf

References

Adams, J. and Smith, D. (2004) *Research and the Regions: An Overview of the Distribution
    of Research in UK Regions, Regional Research Capacity and Links between Strategic
    Research Partners.* Oxford: Higher Education Policy Institute.
AUT (Association of University Teachers) (2003) *The Risk to Research in Higher Educa-
    tion in England.* London: AUT.
Barnard, C. (2004) One trick pony won't win race, *The Times Higher Education Supple-
    ment* (online), 12 November.
Baty, P. (2005) Ratings drive hits teaching, *The Times Higher Education Supplement*
    (online), 18 March.
Bourdieu, P. (1988) *Homo Academicus.* Cambridge: Polity Press.
Boyer, E. L. (1990) *Scholarship Reconsidered: Priorities of the Professoriate.* Princeton:
    Carnegie Foundation for the Advancement of Teaching.
Brown, R. (2000) Teaching is the main event, not a sideshow to research, *Research
    Fortnight*, 12 January.
DfES (Department for Education and Skills) (2003) *The Future of Higher Education.*
    Norwich: The Stationery Office.
DfES (2004) *Higher Education Act.* London: The Stationery Office.
Fazackerley, A. (2004) Russell Group rift over anti-RAE stance, *The Times Higher Edu-
    cation Supplement*, (online), 29 October.
Fisher, M. and Marsh, P. (2003) Social work research and the 2001 Research Assess-
    ment Exercise: an initial overview, *Social Work Education*, 22(1): 71–80.
Gambrill, E. (2002) 'I am not a rubber stamp': my experience as a non-UK RAE
    Adviser, *Journal of Social Work*, 2(2).
Garrick Report (1997) Higher Education in the Learning Society: the National
    Committee of Enquiry into Higher Education, *Report of the Scottish Committee*, July,
    Edinburgh.
Hare, P. G. (2003) The United Kingdom's Research Assessment Exercise: impact on
    institutions, departments, individuals, *Higher Education Management and Policy*,
    15(2): 43–61.
Harley, S. (2002) The impact of research selectivity on academic work and identity in
    UK universities, *Studies in Higher Education*, 27(2): 187–205.
Hattie, J. and Marsh, W. (1996) The relationship between research and teaching: a
    meta-analysis, *Review of Educational Research*, 66: 507–42.
HEFCE (2004) *Quality Profile Will Provide Fuller and Fairer Assessment of Research*, HEFCE
    Press Release, 11 February.
HEFCW (2002) *Paper for National Assembly of Wales Review of Higher Education.* www.
    wfc.ac.uk/**education**/   hefcw/**nawreview**/pdfs/wfcevid_e.pdf   (accessed   30
    March 2004).
Henkel, M. (2000) *Academic Identities and Policy Change in Higher Education.* London:
    Jessica Kingsley.
House of Commons Science and Technology Committee (2004) *Research Assessment
    Exercise: A Re-assessment: Eleventh Report of Session 2003–04.* London: The Station-
    ery Office.

Jenkins, A. (2004) *A Guide to the Research Evidence on Teaching-Research Relations*. York: HE Academy.

Jongbloed, B. and Vossensteyn, H. (2001) Keeping up performances: an international survey of performance-based funding in higher education, *Journal of Higher Education Policy and Management*, 23(2): 127–45.

Lewis, J. (2002) Assessing the Research Assessment Exercise: an expensive [mad] lottery? Presentation to the AUA annual conference, April.

Lucas, L. (2001) The research game: a sociological study of academic research work in two universities, Unpublished PhD, University of Warwick.

Lucas, L. (2003) Reclaiming academic research work from regulation and relegation, in M. Walker and J. Nixon (eds) *Reclaiming Universities From A Runaway World*. Maidenhead: SRHE/Open University Press.

Lucas, L. (forthcoming) *The Research Game in Academic Life*. Maidenhead: SRHE/Open University Press.

MacGregor, S. (2003) We did not simply mimic received opinion, *Journal of Social Work*, 3(1).

MacLeod, D. (2004) This could be the last time, *Guardian Unlimited* (online), 9 November.

McNay, I. (1997) *The Impact of the 1992 Research Assessment Exercise on Individual and Institutional Behaviour in English Higher Education*. Chelmsford: Anglia Polytechnic University.

McNay, I. (2003) Assessing the assessment: an analysis of the UK Research Assessment Exercise, 2001, and its outcomes, with special reference to research in education, *Science and Public Policy*, 30(1): 1–8.

McNay, I. (forthcoming) Research assessment; researcher autonomy, in C. Kayrooz, G. Akerlind and M. Tight (eds) *Autonomy in Social Science Research* (submitted to SRHE/Open University Press).

Newby, H. (2001) The Research Assessment Exercise 2001. Paper presented to conference 'RAE 2001: Review, Reflection … Reformulation?' University of Greenwich, London, 11 April.

Orr, D. (2004) Research assessment as an instrument for steering higher education – a comparative study, *Journal of Higher Education Policy and Management*, 26(3): 345–62.

Ozga, J. (2005) In the public interest? Research, knowledge transfer and education policy, Professorial Inaugural Lecture, Centre for Educational Sociology, Edinburgh, 25 January.

Roberts, G. (2003) *Review of Research Assessment*. Bristol: HEFCE.

Sharp, S. (2004) The Research Assessment Exercises 1992–2001: patterns across time and subjects, *Studies in Higher Education*, 29(2): 201–18.

SHEFC (Scottish Higher Education Funding Council) (2004) *Higher Education in Scotland: A Baseline Report*. Edinburgh: SHEFC.

Thomson, A. (2004) Scrap the RAE, says report, *The Times Higher Education Supplement* (online), 10 September.

Universities UK (2003) *Funding Research Diversity*. London: UUK.

Wojtas, O. (2004) Scots team up to fend off global competition, *The Times Higher Education Supplement* (online), 10 September.

Zaman, M. Q. (2004) *Review of the Academic Evidence on the Relationship Between Teaching and Research in Higher Education*. London: DfES.

11

Mainstreaming the Third Stream

Marilyn Wedgwood

Introduction

Particularly since the 1990s, universities have tried, encouraged by governments, to get more closely involved with the economy and with society. Pursuing that has evolved into a third strand of academic activity alongside teaching and research, the 'third stream'.[1] Additional public funding (combined with a rationalization of a variety of schemes that support the third stream) has been allocated to advance this closer involvement.

It is now time to recognize that such engagement is not an extra but mainstream; indeed engagement might be a way of pursuing teaching and research. It is timely for universities and governments to assess how they are progressing towards fruitful third strand engagement to inform future policy, strategy and activity within a mass system of provision.

Presented in this chapter are two models which illustrate the spread of a university's activities and the degree to which they interact, or not, with broader social and economic concerns. They aim to provide some of the conceptual clarity essential for making effective policy in this area, and to allow actors in the system to position themselves over the next decade.

Model 1 shows how engagement with society and the economy is meaningful not just for science, engineering or business departments, but across the whole range of academic disciplines. It allows us to examine the depth and variety of involvement in the different agendas that are important for the development of an equitable society in a thriving economy.

Model 2 illustrates the degree to which activities are steered or driven by the traditional academic criteria or by external societal imperatives. This model provides a 'map' by which one can plot a university's, department's, discipline's or individual academic's 'position' in terms of their engagement with academic and societal issues. This in turn shows how an HEI responds to the relevant influences on it and makes clear how current 'esteem' quality measures have limited coverage with the net consequence that the higher education sector is 'driven' in particular directions.

The policy challenge

Government needs clarity and to speak with a single voice. But there are tensions in national policy directions and tensions for the institutions themselves in the implementation of the policies.

The dominant policy perspective is that the 'third stream' is about stimulating business growth through enhanced business competitiveness, productivity and performance, wealth creation and business start-up. The underlying objective is to support economic growth. There is, therefore, significant focus on the exploitation of the science base. Much of the impetus for this is from a desire to grow the knowledge economy and to increase innovation and investment in research and development (R and D) by companies. The strengthening of the science base and the commercial exploitation of research are major parts of this agenda. For the universities this provides resource support for science research and an income stream from its commercialization. This agenda is primarily championed by the Office for Science and Technology (OST) and the DTI, with significant support from Treasury (HM Treasury, DTI, DfES, 2004).

Another perspective is that the third stream agenda is about the contribution universities can make to society more generally – the underlying objective being the best way to achieve public good. It is therefore all-encompassing: it involves a wider range of academic disciplines, a wider range of local and national government agendas and a wider range of stakeholders beyond business, such as regional agencies, local government, the police, the education services, communities, voluntary services, the health services. This broader perspective encompasses enduring agendas of governments both to stimulate the economy and to generate an inclusive society and reflects more closely economic development plans produced in the regions and sub-regions. These address social, cultural, environmental and infrastructure issues as well as business competitiveness and wealth creation. HEFCE considers the civic responsibilities of universities an additional part of the third stream agenda. The wider interpretation also encourages diversity with excellence in the HE system: each institution is able to build on and work to individual and distinctive strengths in the different disciplines contributing to a range of societal agendas. This wider interpretation is signalled in the HE White Paper (DfES, 2003), championed by HEFCE in its Strategic Plan (HEFCE, 2004) and through its Business and Community Committee and evident throughout the sector in, for example, recently successful Higher Education Innovation Fund 2 bids. In Wales, the plan for regional clusters of institutions is about community regeneration, not just the economy. In Scotland, the Enterprise portfolio is twinned with Lifelong Learning in a single ministry. After the 2001 RAE, the Northern Ireland Office gave £10m to supplement research funding for work relevant to the economic and community development.

Whatever the interpretation, the defining characteristic of the third stream is that it demands a demonstrable connectedness, an engagement, with the concerns and issues of society, be they economic, social, cultural or environmental. Knowledge transfer (two-way) is therefore fundamental to it. One consequence is that HEIs have to interact more professionally with stakeholders – growing that market, and developing new skills, behaviours and organizational structures to interact with it. Mainstreaming the third stream will challenge notions of what it is to be an academic in the twenty-first century and what it is to be a university. It will generate new demands for management and administration in the institutions and in the skills of the staff. It will challenge the businesses and institutions outside academe to reflect on how and why they engage with the HEIs.

Government and its agencies must make clear that technology transfer, start-ups, licensing, etc., are only a small segment of the broad spectrum of engagement. What is to be encouraged is debate, exchange of ideas, comparison of theory and practice, a mutual valuing of theorists and practitioners across the board and recognition of the breadth of contribution HE can make to society. Mainstreaming the third stream requires a 'freeing up' from individual government departments' specific interests and a forward looking view about how to maximize the public investment in the knowledge base for the good of society as a whole in a way that enriches the quality of the academic institutions.

The models

The models below present a holistic approach. They take account of the fact that since the mid-1980s, governments have placed more demands on HE to deliver on societal agendas beyond the provision of learning programmes and academic research. Those demands include direct involvement in economic development, regional development, and social inclusion through widening participation; sector skills developments; continuous professional development; exploitation of the research base; business innovation and competitiveness; and graduate employability. The models concentrate mainly on the value of 'intellectual assets' in HE to support such agendas, not the broader civic responsibilities of HEIs as corporate institutions in defined localities.

They work from the general principle of inclusiveness – the involvement of all academic disciplines and the involvement of non-commercial businesses and organizations as well as commercial business. The models are conceptual frameworks for analysing the potential capability of the third stream, and as such they provide some insight about the implications of present and future policy and strategy decisions.

The optimization model

This mainly addresses third stream issues from a government perspective (see Figure 11.1). It exemplifies the value and role of the HEIs' intellectual resources in underpinning the economy and in promoting a good quality of life. It recognizes that economic success depends on a blend of economic, social and cultural and infrastructure inputs that both public and private sectors can benefit from, and that HE has intellectual resources that can contribute in meaningful ways.

The model unfolds from the original perspective of HEFCE – Higher Education Reaching Out to Business and the Community (HEROBAC). This approach addresses two major, enduring concerns of governments: one to generate and sustain a strong economy (wealth creation), the other to generate a strong equitable society (quality of life). The former is the domain of private business; the latter has particular relevance to public service delivery. Whilst each of these issues is powerful and important in its own right, each impacts on the other. National and local governments are concerned that economic development should be inclusive, benefiting citizens in all strata of society. The quality of life factors are affected by economic strength. Local conditions affect business success through the quality of the infrastructure to do business, the availability of skills, the quality of life that attracts and retains employees, or the quality of the transport or ICT systems. This synergy between the development of the economy and of society for growing the knowledge economy, is recognized in work by van Winden and van den Berg (2004) for the Dutch Ministry of the Interior and Kingdom Relations, in collaboration with France, the UK and Germany.

Each level of government and each new administration addresses these two major issues in different ways. Figure 11.1 highlights some of the areas that have prominence in national, regional and local policies, and that emerge as part of economic development plans at these levels, such as those for the North West Development Agency (NWDA, 2003) and the Greater Manchester Economic Development Plan (Manchester Enterprises, 2004). It is fascinating to reflect on these areas and to recognize that within HE, there is expertise relevant to these various societal agendas through the broad range of academic disciplines. Science, engineering technology, the social sciences, education, the humanities and arts all have a contribution to make across the range. They give insight into issues such as human behaviour, government and citizenship, knowledge, communication and learning, lifestyles, health, social stability, human productivity, social justice and exclusion, work and organization, scientific discovery, technological advances, and cultural development. All these insights and understandings are fundamentally relevant to a vibrant society. They provide the seed corn of creative talent for driving improvements in society and the economy. At the base of Figure 11.1 various Whitehall departments are roughly positioned with respect to their areas of interest; this would be replicated in devolved administrations.

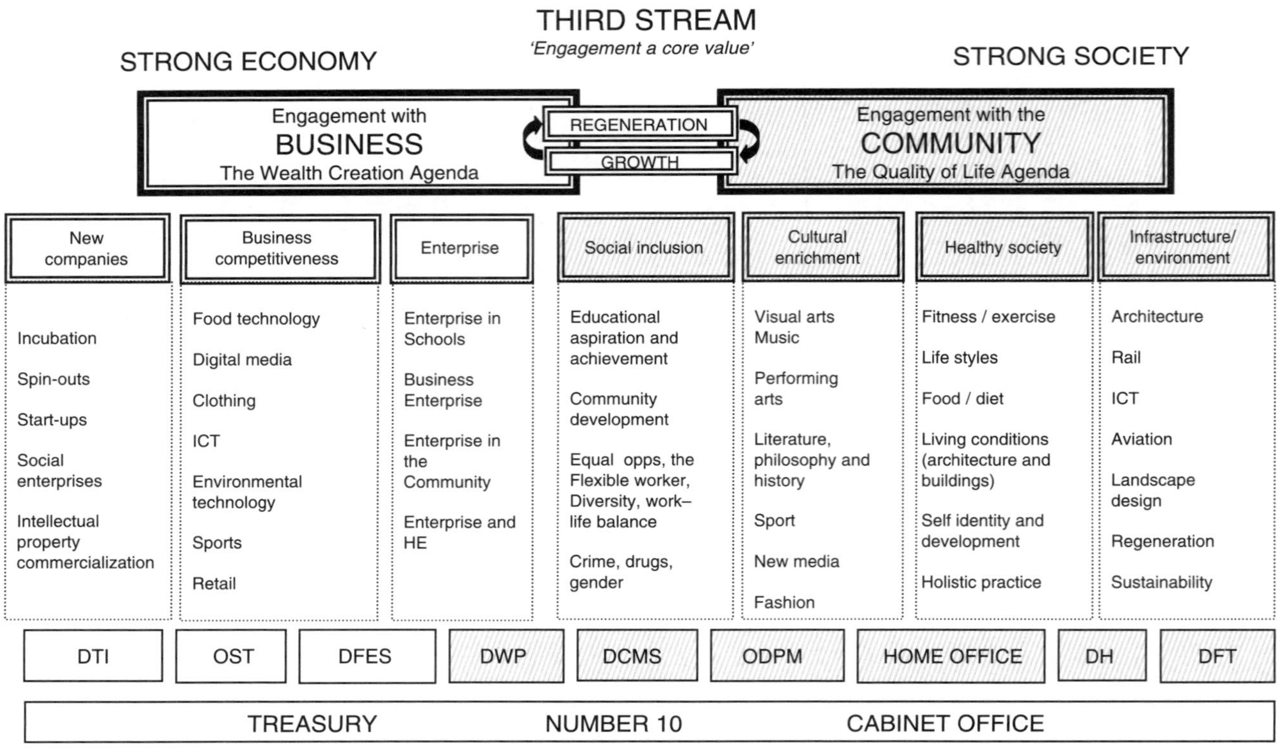

THIRD STREAM
'Engagement a core value'

STRONG ECONOMY   STRONG SOCIETY

Engagement with BUSINESS — The Wealth Creation Agenda			REGENERATION / GROWTH	Engagement with the COMMUNITY — The Quality of Life Agenda			
New companies	Business competitiveness	Enterprise	Social inclusion	Cultural enrichment	Healthy society	Infrastructure/ environment
Incubation	Food technology	Enterprise in Schools	Educational aspiration and achievement	Visual arts	Fitness / exercise	Architecture
Spin-outs	Digital media	Business Enterprise	Community development	Music	Life styles	Rail
Start-ups	Clothing	Enterprise in the Community	Equal opps, the Flexible worker, Diversity, work–life balance	Performing arts	Food / diet	ICT
Social enterprises	ICT	Enterprise and HE	Crime, drugs, gender	Literature, philosophy and history	Living conditions (architecture and buildings)	Aviation
Intellectual property commercialization	Environmental technology			Sport	Self identity and development	Landscape design
	Sports			New media	Holistic practice	Regeneration
	Retail			Fashion		Sustainability

DTI	OST	DFES	DWP	DCMS	ODPM	HOME OFFICE	DH	DFT
TREASURY				NUMBER 10		CABINET OFFICE		

Figure 11.1 The Optimization model

Figure 11.1 aims to capture this point, with reference to the contribution Manchester Metropolitan University (MMU) can make from its academic discipline and expert base. All institutions could undertake similar mapping. Tables 11.1 and 11.2 further exemplify the value and impacts of academic disciplines in relation to different societal agendas.

Professional activities that build on the knowledge base are the tools by which capability is 'released' and made available to a non-academic 'audience'. Such activities are broadly described as 'knowledge transfer' and involve students and staff. They include activities such as the commercializa-

Table 11.1 The Optimization model in relation to Art and Design

	INTELLECTUAL CAPITAL *The resource base*	WEALTH CREATION	QUALITY OF LIFE
ART and DESIGN	**130 Academic staff**	○ People into Creative Industries (CIS) ○ Creative Industry start-ups and spin-outs	○ Performers and producers ○ Public exhibitions, displays, performances and facilities
	Over 1000 Graduates per year	○ Design for competitive products in all sectors	○ Public art
	Expertise is contained within the schools of:–	○ Creative expert advice and consultancy in CIS	○ Arts for health
	Architecture	○ Sophisticated consumers	○ Creative arts in communities to address deprivation and inclusion
	Art	○ Archived reference material for competitive products	○ Saving and maintaining museums as a community resource
	Design	○ Museums and collections for tourism	○ Advice and support on the development of conducive environments
	History of Art and Design		○ Heritage ○ The built environment

Note: This takes the optimization model further by identifying the contribution of a Faculty's work (Art and Design) to the wealth creation and quality of life agenda. Similar examples can be developed for other discipline areas.

Table 11.2 Example impacts of third stream work for different subjects, on 'Quality of Life' issues

	Issue	*Work in the HEIs*	*Impact*
Architecture	Physical environment	New use of historic gardens	Improved community resource
Sport	High levels of heart disease	Daily regime of physical activity	City protocols and schemes adopted by GPs that are also quality assured
Community Studies	Old age inclusion	Pension seeking behaviour of ethnic groups	Pension tracking pack to help pensioners
Psychology	Prisoner rehabilitation	Working with prisons with offenders	Reduced rate of offending
Health Care Studies	Health promotion on HIV and AIDS	Perspectives in African Caribbean communities	Increased understanding of cultural and language issues in take up of advice

Note: This shows the way in which examples of work by academic staff with the non commercial sector, relate to issues within economic development plans, and indicates the impact of the work.

tion of Intellectual Property through spin-out companies and licences, student placements, contract research and teaching, collaborative research and teaching, expert advice, consultancy and specialist technical and advisory services (CBI, 2001). The third stream, in its broadest conception, would also include other professional activities such as being a non-executive on the board of a company, or an adviser to the public sector, or an expert witness, or writing reports, policy papers or books.

On the whole, such knowledge transfer activities have concentrated on the wealth creation/strong economy (left-hand side) part of the model presented in Figure 11.1. However they also have validity for the quality of life agenda that is represented on the right-hand side of the model. Often the methods of engagement and skills required to engage in such agendas are directly transferable: enabling access, managing stakeholder interests, negotiating 'deals' and setting up contracts. The significant understandings and experiences about business–university interactions in the HE system are similarly transferable.

Policy implications of the model

The model illustrates the breadth of capability and potential in the HE system to engage with societal agendas to generate a strong economy and society and the kind of return governments could achieve from their investment in HE. The prime policy decision is whether to embrace this breadth or to restrict the focus.

It is interesting to note that in the report of the consultation process for the development of HEIF2 (HEFCE, 2003b; HEFCE, 2003c) 'There was broad support for the wider brief beyond science and technology' and support for 'explicit recognition of the public service, civic and community related outcomes, and an applauding of the acknowledgement of the potential for HEIF activities of the arts, humanities and creative industries'. Such breadth is also applauded within the HEFCE Strategic Plan 2003–08 (HEFCE, 2004).

A further decision then relates to the nature and extent of strategic partnership arrangements between HEM and different governmental departments. A strategic partnership between HEFCE and the DTI and OST already exists. The Office of the Deputy Prime Minister (ODPM), the Home Office, the Department of Health and the DfES can also benefit in the delivery of their agendas from similar partnership arrangements that either generate new or expand existing arrangements. Their involvement would help to capitalize on the expertise in HE for the departments' agendas and give recognition to the value of work that engages stakeholders outside the private sector.

Underlying such decisions is a fundamental principle about what return governments expect from their investment in terms of the wider contribution to society. An inclusive approach will optimize that return.

Diversity with Excellence model

In embracing the third stream, institutions have to understand where and how it fits with their mission, their traditions, their culture and their organization structures. The Diversity with Excellence model aims to do this through a series of unfolding figures (11.2–11.9). A central tenet of the model is that teaching and research are the two core activities of HEIs, developed and delivered in a context. The horizontal line in Figure 11.2 represents the core activity and the vertical one the context. One end of the context line is the academic one, where the academic disciplines define and set the standards, approaches and methodologies. The relationships are with the peer academic community who codify, verify and validate the quality and value of the work. The context is an academic theoretical one. Academic achievement and value are the drivers. The other context incorporates those communities who operate outside of academe. It is labelled societal (context) in Figure 11.2. The value and quality of the teaching and research at the societal end are measured by the wider community's interests, standards,

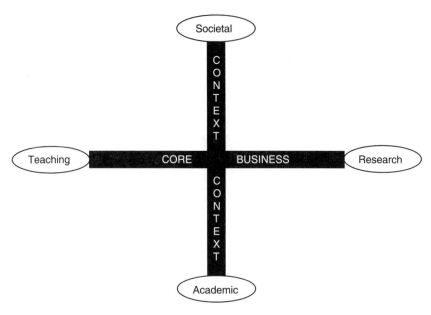

Figure 11.2 The basic Diversity with Excellence model

requirements and values. Teaching and research, in this context, are practice-informed, practice-relevant, and both draw on and contribute to the issues that arise out of 'practice'. They are driven by the concerns of the external community. They are similar to the quadrants in McNay's (2003) model labelled 'collegium' and 'enterprise', and also echo the Mode 1/Mode 2 debate in research and knowledge production (Gibbons, 2003).

The context line in a sense reflects 'public good'/ 'public service'. It aims to capture the breadth and variety of the value the core activities of teaching and research can bring to society outside of academe, if focused to do so.

At each of the contextual ends the teaching and research are still excellent, still subject to the principles, values and approaches of the higher education environment such as rigour, objectivity, originality, creativity and evidence. What is different is the 'driver'. At the societal end the inspiration comes from the concerns, and issues of practice, whereas at the other end the drive is from the academy. Each is legitimate, each interacts with the other, but the third stream is about deliberate engagement with society's issues and concerns, activities that relate to the top half of the diagram. It is this area that encapsulates the third stream and that is the focus for mainstreaming the third stream.

The broad missions/priorities of HEIs (or of departments, faculties or individuals) can be explored through the model as exemplified in Figure 11.3. Clearly in the top half of the diagram the way the HEI conducts its core business is coincident with being engaged with society. In contrast, engagement with society could undermine the core direction for those positioned

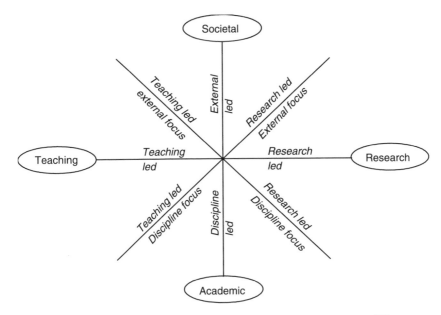

Figure 11.3 Diversity with Excellence model showing the continuum of different models for institutions, faculties, departments or individuals

in the lower half of the diagram. (Commercialization of IP is a decision about generating income rather than being about 'mission'.)

Figure 11.3 also exemplifies the commitment of the New Labour government to institutional diversity made clear in Blunkett's Greenwich speech in February 2000 (Blunkett, 2000): 'Our objective is expansion with diversity and excellence throughout the sector', and echoed in one Funding Council's Strategic Plan for 'a sector working to common standards of excellence to achieve shared goals across a wide range of activity' (HEFCE, 2004).

Figure 11.3, as well as being relevant to the range of HEIs in the UK, also has relevance to different subject disciplines within institutions. For some, the engagement with practice is an integral part of the subject discipline. The practice of law informs the research, which informs the practice in a virtuous circle. The practice of engineering often informs the theory which informs the practice. For other subjects links can be made where the input of academe enlightens and supports the practice, whether through a scientific discovery being exploited to produce a competitive product, a historian enhancing the success of an archaeological amenity for the public, or a town planner assessing the impact of new housing policy. Different faculties or different departments will have different emphases.

Figure 11.4 develops the model further by identifying and positioning different agendas HEIs have to deliver. Clearly the top half of the diagram relates to the third stream. Most of the time, however, third stream work is interpreted in relation to research, and therefore the top right-hand side

Figure 11.4 Diversity with Excellence model showing different agendas HEIs are expected to address in relation to their position in the model

only. Figures 11.5 and 11.6 make more explicit the differentiation of the top half of the diagram. Figure 11.5 identifies the impacts that teaching and research have when pursued in different contexts. Figure 11.6 identifies the stakeholders with particular interests in these areas. Though the diagrams highlight the societal benefit, the HEI also benefits at both an institution level and at the level of the individual academic or student. The wider range of stakeholders that the third stream work engages provides a bigger pool of investment into the university. That investment, as well as bringing in funding, generates relationships that enrich teaching and research by providing different contexts, insights and resources. Such insights can generate new learning experiences for students and new discoveries that contribute both to the academic research base and to practice. In pragmatic terms, third stream work, carefully managed, contributes to the assessments of research and teaching and learning.

The model is developed further by exploring the quality esteem measures in Figure 11.7, and the current main funding methodologies in Figure 11.8 (see page 147). For research there is a quality and esteem measure in the form of the Research Assessment Exercise (see Lisa Lucas's chapter in this volume). The Teaching Quality Assessment (TQA) process – now revised – gave quantitative measures from peers. Greater emphasis is now placed on auditing institutions and judging their quality through an institutional self-evaluation process and discipline audit trails. The work is organized by the Quality Assurance Agency (QAA) and reviews are undertaken by peers.

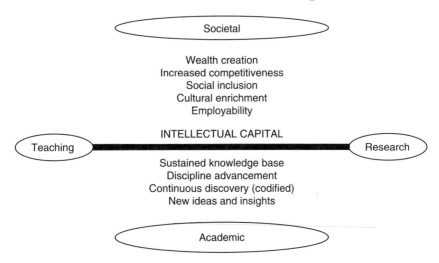

Figure 11.5 Diversity with Excellence model showing impacts of endeavour focused on societal or academic issues

Figure 11.6 Diversity with Excellence model showing the main stakeholders for academic endeavour in a societal and academic context

Figure 11.7 shows starkly that there are no national 'strategic' quality and esteem measures for measuring the quality of third stream activity on a par with those for research or for learning and teaching (though some aspects of the RAE and TQA and the new QAA processes provide some acknowledgement). Institutions do not have a means of expressing their excellence in engaging with society through formalized esteem measures that are published 'kite marks' of excellence. Instead of having one national measure of

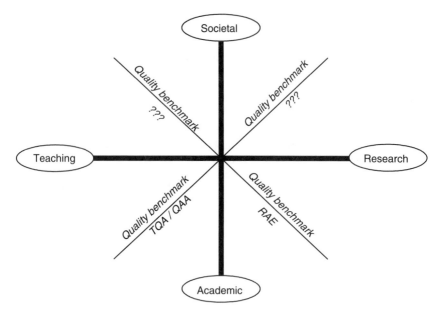

Figure 11.7 Diversity with Excellence model showing measurement scales for esteem measures defined by the quality benchmark

esteem there is a range of performance measures that indicate performance for a bidding competition or more generally. Examples include HEBIS published by HEFCE (HEFCE, 2003a); performance measures for different bids such as HEIF2; and widening participation enrolments from HEFCE. These are not yet organized into national measures of esteem. Those institutions that excel in these areas, as a recognized professional area of endeavour within the sector, or seek to excel in them, do not achieve recognition. In some countries, e.g. Germany and the Netherlands, such engagement *is* part of a review process (Orr, 2004)

There would be value to be gained in mainstreaming the third stream to work through esteem measures that aim to provide quality benchmarks on a par with those for research and learning and teaching. Each of these address a mixture of indicators in relation to institutional perspectives on strategy and management as well as output and performance. The key characteristic is that the measures are contained within an overall framework (and process) for assuring and recognizing excellence and quality. The measures are above and beyond simple indicators of activity or performance. There is work underway on metrics for the third stream working through OST, the Research Councils and HEFCE. Though the HEBIS has developed out of the DTI over a number of years to monitor different types of third stream activity quantitatively and qualitatively, it has a long way to go before it becomes a measure of quality and esteem. SHEFC (2003) has also addressed metrics developing a 'university-centric' model based on income to the university.

The income is weighted according to the income source (which is itself a proxy measure) which attempts to recognize that some activity is undertaken for the public good whilst other activity, such as venturing, generates income. The latter, as a result, has the lowest rating. The development of metrics is difficult whilst there remain policy tensions identified earlier. There is no clear consensus on their focus, their type or the degree to which they should embrace a narrow or wide agenda for the third stream. However, since 'what gets measured is what gets done', getting them right in terms of the 'end points' required in the institutions, in the economy and in the organizations external to the universities is critically important for driving the third stream forward in the right direction. Clearly, esteem measures would help legitimize and validate the importance of third stream work.

The third stream has not yet evolved into a core area of work. The lack of esteem measures exemplifies this as do the funding methodologies. Funding for work that engages with societal agendas (defined in the top half of the model) is generally approached in a piecemeal way (Figure 11.8). The funding for teaching and research is 'core' and sustained whereas that for the third stream is mainly based on 'time-defined' initiatives and projects. A commitment to core funding was made in the HE White Paper (DfES, 2003) through the Higher Education Innovation Fund (HEIF). Though it is not formula funded at the present time, but won through competitive bidding, there does appear to be a commitment to allocate a substantial part of the

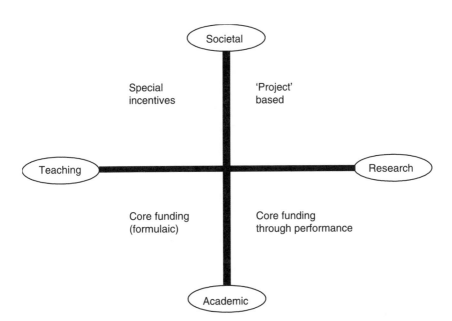

Figure 11.8 Diversity with Excellence model showing the different main funding methodologies for activity that falls within each of the quadrants

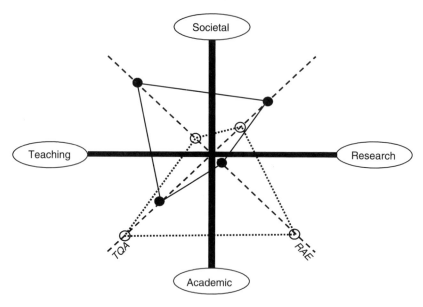

Figure 11.9 Diversity with Excellence model used for 'mapping' activity, performance or aspiration in relation to the country, institution, faculty department or individual

funds through formula funding, while keeping an element of competitive bidding.

Finally, Figure 11.9 aims to show that institutions, individuals or departments can map themselves using the bisecting axes as measures of different parameters such as priority, emphasis, capability, performance or excellence.

Policy implications of the Diversity with Excellence model

The model emphasizes the diversity in the HE system. It draws attention to the fact that institutions have different histories, cultures, traditions and strengths that determine their own particular identities and 'personalities' in their geographical locations.

A fundamental policy decision is about how diverse the HE system should be to meet the requirements in the twenty-first century. A decision to embrace the diversity of the HE system in mainstreaming the third stream would release significant potential for institutions and disciplines to contribute to a variety of major government agendas. Such a decision would help to inform the breadth and diversity of the third stream developments and encourage new futures for a wider range of institutions and diversity of mission that yields many excellences.

Related to that decision is one about the relative importance of ensuring that the HE sector engages with society, and whether that should include the whole sector or parts of it. Open engagement with communities is a characteristic of Trow's 'universal' level of provision.

Perspectives on mainstreaming the third stream

A revised landscape for higher education? What is the 'end game'?

The significant challenge is to achieve a cultural shift where higher education and the stakeholders are routinely engaged with each other as a normal part of their professional activity, bringing mutual benefits that support the growth of a strong economy and society, with high professional standards. The activity is not new, but what is new is the re-positioning of the activity as a core area of work for HE. That repositioning, sustained with core funding, should address many of the concerns about making the interface effective between HE and its stakeholders. The routine working will generate improved mutual understandings and with it respect and trust that fuels continuation and sustainability. The market for HE will be more confident and further bolstered through measures that assure high quality professional standards. Partnerships with other government departments, besides the DTI, will ensure the relevance of the third stream to government agendas, and specific initiatives can address market failures.

New interpretations

The new climate will challenge some existing notions and perspectives on a university of the twenty-first century. New ways of seeing and doing things will inevitably result.

Already there is a shift in thinking from 'technology transfer' to 'knowledge transfer' to 'knowledge exchange and interchange'. This shift recognizes that knowledge flows are multiple and not just from academe to industry. The innovation system is complex, not linear as SURF (Centre for Sustainable Urban and Regional Futures) points out: 'new theories of innovation, which reject a linear firm-based approach, see that the relationships between firms, universities and their wider environments is critical in leading to improved economic performance' (House of Lords, 2003:). The importance of relationships is emphasized in the Lambert Report (Lambert, 2003). In practical terms the policy decisions must create an environment – a context and climate – where such interchange and relationship building is easy.

Mainstreaming the third stream will modify the climate of HE and the way it does its business. Engagement will be a more valued activity that becomes increasingly recognized as a legitimate professional area of work for the academic and the HEI. Core funding will enable the development of specialist staff to promote, facilitate and broker engagement. It will buy time for academic staff to engage. It will facilitate the development of new systems and procedures that improve access for the stakeholders; it will assure quality; it will provide a professional career path for staff; it will encourage the development of new skills, for example, in stakeholder management; and it will generate confidence in the market of the commitment and ability of HE to engage.

Higher education will actively develop new markets with new products and services whilst still maintaining the integrity of its fundamental mission of research and teaching. But the market is a complex one for the third stream as for other areas of HE. Government clearly wants to improve the competitive position of companies through innovation, and provides resources to HE to address this. It basically wants HE to get involved in a marketplace (small and medium enterprises, for example) where the return is not necessarily cost-effective. The development of new markets will continue to create tensions for universities in achieving the balance between providing a public service and being commercially viable. The increasing reliance on private funding and income generation will change the dynamics in universities in relation to their public service role. Those most heavily reliant on public funding could reasonably be expected to fulfil their public service role. However as the income base diversifies and the balance between public funding and private funding/income generation (from IP exploitation) changes, so too does the relative importance of public service delivery, as universities become more independent of the 'public purse'.

There will be a major challenge in setting up quality and standards. Much of the emphasis at the present time is on metrics, performance measures that justify the return on government investment. But the third stream is about long-term change, long-term development, where metrics might help drive the change and the direction. However, producing metrics outside of a wider framework of quality and standards seems misplaced where the policy is to mainstream the third stream for sustainable impact. Decisions about what such a quality framework might be in which metrics fit will be critical in driving the third stream in particular directions as it is mainstreamed. Such a framework must identify the strategic aims, objectives and goals of the third stream. Ideally it would address institutional leadership and management processes, a strategic plan by institutions with goals, activities and the impacts that relate to the different stakeholders – the university itself, the businesses or other user organisations, and governments – local or national. The framework will set the reference point, the direction, if the focus and breadth of the third stream are agreed. Outcome and impact measures can then fit in the frame in relation to different time scales and geographical emphases.

Currently there is work underway by HEFCE, by OST as part of HEIF and the research councils to further develop metrics/performance measures from each of their different perspectives for activities that broadly relate to knowledge transfer. Such metrics seem driven by accountability to justify investment. They are mainly informed by ideas on measures that relate to the impact of third stream activity on R and D investment by companies: the Science and Innovation Investment Framework (HM Treasury, DTI, DfES, 2004) identifies increased investment in R and D in the economy as a strategic aim. Such measures are neither the best nor most appropriate for the range of activities and impacts that engagement by many academic disciplines generates. Even the development of social, civic and cultural indicators by HEFCE seem to reflect such an approach. But contribution to the PSA (Public Service Agreement) targets that are required of public service deliverers would seem very appropriate for work with the non-profit sector.

Powell (2004) argues for a more sophisticated and forward thinking approach to the development of competency, capability and quality in third stream activities. He has led a group of 11 universities in developing the UPBEAT project which allows competency to be progressively monitored and measured through the development of mastery in defined attributes, behaviours and results. Wedgwood (2003) presents an approach that draws on balanced score card methodologies that start from the fundamental point of what the strategic aims, objectives and goals of the third stream are.

An interesting reflection is whether engagement becomes a 'core value', not just a core activity. The concept has been explored and championed by the Association of Commonwealth Universities (ACU, 2002; Bjarnason and Coldstream, 2003). Coldstream emphasizes the importance of engaging with wider society 'not as an adjunct to but a sine qua non of their central purpose'. He argues that a debate about engagement (third stream in the context of this chapter) is

> about how universities may understand society's expectations, try to anticipate and to help form them, take the fullest account of the anxieties within them, learn, listen and respond to them – often rather uncomfortably in the well-lighted drama of public controversy.
>
> (Coldstream, 2003: 4)

The third stream is already generating new behaviours, new skills, new relationships and new perspectives that will be embedded in the heart of the institutions themselves. Individual members of academic staff will be involved in three core areas of work – teaching, research and engagement (third stream). Synergies will generate new insights, understandings, relevancies and expectations. Brown (2002), examining the literature on scholarship, addresses concepts of academic professionalism that reinforce the notion of synergistic relationships between the activities that constitute academic professionalism. Gibbons (2003) explores the nature of the social contract between society and the institutions in relation to the requirement of society for knowledge and the way in which it is changing and could change as institutions embrace engagement as a core value. He concludes that unless the universities become more involved in, and devote more resources to, the production of socially robust knowledge, they will be unable to maintain their part of the bargain under the new social contract; that is, they will be not able to sustain either the autonomy they seek or put on a sound footing their role as conscience of society and protector of public good.

(Gibbons, 2003: 50)

The policy choices

The third stream is in transition from a projects based approach with highly specific metrics, to a core routine area of work by HEIs, core funded alongside teaching and research, and quality assured through defined quality and standards processes and esteem measures. Exploitation of the science and technology base for economic growth, and innovation through investment in R and D, are an integral part of its development, to strengthen the UK's competitive position in the global knowledge economy.

Where the policy is much less clear is in relation to the wider economic agenda, and to the social agenda. The positioning of HEIF 3 in the Science and Innovation Framework places emphasis on the science and innovation aspects bringing into question the 'place' of the wider agenda. It questions whether the contribution HE can make to the social, cultural, infrastructural and environmental components that permeate economic development plans can be released because they are insufficiently recognized.

Mainstreaming the third stream generates many questions for policymakers to address. The choices and decisions will shape the future focus, emphasis and approach. Figure 11.10 attempts to capture this. It identifies

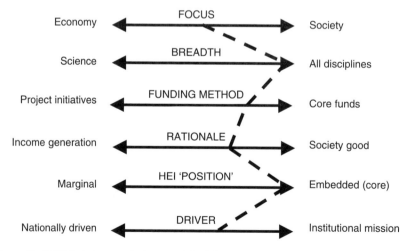

Figure 11.10 Third stream choices and decisions

broad areas (through horizontal lines) where decisions have to be made about the relative focus of third stream activity. The figure has relevance at national and institutional level. If the national decision is one that incorporates all these aspects, then individual institutions could define their own emphases in relation to their mission, their history, their cultures and their strengths. The lines also highlight in many ways the tensions in policy noted at the start of this chapter.

Challenges to policy decision-makers

The third stream is at a critical time in its development. There is a significant opportunity to stand back and look at its potential and its place in the HE sector. For policy-makers there are real challenges about the nature and breadth of the third stream, the process of implementation and the relative importance of such activity within the sector. Some key messages of this chapter are summarized below.

Embrace the breadth – make it inclusive

Enabling the full range of academic disciplines and stakeholders to be intimately involved in the third stream optimizes its potential, stimulates a new culture of engagement between the sector and its stakeholders, gives the greatest level of return on government investment, capitalizes on and gives renewed momentum to interest and capability that already exists and encourages diversity with excellence in the sector to reflect different requirements of students, private and public sector organizations and future employers.

Aim for quality and standards not just metrics

The delivery of the third stream, like the delivery of teaching or research, requires a complex mix of: quality institutional support systems and processes; quality activities and outputs; and an overall framework of quality and standards. The long-term aim is to generate high quality institutional development and change that raises competency and capability to high professional standards. The impact of third stream activity, in its range and complexity, on business performance, on public sector delivery and on society generally, demands and justifies serious endeavours to solve the issue. Many measures are in place in terms of business performance and productivity, of social cohesion and public service delivery. HE's contribution can be more fully explored and exploited. The drive to get the metrics right for the end game must continue.

Set the third stream in an enabling framework

Each HEI has its own history, culture, strengths, relationships, mission and geographic locality that mean the third stream will be delivered in different ways with different emphases. Too high a regulatory framework by governments will constrain the capability of the sector, but a framework that sets the overall direction whilst enabling institutions to deliver to their strengths is emancipatory. Interventions can be made where a specific impact is required or where attention needs to focus to bring about change. An enabling policy framework, with the opportunity to interpret locally would be a compass, not a road map. The sector is richly diverse: that richness and diversity provides a very valuable resource base for the multitude of stakeholders who have different requirements for research, teaching and learning, and third stream activity.

Conclusions

Society is faced with continual challenges. Within higher education there is a rich and diverse pool of internationally connected academics who, through their professional work, constantly challenge the existing status of society's knowledge, to generate new insights, discoveries and inventions that can enable the development of society in all aspects. The third stream can release that capability, but it requires an enlightened approach that recognizes and understands how the range of subject disciplines as they continuously evolve, contributes; one that uses the public funded knowledge base in a sensible way to help address the significant issues faced by society and governments at national or local level.

At the heart of the mainstreaming of the third stream are individuals, the academic staff and members of support teams. It is those individuals who will deliver higher education within the framework set by institutions and governments. They are the central focus. They will be the 'integrators' who find their own individual ways of accommodating the different demands being made within an academic professional context. They will develop their own expertise, knowledge, skills, networks and contacts that then become manifest in teaching, research, third stream and other professional activities. Some will be specialists in one of these areas, but many will recognize and become expert in capitalizing on the synergies between these different components, developing themselves and enriching the quality of higher education. But all this will happen only if the policy context is the right one and if the policy-makers make it possible.

Much of mainstreaming the third stream is about rediscovering a traditional area of academic professionalism that is not recognized in the current regulatory and accountability framework. It is about giving freedom to excel. The models begin to tease out the richness of academic professionalism and the impacts of policy on strengthening or undermining its expression and value. Public funding, informed by the policy-makers, will shape the future of the third stream to be engaged with society in all its variety and richness or not. Society deserves the very best return for its investment in the higher education infrastructure of the UK.

Note

1   The third stream as a third core objective for universities emerged in the mid-1990s. It grew out of an increasing recognition that universities had a role to play in the development of local economies (Gray, 1999) and whilst led in England mainly by HEFCE, involved the DTI. Their dialogue resulted in competitive bidding rounds for the third stream/mission. HEROBAC (Higher Education Reaching out to Business and the Community, HEFCE, 1999) was the start and provided funding from 2000–2004. From the start, HEFCE recognized the breadth of contribution that HE could make to the development of society. It therefore ensured that the 'third leg' agenda addressed knowledge transfer in the context of society more generally rather than just in economic terms. The HEACF (The Higher Education Active Community Fund) was instigated in 2002 and followed up in 2004. It was a partnership with the Home Office to support volunteering. This action further reinforced the breadth of focus of the third stream. HEIF 1 started in 2001 and incorporated more funding and more of the work of the DTI. (It incorporated initiatives such as University Challenge and Science Enterprise Challenge – both concerned with generating spin-out companies from research). The Higher Education White Paper followed in 2003 (DfES, 2003), making a commitment to a permanent third stream of funding through HEIF. It set out its vision in Chapter 3 entitled 'Higher education and business-exchanging and developing knowledge and skills'. In 2003 HEFCE (HEFCE, 2004) introduced four strategic themes in its strategic plan. One of these was 'To support all HE institutions in making a significant and measurable contribution to economic development and the strength of communities'. A committee was established reporting to the HEFCE board advising on such matters.

During 2003/4 Treasury worked with other Whitehall departments (mainly the DTI but also including the DfES) to produce a series of reports that had direct relevance to the third stream (The Lambert Report on Business University Interactions and the Innovation Review). In 2003 HEIF 2 was launched in December, to provide funding from 2004–2006. Though managed by HEFCE there was very significant input from OST in managing the process. After consultation, the bidding document incorporated a broader focus for HEIF 2 (HEFCE, 2003b).

During the whole of this period of development from the mid-1990s there was also significant growing emphasis on the importance of science and of innovation in driving the economy and of the engagement of HEIs in that agenda. This is exemplified by a whole series of reports such as the *Innovation Report* (DTI, 2003), Roberts Report (Roberts, 2002) and The House of Lords Science and Technology Select Committee Report in 2004 on SETting the Regional Agenda. Attention too was given to fiscal and other incentives that engaged business in innovation. In 2004 the third stream became embedded in the Science and Innovation strategy and work began to address a formulaic funding methodology.

In summary, having started from a broad focus through HEFCE, third stream developments are positioned in the science and innovation framework of the DTI/OST and Treasury, which have remits covering all four countries of the UK.

References

ACU (Association of Commonwealth Universities) (2002) *Engagement as a Core Value for the University: A Consultation Document.* London: ACU.

Bjarnason, S. and Coldstream, P. (eds) (2003) *The Idea of Engagement: Universities in Society.* London: Association of Commonwealth Universities.

Blunkett, D. (2000) *Modernising Higher Education: Facing the Global Challenge.* Speech at the University of Greenwich, 15 February. London:DfEE.

Brown, R. (2002) Scholarship, in *On Learning Teaching and Higher Education Vol. 1,* working paper No 16. Southampton: Southampton Institute.

CBI (Confederation of British Industries) (2001) *Partnerships for Research and Innovation – Between Industry and Universities.* London: CBI. www.auril.org.uk.

Coldstream, P. (2003) Engagement: an unfolding debate, in S. Bjarnason, and P. Coldstream, (eds) *The Idea of Engagement: Universities in Society.* London: ACU.

DfES (Department for Education and Skills) (2003) *The Future of Higher Education,* Cm 5735. London: The Stationery Office.

DTI (Department of Trade and Industry) (2003) *Innovation Report: Competing in the Global Economy: The Innovation Challenge.* London: DTI Publications. (The review can be viewed online or downloaded in Adobe Acrobat PDF format from http://www.dti.gov.uk/innovationreport/)

Gibbons, M. (2003) Engagement as a core value in a Mode 2 society, in S. Bjarnason and P. Coldstream, (eds) *The Idea of Engagement: Universities in Society.* London: ACU.

Gray, H. (1999) Re-scoping the university, in H. Gray (ed.) *Universities and the Creation of Wealth.* Buckingham: SRHE/Open University Press.

HEFCE (Higher Education Funding Council for England) (1999) *Higher Education Reach Out to Business,* Community Fund round 1 (HEFCE 99/40). Bristol: HEFCE.

HEFCE (2000) *Higher Education Reach Out to Business,* Community Fund round 2 (HEFCE 00/05). Bristol: HEFCE.

HEFCE (2001) *Higher Education Innovation Fund: Invitation to Bid* (HEFCE 01/43). Bristol: HEFCE.

HEFCE (2003a) *Higher Education business Interaction Survey 2000–01* (03/11). Bristol: HEFCE.

HEFCE (2003b) *Higher Education Innovation Fund: Invitation to Bid* (HEFCE 03/58). Bristol: HEFCE.

HEFCE (2003c) *Higher Education Innovation Fund Consultative document* (HEFCE 03/34). Bristol: HEFCE.

HEFCE (2004) *Strategic Plan 2003–2008* (revised April 2004). Bristol: HEFCE. www.hefce.ac.uk/Pubs/hefce/2004/04_17/04_17.pdf

HM Treasury (2001) *Productivity in the UK: 3 – The Regional Dimension.* www.hm-treasury.gov.uk/Documents/Enterprise_and_Productivity/productivity_in_the_UK_3_the_regional_dimension/ent_prod3_index.cfm

HM Treasury/DTI (Department for Trade and Industry)/DfES (Department for Education and Skills) (2004) *Science and Innovation Investment Framework*

2004–2014. Norwich: TSO. www.hm-treasury.gov.uk/medi/95846/spend04-siencedoc–1–090704.pdf

House of Lords, Select Committee on Science and Technology (2003) *Science and the RDAs – SETting the Regional Agenda*. London: The Stationery Office.

Lambert, R. (2003) *Lambert Review of Business-University Collaboration*. London: TSO. www.hmtreasury.gov.uk/consultations_and_legislation/lambert/consult_lambert index.cfm

McNay, I. (2003) *Developing Higher Education Senior Managers Strategically*. Sheffield: HESDA Universities Scotland.

Manchester Enterprises (2004) *Greater Manchester Economic Development Plan*. Contact Susan Jarvis@Manchester-Enterprises.co.uk

NWDA (North West Development Agency) (2003) *Regional Economic Strategy 2003*. www.nwda.co.uk and www.englandsnorthwest2020.com

Orr, D. (2004) Research assessment as an instrument for steering higher education – a comparative study, *Journal of Higher Education Management and Policy*, 26(3).

Powell, J. A. (2004) Measuring success in non-traditional university-business-community reach-out, in *Proceedings of the UPBEAT Conference*. Salford: Salford University.

Roberts, G. (2002) *SET for Success – The Supply of People with Science, Technology, Engineering and Mathematics Skills*. The Report of Sir Gareth Robert's Review. London: The Stationery Office. www.dti.gov.uk

SHEFC (Scottish Higher Education Funding Council) (2003) *Knowledge Transfer Grant: Collection of Activity Data*. Circular letter HE/43/03.

van Winden, W. and van den Berg, L. (2004) *Cities in the Knowledge Economy: New Governance Challenges*. Rotterdam: European Institute for Comparative Urban Research.

Wedgwood, M. A. (2003) Making engagement work in practice, in S. Bjarnason, and P. Coldstream (eds) *The Idea of Engagement: Universities in Society*. London: Association of Commonwealth Universities.

Part Four

Staff and system issues

12

Managing Institutions in a Mass Higher Education System

Ian McNay

Introduction

The first chapter presented a picture of a stratified system under strain from trying to deliver competing, contradictory, even conflicting objectives. There is a similar picture at institutional level. This chapter draws on presentations to the seminar series by Stephen Rowland, Robin Middlehurst and Ian McNay to explore issues within HEIs trying to meet too many objectives, and risking falling short on them all. In doing so, the risk is that the community will be divided in several ways. The Leadership Foundation is reported to be concerned about the quality of top management in the HE sector (Baty, 2005), where academics have an anti-managerial culture, so that the best do not aspire to roles as organizational leaders. Middlehurst (1993) had earlier identified anti-learning cults among such managers.

That mind-set may be not only at the top. Work by Archer (2005) found that heads of universities believed that they, and their top management teams 'were aligned with the direction and ambition of the institution'. They, and their senior HR staff were confident in their own competences and practices, but they were critical of others:

> Looking beyond the top team, the story changed. Heads of institutions and HR alike spoke of the challenges of getting managers throughout the organisation to manage. However clear the vision from the top management team, the frustration voiced by HR heads was of what one described as 'a thick layer of cloud below'. The recurring description of middle management was of staff in positions of leadership who did not find it easy to lead and whose loyalties often lie primarily with their subject or their teams; and of a highly resilient anti-management culture – even amongst managers.
>
> (Archer, 2005, para. 22)

That is reminiscent of a vice-chancellor whom I interviewed. He claimed (almost declaimed) that 'we [the executive team] are good at policy development; *they* are poor at delivery'. 'They' were the deans and heads of department. The University Secretary commented on their behaviour: 'if they do not attend academic board, or if present, do not speak in support of the executive recommendations, they will never be implemented at faculty level'. McNay (2003: 56) notes that 'in managing change, leaders make it *wanted*; managers make it *happen*; academics, administrators and ancillary staff make it *work*'. In many institutions, the iterations and articulations among those levels are not in place. This chapter explores some of the gaps.

Organization culture . . . and organized anarchy?

Previous work has developed a model of organization culture (McNay, 1995; 1999) and explored how, within different cultures, the competing needs of equity, excellence and enterprise can be met (McNay, 2002) and a common sense of community developed (McNay, 2005b). Here, I locate the cultures within the policy context outlined in Chapter 1, and the models of institutions in mass provision. Scott (1995) saw institutions moving through a managerial culture to a strategic, 'reflexive' culture of management in tune with system movement through mass to universal provision. They are not there yet. Trow (1973), summarized in Brennan (2004), saw a movement through institutions with academics as amateur managers and a large bureaucracy to the development of a cadre of specialist full-time professionals. He also saw a breakdown of internal consensus, making institutional governance insoluble, with decision-making flowing into the external political authority. That may be happening in Wales, where funding is being used to drive an agenda of regional clusters of institutions and mergers, and where a national bursary scheme linked to fees is mooted, in contrast to the variety of access agreements in England. Some of those anticipations are borne out by the work reported here.

My previous work established four 'cultures' of HE institutions, plotting the degree of central control over policy development (tight/loose) against the degree of central control over practice/delivery. In contingency theory, the axes might relate to degrees of agreement over ends and means, with consequences for decision-making. I gave the four quadrants labels of collegium, bureaucracy, corporation and enterprise. My findings support those of Shattock (2003) and Clark (1998, 2004) that the 'best' institutions have, first, a strong sense of identity/mission, and, second, a culture where the collegial enterprise is the norm. The first characteristic is necessary to avoid the worst aspects of March's organized anarchy, and garbage can model where choices are made without clear objectives, by groups/committees with changing participation and unclear remits and authority (Pugh and Hickson, 1996).

The collegial enterprise relates to *service needs* of clients and partner communities as a driver. It tends towards devolved structures, diverse products and processes and a development agenda. The corporate bureaucracy faces the other way: it has *system imperatives* as drivers. It tends towards dependency and an agency role, with low risk strategies and a culture of centralization, conformity, compliance and control, reflecting a perception of the external policy environment, with an assertive interventionist and regulatory state (Moran, 2002; 2004). The internal culture often derives from a lack of institutional confidence, perhaps linked to lack of felt competence in senior staff. It leads to a lack of trust in colleagues and a closed system where, despite pressures for open accountability to the outside world, there is poor communication inside, and strong control over data, especially given the provisions of the Freedom of Information Act. The poor sense of institutional identity means that senior staff become *managers,* even administrators, of the *implementation* of government initiatives, not *leaders* of academic *innovation and enterprise* by staff. There is a very porous strategic filter from the policy environment, leading to poor selectivity of what to pursue, and what not. This runs counter to Clark and Shattock who both urge self-reliant autonomy, though Deans (2005) suggests they differ in their reasoning. He suggests that Clark uses the positive idea of freedom (Berlin, 1969) – the 'freedom to' be what you want to be, whereas Shattock emphasizes autonomy, 'freedom from' the state with its unpredictability, even when the same party is re-elected. Ministerial changes can lead to sudden shifts in policy priorities.

The enterprise culture can, of course, be just as indiscriminate, and the market can be just as unpredictable. Indeed, the state can now be seen as a major customer, always right and sometimes fickle. The agreements between ministers and funding councils and then between councils and institutions underline the customer-contractor relationship. In the 'hard' enterprise culture, linked to the corporate quadrant, enterprise is often equated to marketing. The access agreements in England, approved through Office for Fair Access (OFFA) as a condition of allowing higher fees, reveal this – many plan to invest extra income in 'selling' in a saturated market. There is less emphasis on quality of service to a diversified mix of students, or development of relevance as a criterion of excellence. The drive is financial with the risk of admission of weaker students, without support and of lower standards (see Chapter 1). Indeed, I have experience of offers being made by a senior member of staff to weak students rejected by departmental academic admissions officers. The justification was the need to meet contract numbers and avoid financial penalties, with little regard for the impact on the individual students or the resultant demands on teaching staff. There is also a risk to the integrity of research. Seventy per cent of academic staff in a sample of nearly 300 across the UK thought it had been compromised (McNay, 2005a). Hancock and Hellawell (2003) suggest that the competitiveness in the enterprise quadrant can lead to concealment tactics even in-house among colleagues who need to know.

There are risks in the corporate bureaucracy, too. Seventy-seven per cent of academic staff believe that 'quality assurance processes have encouraged low-risk conformity at the expense of innovation, independence and difference in teaching', though the figure for research is lower (51 per cent). They also have concerns about freedom. Seventy-nine per cent agreed that 'there is a fear of sanctions against those who "speak truth to power", with corporate management approaches verging on a culture of "bully and blame" ' (McNay, 2005a). The 'hard' bureaucracy of rules, regulations and the use of performance indicators for summative judgement by the corporate management, has displaced the 'soft' bureaucracy of committees, representative democracy and collective governance. So, communication is one way – downwards and then only selectively – without representation upwards. And the citizens of the academic community have no electoral opportunity to change things, nor a judiciary to moderate executive excesses. E. M. Forster ([1951] 1972:67) gave 'two cheers for Democracy: one because it admits variety [= diversity] and two because it permits criticism'. He articulated some of the themes of this chapter:

> It does start from the assumption that the individual is important, and that all types are needed to make a civilisation. It does not divide its citizens into the bosses and the bossed – as an efficiency-regime tends to do. The people I admire most are those who are sensitive and want to create something or discover something, and do not see life in terms of power . . . [they] need to express themselves; they cannot do so unless society allows them liberty to do so, and the society which allows them most liberty is a democracy. Democracy has another merit. It allows criticism, and if there is not criticism, there are bound to be hushed-up scandals.
>
> (Forster [1951] 1972: 67)

And, indeed, there have been such scandals in HE institutions.

Fissures, fractures and fragments

That leads to stratified institutions, with a strongly corporate 'leadership', separated from an operational workforce striving to retain a human face to the enterprise and collegial working with colleagues in course teams and research groups in their version of the HE 'project'. So, a 'corporate collegium' develops, with little iteration between the levels. More positively, administrators are adapting (see Whitchurch, 2004, and this volume). Burrell (2003) noted an expectation of HR staff that they would move from processing, through policing compliance to partnership in strategic development, working with academic units in a devolved structure. This contrasts with the enduring 'us and them' divisions described by Dobson (2000) in Australia. Another of my students, investigating equal opportunities policy, concluded that 'we police compliance; we do not promote commitment'. Even within the senior management team, there is a lack of a collective culture. In universities I have studied, there is an unwillingness to engage with the portfolios of other members, a mutual pact based on *noli me tangere*. This leads to a silo mentality and the lack of strategic integration noted by HEFCE (2001).

Rowland (2004: 2) identifies 'fractures and fault lines that divide aspects of our academic lives, which we must struggle to bring into more productive relationships through contest and debate'. These include divisions

- on the purposes of higher education, where the economic instrumentalism of governments worldwide (Rowland, 2003), shared by most students in the 'Age of Delivery', contrasts with the (often tacit) assumptions of academic staff about 'discovery', curiosity', 'excitement'.
- on teacher–student roles and relationships, following from the first fracture. Is it guru to disciple, service provider and client (as implied by satisfaction surveys)? If the curriculum is 'student-centred', how far does this mean a lack of challenge to student values and of a challenge to change?
- between teachers and managers, as in the corporate-collegium conundrum described above, and the balance of autonomy and accountability, compliance and challenge, policy debate or simply delivery.
- between teaching and research, given differential esteem and financial rewards, a view of them as discrete functions conducted in separate structures, and a failure to move from emphasis on difference to a recognition of their complex interdependence.
- the fragmentation of knowledge, the state of flux in the boundaries between disciplines and the development of specialized 'local' sub-disciplines. He cites Clark's work (Clark, 2000) which calculated the growth of articles in chemistry as more then 500,000 per year in the 1990s, needing four full-time research assistants simply to keep up with reading the titles, never mind engaging with the 8500 science specialities identified in the same study.

Rowland claims that 'policy initiatives have tended to aggravate, rather than ameliorate these fractures' (and others that he lists but does not develop). He urges a series of 'critical conversations' across the divides as part of developing a new professionalism, a new identity and new roles for academic professionals, as they

> . . . struggle to form new relationships across the fault lines of their fragmented world. This is characterised by an 'intellectual sociability' in which academics, students and the wider community think together for the common good, whilst recognising difference and diversity. The first and foremost subject of this thinking together must concern the purposes of higher education itself.
>
> (Rowland 2004: 21)

Some of those issues of roles and identity are developed by Saunderson (this volume) and have been a major concern of Henkel (2000).

Diverse, distributed, devolved, democratic – a model for the mass/universal university?

The idea of a fragmented organization is not new. Mintzberg (1989) saw it as the normal future model. Deal and Kennedy (1988) in mainstream management and Schuller (1992), in his vision of the academic community, call it 'atomised'. Its features include:

- small task-focused groups;
- each unit with budgetary authority and managerial control over its own destiny;
- links with larger entities through benign computer and communication networks;
- strong cultural bonds within larger organizations.

(adapted from Deal and Kennedy, 1988)

Knight and Trowler (2001) suggest that universities and colleges might best be treated as 'constellations of communities', where staff find different roles and identities related to different activities with their different structures and processes.

Robin Middlehurst (2004a, 2004b), in discussing governance, leadership and management, built on McNay's ideal organization cultures (see above), and related his leadership styles to the work of Clark and Shattock. These imply a movement towards the collegial enterprise in a cyclic pattern that recognizes the need for a moderated collegial model. The progression is from:

> consensual, participatory, often informal, 'servant' leadership in the original collegium, through
>
> formal/rational modes in representative committees and through management by objectives,
>
> political/tactical approaches using power and other resources in a transformational leadership, often with an 'heroic' model, to
>
> project teams where leadership is devolved, distributed and adaptive.

That last will need new processes (e.g. activity based costing) and structures and roles. She recognized the dilemmas and tensions in trying to pursue a diversity of styles in complex organizations with multiple missions.

Her analysis of job advertisements in the *Times Higher Education Supplement* showed a strengthening of the central steering core, with highly paid executive level posts, but with separation of leadership by function – teaching, research, knowledge transfer, service functions. Within some of those remits, new roles emerge relating to new functions such as e-learning and intellectual property exploitation. These reflect the increased expectations of academics to pursue diversified roles, so creating tensions about linkages and priorities, about future career paths and about identity within diversity, as well as risking stress from overload.

She also identified a strengthening of Clark's 'developmental periphery', with posts covering partnerships, community relations, business liaison, outreach and widening participation. She recognizes the tensions these strengthening elements can create within a diverse and extensive set of expectations. She resists the new public management approach with stronger managerialism recommended by the Lambert report (see Shattock, this volume), recommending models that encourage networks and engagement to build intellectual capital of individuals and political capital of institutions. Alignment of processes and structures with agreed strategy helps bridge between the two. And . . .

> because universities are places where ideas and values are deeply integrated with structures, functions, roles and cultures, change processes must address the socio-emotional and symbolic aspects of institutional life as well as the instrumental aspects of the business.
>
> (Middlehurst, 2004b: 278)

Conclusion

The agenda for the next phase of the life cycle is, then, one of internal change to respond to external turbulence and political threat. Such change needs learning, and unlearning to get rid of the inhibitors of the past – excessive hierarchy and bureaucracy, ingrained routines, weak communication, defensive territoriality and conservative risk aversion (Middlehurst, 2004b). The organizations with learning as their business need to become learning organizations (Garratt, 2000; Pedler *et al.*, 1997; Rowley, 1998). They have not performed well as such in the past – ideas may be encouraged but not rewarded, learning encouraged but not funded. Disputation, the essence of disciplinary development, is seen as dissent when policy is presented for delivery, and scant allowance is made for diversity. More emphasis is put on blame for mistakes than on the lessons from them. Little attention is given to low paid staff who are at crucial access points to students and the public, their attitudes and opinions. Security, reception, catering and cleaning are often outsourced, yet those who work in these functions are a crucial intelligence network. Use of evaluative tools with HE staff regularly produces scores on their institutions as learning organizations well below 50 per cent (McNay, 2003). There is a need for a better flow between ideas, policy, operational framing and activity, so that there is a dynamic developmental energy based on iterative feedback (Pedler *et al.*, 1997). Perhaps the first requirement is a willingness to learn, which requires a humility not often associated with the academic culture (Phillips, 2005).

The messages for senior managers, then, echo those for government in Chapter 1. At both levels there needs to be a recognition that the span of control is too big to allow presidential corporate micro-management of the levels below. There needs to be a clear statement of institutional identity, shared by staff and within which they can find a personal and professional identity. Assertion of institutional autonomy must be accompanied by recognition of appropriate professional autonomy: top managers need to learn to trust and 'let go'. Development at the periphery means sponsored experimentation and innovation with allowance for failure. Thus, there may be an inner diversity to match a system level diversity. All this will be helped by inclusive, collective decision-making and open communication: Forster's democracy. There is a need, too, for staff and their unions to move away from a defensive agenda dominated by conditions of service, to a development partnership with other stakeholders along European models.

Feel the fear, but do it anyway!

References

Archer, W. (2005) *Mission Critical? Modernising Human Resource Management in Higher Education.* Oxford: HEPI.

Baty, P. (2005) Manager roles fail to attract core staff, *Times Higher Education Supplement,* 11 February.

Berlin, I. (1969) *Four Essays on Liberty.* Oxford: Oxford University Press.

Brennan, J. (2004) The social role of the contemporary university: contradictions, boundaries and change, in CHERI *Ten Years On, Changing Higher Education in a Changing World.* London: Centre for Higher Education and Information at the Open University.

Burrell, C. (2003) MSc dissertation, University of Greenwich.

Clark, B. R. (1998) *Creating Entrepreneurial Universities: Organizational Pathways of Transformation.* Oxford: IAU Press/Pergamon.

Clark, B. R. (2000) Collegial entrepreneurialism in proactive universities, *Change.* 10–19.

Clark, B. R. (2004) *Sustaining Change in Universities: Continuities in Case Studies and Concepts.* Maidenhead: SRHE/Open University Press.

Deal, T. E. and Kennedy, A. A. (1988) *Corporate Cultures: The Rites and Rituals of Corporate Life.* London: Penguin.

Deans, P. (2005) Assignment: MBA in HE Management. London: Institute of Education.

Dobson, I. R. (2000) 'Them and us' – general and non-general staff in higher education, *Journal of Higher Education Policy and Management,* 22(2): 203–10.

Forster, E. M. ([1951] 1972) What I believe, in *Two Cheers for Democracy.* London: Edward Arnold.

Garratt, B. (2000) *The Learning Organization: Developing Democracy at Work.* London: HarperCollins.

Hancock, N. and Hellawell, D. E. (2003) Academic middle management in higher education: a game of hide and seek, *Journal of Higher Education Policy and Management,* 25(1): 5–12.

HEFCE (Higher Education Funding Council for England) (2001) *Review of Strategic Plans and Financial Forecasts.* Bristol: HEFCE.

Henkel, M. (2000) *Academic Identities and Policy Changes in Higher Education.* London: Jessica Kingsley.

Knight, P. and Trowler, P. R. (2001) *Departmental Leadership in Higher Education.* Buckingham: SRHE/Open University Press.

McNay, I. (1995) From the collegial academy to corporate enterprise: the changing cultures of universities, in T. Schuller (ed.) *The Changing University?* Buckingham: SRHE/Open University Press.

McNay, I. (1999) Changing cultures in UK higher education: the state as corporate market bureaucracy and the emergent academic enterprise, in D. Braun and F-X. Merrien (eds) *Towards a New Model of Governance for Universities: A Comparative View.* London: Jessica Kingsley.

McNay, I. (2002) The E factors and organisational culture, in G. Williams (ed.) *The Enterprising University: Reform, Excellence and Equity.* Buckingham: SRHE/Open University Press.

McNay, I. (2003) *Developing Higher Education Senior Managers Strategically.* Sheffield: HESDA and Universities Scotland.

McNay, I. (2005a) Shifting values and standards in academic life. Consultative conference on 'Higher education and human good', Sarum College, March.

McNay, I. (2005b) Higher education communities: divided they fail?, *Perspectives,* 9(2): 39–44.

Middlehurst, R. (1993) *Leading Academics.* Buckingham: SRHE/Open University Press.

Middlehurst, R. (2004a) Revolving doors or permanent ways? Presentation to ESRC/SRHE seminar series 'From mass to universal higher education: building on experience', London, February.

Middlehurst, R. (2004b) Changing internal governance: a discussion of leadership roles and management structures in UK universities, *Higher Education Quarterly,* 58(4): 258–79.

Moran, M. (2002) Review article: understanding the regulatory state, *British Journal of Political Science,* 32(2): 391–413.

Moran, M. (2004) *The British Regulatory State: High Modernism and Hyper-innovation.* Oxford: Oxford University Press.

Pedler, M., Burgoyne, J. and Boydell, T. (1997) *The Learning Company: A Strategy for Sustainable Development,* 2nd edn. London: McGraw-Hill.

Phillips, S. (2005) Some people are just too clever for their own good, *Times Higher Education Supplement,* 25 March.

Pugh, D. S. and Hickson, D. J. (1996) James March, in *Writers on Organizations,* 5th edn. London: Penguin.

Rowland, S. (2003) Teaching for democracy in higher education, *Teaching in Higher Education,* 8(1): 89–102.

Rowland, S. (2004) Overcoming fragmentation in academic life and the questions it poses. Presentation to seminar 'Changing systems,changing roles: expectations and experiences of staff', one of the ESRC/SRHE series, From mass to universal higher education: building on experience, UCL, London, January.

Rowley, J. (1998) Creating a learning organisation in higher education, *Industrial and Commercial Training,* 30(1): 16–19.

Schuller, T. (1992) The exploding community? The university idea and the smashing of the academic atom, in I. McNay (ed.) *Visions of Post-compulsory Education.* Buckingham: SRHE/Open University Press.

Scott, P. (1995) *The Meaning of Mass Higher Education.* Buckingham: SRHE/Open University Press.

Shattock, M. (2003) *Managing Successful Universities.* Maidenhead: SRHE/Open University Press.

Trow, M. (1973) *Problems in the Transition from Elite to Mass Higher Education.* Berkeley, CA: Carnegie Commission on Higher Education.

Whitchurch, C. (2004) Administrative managers – a critical link, *Higher Education Quarterly*, 58(4): 280–98.

13

Academic Staff in a Mass Higher Education System: The State We're in

Stephen Court

Introduction

This chapter looks at the expansion of higher education in the UK since 1960, and the implications of that for academic staff in terms of the intensification of their work, their working hours and the activities they undertake. Academic work is also diversifying because of increased links between higher education and the wider community, particularly the business sector. These factors – and comparatively low levels of remuneration – are likely to be contributing to the high levels of occupational stress reported by academic staff. While academics continue to demonstrate high levels of commitment to their work, there are concerns about the toll stress is having on health and work–life balance. Finally, some ways of improving the working lives of academics are considered, including a reduction in the student:staff ratio; increasing use of academic and related and support staff; greater use of information and communication technology; clear guidance on best practice when academics are involved in commercializing intellectual property, and greater financial incentives for universities to allow academics to be involved in this area.

Expansion

In Hilaire Belloc's vitriolic poem *Lines to a Don*, dons were either 'remote and ineffectual', or 'regal', sailing 'in amply bellying gown enormous through the Sacred Town'. Probably neither description would fit today. Academics, whether Oxbridge dons, redbrick researchers or lecturers in the former polytechnics, are key workers toiling in one of society's biggest recent growth areas – and a major earner of income from abroad (fee payments by international students studying in the UK generated £2.7 billion in export earnings in 1999/2000; Universities UK, 2004). Academic staff are involved in a spectrum of professional activities, including teaching, scholarship, research, outreach to the community, consultancy, development of intellectual property, commercializing research and setting up spin-off companies. There is no room for the ineffectual or time for the regal. Student numbers have grown exponentially, while the increase in academic staff numbers has failed to keep pace.

In 1960 there were 111,000 full-time undergraduate and postgraduate students in UK universities. Alongside them were a further 74,000 students in the non-university higher education sector (Table 13.1). Forty years later there were slightly more than 1.25 million full-time higher education students (Table 13.2), and more than two million students in all. Although much has been heard of the expansion of UK higher education in the 1990s, the decade which saw the greatest percentage rise in student numbers was 1960–70. Partly aided by the impetus given to the expansion of higher education by the Robbins report of 1963, this decade saw the establishment of more than twenty universities – some as entirely new institutions – as well as numerous Oxbridge colleges, and the creation of 26 polytechnics. Between 1960 and 2000, the proportion of young people in higher education as full-time undergraduates rose from one in 20 to one in three (Table 13.3).

Academic staff numbers have increased, but at a slower rate than student numbers. In 2002–3[1] the Higher Education Statistics Agency reported a total of 146,000 academics in the UK, of whom 85,000 undertook both teaching and research, 46,000 were employed on research-only contracts, and 15,000 were on teaching-only contracts.[2] In terms of full-time staff at universities

Table 13.1 Full-time higher education students by sector, UK

	Universities*	Non-university sector#
1960	111,000	73,800
1970	235,300	221,300
1980	307,000	228,000
1990	370,000	378,000

* undergraduate and postgraduate
\# includes: colleges of education (teacher training); advanced courses in FE institutions
Source: DES; USR

Table 13.2 Full-time higher education student totals, UK

	Total	Change %
1960	184,800	
1970	456,600	147
1980	535,000	17
1990	748,000	40
2000	1,276,300	71

Source: DES; USR; HESA; author

established before 1992 who were wholly financed by their institution – that is, mainly 'traditional' academic staff engaged in both teaching and research – there was a large increase in the 1960s, but a decline in the 1980s (Table 13.4). This is reflected in the change in student to staff ratios. The student: staff ratio held fairly constant in the 1960s and 1970s, but increased sharply in the 1980s (Table 13.5). When academic staff from the university and non-university (i.e. former polytechnic) sectors are added together, there was an increase in staff numbers of more than 40 per cent in the 1990s, but that decade also saw a marked deterioration in the student:staff ratio.[3]

The all round increase in the number of academic staff in the UK – including academics on research-only and teaching-only contracts, as well as on teaching-and-research contracts – has seen some marked changes in their biographical profile. The most significant changes concern the gender of staff, mode of working and terms of employment. In short, there are more female academics, more academics are working part time, and more are on fixed-term contracts. In 1982–3 14 per cent of full-time academic staff in UK universities (excluding the polytechnic sector) were women; by 2002–3 39 per cent of *all* UK academics (full-time and part-time) were women. In 1982–3, one in 20 university academics worked on a part-time basis; 20 years later, the proportion of academics working part time was almost to one in five, with

Table 13.3 Age Participation Index, Great Britain

	%
1960	5
1970	14
1980	13
1990	19
2000	33

Home initial entrants, under the age of 21, to full-time under-graduate HE, expressed as a percentage of the average number of 18- and 19-year-olds in the GB population.
Source: NCIHE (1997); HESA

Table 13.4 Full-time wholly institution financed academic staff, UK

	Universities	*Non-university sector*	*Total*
1960	13,900	n/a	
1970	28,700	n/a	
1980	34,300	n/a	
1990	31,900	25,200	57,100
2000			80,400

N/a = not available
Source: DES; USR; HESA

Table 13.5 Student: staff ratios, UK HE

1960	8 : 1
1970	8 : 1
1980	9 : 1
1990	13 : 1
2000	16 : 1

Full-time students : full-time wholly university funded academics
Source: USR; HESA; author

women comprising the majority of part-time workers. In 1982–3, 24 per cent of university academics were employed on a research-only basis; by 2002–3, that proportion had increased to 32 per cent. Published data are not available for the proportion of academic staff in 1982–3 who were employed on a fixed-term contract. However, in 1995–6, 41 per cent of academic staff were employed on a fixed-term contract (with virtually all research-only staff on fixed-term contracts); by 2002–3 the fixed-term proportion had risen slightly to 42 per cent (AUT, 2004).

Intensification

Academic work has intensified. That much is evident from the rise in student numbers and in the student:staff ratio. Another measure of this is the use of time, which shows that the average working week for academic staff has got considerably longer. In the early 1960s academics employed on a full-time basis worked just over 40 hours on average in a term-time week. Three decades later the term-time working week had stretched by more than one-third, to just under 55 hours (Table 13.6). The tasks carried out by academics have also changed. Comparison of the survey of academic staff use of time conducted for the Robbins report in 1962 and the survey conducted by the Association of University Teachers in 1994 indicates a similar proportion of time spent in teaching, a reduction in time spent on research, a reduction in the time spent on private study or 'internal academic' matters, and a big rise in the time spent on administration (Tables 13.7 and 13.8). One of the reasons for more administration is the work relating to the greater number

Table 13.6 Average hours worked per week by academic staff

Survey for/by	Survey date	Hours	Method	Period
Robbins report	1962	40.5		Term-time
CVCP	1970	50.5	Diary	Weighted average
AUT	1994	54.8	Diary	Term-time

Source: Court, 1996

Table 13.7 Academic staff use of time: Robbins term-time survey 1962

Teaching	34%
Research	28%
Private study	11%
Administration	11%
Other work within university	10%
Work outside university	6%

Source: Court, 1996

Table 13.8 Academic staff use of time: AUT term-time survey 1994

Teaching	35%
Research	20%
Internal academic	5%
External academic	7%
Administration	33%

Source: Court, 1996

Table 13.9 The higher education audit explosion

1986	First RAE
1989	Second RAE
1992	Third RAE – the first covering all institutions
	Start of institutional audit under the Higher Education Quality Council on 5-yearly cycle
1993	Start of quality assessment in teaching departments on 5-yearly cycle
1996	Fourth RAE
2001	Fifth RAE

of students in higher education; another, perhaps more significant, reason is the 'audit explosion' there has been in the sector.

In what some would describe as an essential exercise in accountability, and others would say was an assault on professional status, academics have been subject to two decades of intense audit (Table 13.9). Every university department in the UK has undergone rigorous examination of teaching quality. Universities' quality assurance mechanisms have been audited at the institutional level. There have been five UK-wide Research Assessment Exercises (RAEs), monitoring the standard of output in every research-active department. In addition, universities have had to comply with the quality assurance requirements of professional and statutory bodies involved in validating degrees in a range of subjects.

Academic staff, as well as teaching more students, and satisfying the demands of quality assurance, are continually required to 'raise their game' in research (see Lucas, this volume). Increasingly higher standards are needed simply to have recurrent funding rise at the level of inflation. To attain the research assessment rating which will bring any recurrent research funding whatsoever, academics need to produce work that will receive a 4 rating, which equates to national excellence in virtually all areas, and some evidence of international excellence. And now in England, at any rate, only research achieving the highest ratings of 5 (international excellence in up to half of research output) and 5* (international excellence in more than half of research activity) will receive recurrent funding increases beyond the rate of inflation.

As well as improving performance in the RAE, academics are under pressure to win research grants and contracts. Between 1995/96 and 2002/03 the amount of income for higher education institutions in the UK from research grants and contracts rose from £1.55 billion to £2.6 billion. Institutions, keen to increase their income in areas that are not tied to funding council formulae, want academics to win more research grants and contracts. This adds to their administrative workload, since grant applications take considerable time and effort to complete (Wedgwood, this volume).

Workload has increased in teaching. There are more students in lectures and seminars, there is more work to mark, more feedback to give (Knight and Yorke, this volume). There is strong pressure to increase further the numbers of students in higher education, and to widen social class access to higher education. The government wants 50 per cent of young people to participate, in some way, in higher education by 2010 – a target already met in Scotland and close to being met in Northern Ireland, but still some way off in England and Wales – and to bring more working-class people into higher education. This will add to workload not simply through bringing in more students, but by bringing in more students who will have arrived in higher education through non-traditional routes, and who will be likely to need extra help with study skills and coping in general with the demands of higher education (Leathwood, this volume).

Diversification

Traditionally academics have had two main functions: teaching and research. But over the past decade in the UK universities and the government have paid increasing attention to linking up higher education and the economy. There is more emphasis on teachers incorporating into courses the skills likely to be of value to graduates in employment after gaining their degrees. Universities now receive considerable sums of government funding to support the transfer of knowledge into the economy. These activities have come to be seen as a third strand in the missions of higher education institutions, in addition to teaching and research (Wedgwood, this volume). The activities range from technology transfer and research collaboration – which are particularly marked in higher education institutions with a higher level of research intensity – to contributing to access to education, supporting small and medium sized enterprises (SMEs) and meeting regional skill needs, which are more marked in institutions with a lower level of research intensity. Institutions with a higher research intensity tend to focus particularly on business sectors/clusters in science, medicine, engineering and technology; institutions with a lower research intensity are particularly active among not-for-profit organizations and in the public sector. Even in the space of one year, from 2000 to 2001, the proportion of institutions with a strategic plan for business support which was developed and being implemented rose from 36 per cent to 47 per cent (HEFCE, 2003: 11). In 1999–2000, UK institutions reported there was a total of 303 spin-off companies with some HEI ownership which were active and had survived at least three years; the following year (albeit with a greater number of institutions reporting), that number had increased to 425. Estimated turnover of active firms with some HEI ownership increased from £98m to £162m (HEFCE, 2003: 34).

So, alongside undertaking teaching and research, academics are finding themselves involved in knowledge transfer activities, ranging in scale from small consultancy projects, to setting up and running a large business. According to research undertaken in 1999, the number of academics engaged to a considerable extent in business related activities was small – less than five per cent of academics reported spending more than 10 hours a week on this area (Coate *et al.*, 2000: 13). But given increased public funding for higher education-business links, and the continuing political pressure for universities to do their bit to improve the economy, it is likely that this figure will grow.

Stress

One unwelcome aspect of employment in higher education, which may well be linked to the intensification and perhaps also the diversification of academic work, is the experience of occupational stress reported by staff. The AUT has undertaken two surveys of occupational stress of its members, in 1998 and in 2004 (Kinman, 1998; Kinman and Jones, 2004).[4] A key finding in the earlier research was that slightly over two-thirds of respondents agreed or strongly agreed with the statement: 'I find my job stressful'; the proportion in the 2004 survey was virtually identical. In the 2004 survey there was a slight reduction in the proportion who felt their workloads were unmanageable, but there were also reductions in the proportion who felt they had ample opportunity to undertake scholarly work, and in the proportion who felt happy with their research quality. Respondents in 2004 reported being under slightly less pressure to increase research or consultancy activity, and to publish, than respondents in 1998. Nevertheless, the more recent survey found staff feeling under greater pressure to obtain research funding. On working hours, the 2004 survey found a slight reduction in the proportion of respondents who reported working long hours. However, it must be a matter of concern that in 2004, 59 per cent of respondents employed on a full-time basis said they worked more than 45 hours a week on average, and 21 per cent reported regularly working over 55 hours a week. Almost one half of respondents in 2004 said they had seriously considered leaving higher education, chiefly because of job insecurity, stress, work overload, excessive bureaucracy, limited prospects of promotion and poor work–life balance. On the last, academic staff said they did one quarter of their work at home: while this helped them perform tasks requiring a great deal of concentration with less interruption than at work, it was nevertheless difficult to achieve an acceptable work–life balance. Most respondents wanted more separation between the two domains.

Overall, according to Kinman and Jones, extremely low levels of psychological wellbeing were found in the 2004 survey: 'Fifty per cent of respondents had symptoms of psychological distress, a level that exceeds the proportion reported in studies of most other occupational groups' (Kinman and Jones, 2004: 3) But no significant difference was found between the overall level of psychological distress found in the 1998 study and the 2004 survey. Kinman and Jones (2004: 5) concluded: 'There is some evidence that employees in the HE sector may have acclimatised to the increasing demands and pressure to be more productive over the last six years; furthermore, slightly higher levels of support from various sources appear to be available to employees than in 1998'.

Reward

The deficiencies in pay for UK academic staff are a matter of public record. During the long-running parliamentary debate prior to the vote on the government's proposed variable fees for students in higher education in England, the Prime Minister acknowledged in the House of Commons that pay for lecturers had increased by only five per cent above inflation over the preceding 20 years. In the same period, earnings in rest of the economy had grown by 45 per cent.[5] This was a reason put forward by the Prime Minister for trying to get more money into higher education. Table 13.10 shows in cash terms the changes in salary for university lecturers, MPs and hospital

Table 13.10 Annual salaries, cash

Year at April	Non-manual average	University lecturer*	MP	Hospital senior registrar ^
1981	£6,958	£12,860	£13,950	£11,900
1990	£15,142	£22,311	£26,701	£23,190
2000	£24,185	£30,967	£48,371	£35,080

* Top of Lecturer B scale (pre-1992 sector)
^ top of scale
Source: National Statistics; IDS; author

Table 13.11 Average pay: academics and comparators (real terms index changes, 1993=100)

Year at April	Higher education teaching professionals	Personnel, training and industrial relations managers	General administrators; national government (HEO to senior principal/Grade 6)	Computer analysts/Programmers	Medical practitioners	Secondary education teaching professionals (England)	Chartered and certified accountants	Non-manual average
1993	100.0	100.0	100.0	100.0	100.0	100.0	100.0	100.0
1994	100.2	99.2	100.6	102.2	98.7	100.0	100.0	100.1
1995	99.7	97.1	104.3	99.6	97.8	98.5	97.1	100.6
1996	96.4	102.1	106.6	101.6	101.9	98.7	99.7	102.5
1997	99.6	102.4	109.2	105.0	106.3	99.4	102.5	104.6
1998	100.6	104.7	107.3	103.9	105.8	98.0	103.1	105.5
1999	100.8	106.4	112.9	104.7	110.1	101.3	107.3	108.2
2000	99.8	105.5	110.2	104.9	108.1	102.0	104.4	109.8
2001	100.8	117.3	114.4	110.9	121.0	108.8	114.0	114.4
2002	104.0	110.9	119.9	111.6	126.0	111.9	115.8	117.8

Source: National Statistics; real terms and index calculations by the author
Note: Data are for full-time employees, both sexes, whose pay was not affected by absence.

senior registrars, as well as in non-manual average earnings. The salaries of academics at the top of the Lecturer B grade on the pre-1992 pay scales (a fairly typical place for academics to be), Members of Parliament and senior registrars (top of scale) were fairly similar in 1981. Twenty years later, MPs had raced ahead, and senior registrars had overtaken lecturers by some distance. Back in 1981 the non-manual average was slightly more than half the salary for lecturers; by 2000 the gap was considerably narrowed.

A similar picture emerges when average pay for academics is compared with average pay for other professional groups in real terms. Over the decade to 2002, average pay for academics sometimes dipped below the rate of inflation, but finally emerged 4 per cent ahead in real terms (Table 13.11). By comparison, average earnings for medical practitioners ran at 26 per cent ahead of inflation; earnings for administrators and relatively senior civil servants rose by 20 per cent in real terms; the non-manual average increased by 18 per cent above inflation; earnings for accountants grew by 16 per cent above inflation, and so on.

Not surprisingly, 40 per cent of respondents to the AUT's survey of its members in 2004 reported being very or extremely dissatisfied with their rate of pay, and a further 24 per cent were moderately dissatisfied (Kinman and Jones, 2004). A particular matter of concern has been the continuing gap between the average salary for female academics working full time and their male colleagues.[6] In 2002–3, the most recent year for which data are currently available, women earned 85 pence for every £1 earned by their male colleagues (Saunderson, this volume). Some progress is being made on these issues through the Framework Agreement on pay and grading structures throughout higher education which was concluded between the employers and the relevant trade unions in 2004, and which is due to be implemented by August 2006. The numerous existing pay scales for different staff groups are being replaced by a single pay spine for all university employees. Through the process of job evaluation, employees will be transferred to the appropriate point on the pay spine. It is hoped that the process of formal job evaluation will reduce if not completely do away with any unfair differences between the rates of pay for men and women academics.

Of course, pay is not the only reward associated with employment. Fifty-eight per cent of respondents to the AUT's 2004 survey of its members reported being moderately to extremely satisfied with their job overall (Kinman and Jones, 2004). More than two-thirds were moderately to extremely satisfied with 'the work itself'. Three-quarters were moderately to extremely satisfied with their opportunites to use their initiative in their present job; and just under three-quarters were moderately to extremely satisfied with the intellectual stimulation they received in their job. Fairly similar levels of satisfaction were expressed by academic staff to questions about the courses they teach, their students and their academic freedom (in terms of the opportunity to pursue their own ideas).

Conclusion

There is something of a paradox in these findings. The AUT's two occupational stress surveys produced some quite widespread evidence of unhappiness and physical symptoms of ill health related to work for academic staff, not least because of extrinsic factors such as low levels of remuneration. But at the same time, academics were able to express high levels of job satisfaction, largely related to factors intrinsic to their work. While many appear to be giving serious thought to finding employment outside higher education, there is also a strong sense that the inherent nature of academic work – the teaching, the contact with students, the scholarship, the comradeship of the discipline, the opportunity for collegial endeavour, the production of new knowledge – exerts a pull strong enough to overcome the shortcomings that come with the job. Although nearly 5000 academics left the UK higher education sector for reasons other than retirement or death in 2002–3, more than twice that number entered employment in the sector in the same year – a pattern that is typical for recent years, and which accounts for the continued growth in academic staff numbers. Yes, recent decades have seen an unprecedented expansion in the number of students and a squeezing of the student:staff ratio; work has intensified; life has become dominated by much-unloved quality assurance mechanisms; and it's hard for academics to find the time – or the funding – for the things they joined the profession for in the first place. And yet there is still a doggedness about the senior common room – as one respondent to the 2004 AUT survey wrote: 'There is a constant expectation to achieve the impossible: deal with more students, find funding for our research, satisfy demands for quality, do our own administration. And we attempt to do it!' Another wrote: 'I could cut down and say no to more work, but my commitment to my subject keeps me motivated'.

Perhaps academic staff are learning to live with the stress and strain of contemporary university life, and to accommodate themselves to a more pressurized professional existence. The concern is that increasing numbers of academic staff will lose their commitment, and identify with the attitude of this respondent, who found the stress of work producing a sense of apathy: 'I am improving my work–life balance simply by being driven on a daily basis further towards just not caring any more about what happens at work. I still do my job, but I am feeling increasingly detached from it'. Even more, there is the danger of an increase in those who are quitting the profession because the external pressures put on higher education: 'My stress is not from the academic pressures I face – these are positive and motivating. I am leaving because of the bureaucratic impositions within HE, which seem to have lost touch with the educational and humanistic aspirations of education'. They may simply want to 'have a life': 'I am leaving as I want to do something more 9–5 where work is not constantly on my mind and I can have a family life', said another.

The future

Kingsley Amis (1960) may have felt, with regard to the expansion of higher education, that 'more will mean worse'. But the consensus in the sector still appears to be that all who are able to benefit from higher education should be given the opportunity to do so, even if that means further increases in student numbers. The policy of the AUT over recent years has been to campaign for increases in government funding for higher education to be channelled into improving the student:staff ratio. With the recent ending of the policy of reducing the unit of resource per student, it should now be possible for there to be a reduction in the student:staff ratio (SSR); without taking action, stress levels are likely to increase. Admittedly, greater use of information and communication technology in teaching might be able to take some of the strain of increased student numbers. But computers will never be a substitute for face-to-face contact between teachers and students, in enabling students to grapple with intellectual problems and staff to apply individual consideration to the intellectual development of students (Conole, this volume). The need for more teacher input per student in the future – rather than less – is a likely outcome of the desire to widen student social class access and enable those from a 'non-traditional' background to have a successful experience of higher education.

It may be time for academic staff to look to recent experience in the schools sector in England and Wales, where a national workload agreement was reached between the government and the majority of trade unions in 2003. According to the agreement, from September 2003

- teachers are no longer required to undertake administrative and clerical tasks on a routine basis;
- improvements are to be made to the work–life balance;
- teachers are to have a reasonable amount of time for management responsibilities; and
- the number of hours a teacher can be required to cover for absent colleagues is limited to 38 hours a year.

From 2005 teachers are guaranteed time for planning, preparation and assessment. Of course, there are many differences between university and school teachers in the way they work. Most academic staff in the pre-1992 sector do not have fixed hours of work specified in their contract, or a requirement that they should be at their official place of work during the working day. But there could be a case for adapting some of the measures now being used in schools for higher education. Although the government's Better Regulation Task Force has recommended ways of reducing the burden of bureaucracy in higher education, there is still more that could be done to cut down the administrative tasks academics have to do. Much greater use could be made of academic related and other support staff – as in schools – in freeing up academics to teach and research. Already academic related staff are increasingly involved in the provision of higher education and the support of students. This includes librarians helping students with finding sources of information (particularly online), with literature searches and project work; administrators being more involved with the practicalities of quality assurance processes; and computer staff developing educational software (AUT, 2001). Greater investment in support staff and information and communication technology could ease the academic workload.

While many academics surveyed by the AUT and the Institute of Education were broadly positive about universities making a contribution to the entrepreneurial vigour of the UK, there are a number of practical and ethical issues that need serious consideration. Although the government continues to increase the amount of public funding to support business links, the amounts available are small in comparison with recurrent funding for teaching and research. Given the relatively small returns institutions have seen so far for their efforts to commercialise their intellectual property, institutions will need to have a strong financial incentive from the government to allow academic staff to be diverted from their core tasks into this area. Academics need to know that time spent on the commercializing of their work will not be expected on top of their usual tasks. More work needs to be done, in the follow-up to the Lambert report (2003), to develop best practice in resolving potential or actual conflict between commercial confidentiality and academic freedom, particularly in terms of publication of research, to give academics confidence when approaching work with the business sector. Institutions need to be developing clear guidelines and best practice for situations where academics might encounter a real or potential conflict of interest between their 'academic' work and any commercial interests. Particular recent cases of commercial sponsorship in the world of higher education have raised sharp conflicts of interests: these too need to be carefully thought through in principle to defend academic freedom. As the conclusion of the 1998 report, *Industry-academic Links in the UK*, noted: 'Successful collaboration is founded upon mutual trust and shared goals with industrial partners, clearly expressed' (HEFCE, 1998: 61).

Notes

1   This is the most recent year for which data were available at the time of writing.
2   Prior to 2003–4 HESA did not collect or publish data on academic staff employed on less than 25 per cent of a full-time equivalent contract.
3   These time series data on student:staff ratios only relate to full-time students and full-time wholly university financed staff; they do not include part-time students, who have grown considerably in number, nor the relatively recent category of teaching-only academic staff, for whom a consistent time series is not available.
4   The AUT has at the time of writing (2004) approximately 49,000 members, the majority of whom work in the pre-1992 higher education institutions; around 80 per cent of AUT members are academics, and 20 per cent are academic related, chiefly administrative, library and computer staff. There were 782 respondents to the 1998 survey (with a 40 per cent response rate) and 1108 respondents to

the 2004 survey (with a 22 per cent response rate); except where indicated, the respondents included academic and related staff.

5   Prime Minister's questions, House of Commons, 27 November 2002.
6   See the AUT report 'The Unequal Academy', Chapter 22, at http://www.aut. org.uk/media/pdf/aut_unequalacademy.pdf

References

Amis, K. (1960) Article in *Encounter*.

AUT (Association of University Teachers) (2001) *Building the Academic Team*. www.aut.org.uk/index.cfm?articleid=148

AUT (2004) *The Unequal Academy*. London: AUT.

Coate, K., et al. (2000) *Academic and Academic Related Staff Involvement in the Local, Regional and National Economy*. London: AUT and Institute of Education.

Court, S. (1996) The use of time by academic and related staff, *Higher Education Quarterly*, 50(4): 237–60.

DfES (Department for Education and Skills) *Education and Training Statistics for the United Kingdom* (series). London: The Stationery Office.

HEFCE (Higher Education Funding Council for England) (1998) *Industry-academic Links in the UK*.

HEFCE (2003) *Higher Education – Business Interaction Survey 2000–1*. March 2003/11.

IDS (Incomes Data Services), *IDS Report* (series). London: IDS.

Kinman, G. (1998) *Pressure Points*. London: AUT.

Kinman, G. and Jones, F. (2004) *Stress and Work Life Balance in Academic and Academic Related Employees in the UK*. London: AUT.

Lambert, R. (2003) *Lambert Review of Business-University Collaboration Final Report*. London: The Stationery Office.

National Statistics, *New Earnings Survey* (series). London: National Statistics.

NCIHE (The National Committee of Inquiry into Higher Education) (1997) *Higher Education in the Learning Society* (The Dearing Report). The Stationery Office: London.

Universities UK (2004) *Achieving our Vision*. London: Universities UK.

USR (Universities' Statistical Record), *Volume One: Students and Staff* (series). Cheltenham: USR.

14

Gender (In)Equity in Mass Higher Education: The Need for Change

Wendy Saunderson

Introduction

Despite the trumpeting of equal opportunities policies and practices across UK higher education institutions (HEIs) since the mid 1990s, the continuing disadvantaged position of female university staff, vis-à-vis their male counterparts, renders equal opportunities (EO) somewhat toothless and ineffectual. For many, EO represents little more than a PR mechanism. The *context* is the vastly changed institutional context of 'corporate colonization'/new managerialism within which EO now operates. The *issues* concern the persistent problems of academic women's inferior position in terms of numerical representation, career progression/promotion, pay, and contractual status. More recently, stress and bullying have emerged as problems. The *empirical evidence* showing an attendant negative impact on academic women's working lives is plentiful: here, a brief account is provided of the author's detailed research evidencing the creation of 'vulnerable' academic identities as a response to coping with the new order. A final commentary on the *future* of EO for female academics offers guidance and recommendations for consideration by policy-makers, senior managers and academic staff.

One proviso: in speaking of equal opportunities – and their necessarily social justice roots – we must recognize that education is no longer a social policy issue, but, as Stedward (2003) argues, has been repositioned to straddle social and economic agendas. It is given a key role in the New Labour analysis of Britain's renewal – to the extent that we can speak of 'education as industrial policy'; therefore, in so far as 'the social and economic are presented as congruent and uncomplicated' (Stedward, 2003: 146), obvious problems arise in reconciling the concept of equal opportunity with the current/prevailing climate of the UK HE sector.

Second, we must acknowledge that 'equal opportunity' cannot be used as a substitute for *equality* (Bunting, M., 2004). Just as New Labour's focus on 'equality of opportunity' as a concrete problem (alongside poverty and social exclusion) may be viewed as a false 'displacement exercise' from the fundamental issue of economic inequality (Jackson and Segal, 2004), we must guard against equal opportunities rhetoric/efforts in our universities being a sticking plaster for gender equality.

Further, the concept itself is often used when opportunities are clearly not equal, no one attempts to make them so, and, although equal opportunity is a variant of equality, it would be more accurate to speak of '*open* opportunities and procedural justice' than to falsely represent them as *equal* opportunities (Hansson, 2004). However, for the purposes of this chapter, 'EO' adopts the 'vision' objective of the Equality Challenge Initiative (ECU, 2004a): that all HEIs work to 'ensure that staff, at all levels, and in all modes of employment are fairly recruited, supported, developed, appraised, rewarded and promoted'.

The context: massification, new managerialism and EO

The issues surrounding and impacting upon women's academic identity and experience of equal opportunities are couched within, and compounded by, the dramatically changed and changing ethos, praxis and pedagogy of UK higher education institutions in the twenty-first century. The new order is variously described as being characterized by rampant entrepreneurialism; regulation and surveillance; corporatism, complicity and collusion; a burgeoning audit culture; increasing 'instrumentalism'; and massification, marketization and managerialism. New Managerialism's benefits are celebrated as producing enhanced levels of the three Es – Economy, Efficiency and Effectiveness – in tandem with accountability. Noticeably, a fourth E – for Equity – is absent (Morley, 1999: 28). As Ball asserts (1994: 125), 'Equity is off the agenda, inequality is a cornerstone of the market.'

The aspect of the 'new managerialism' appearing from the literature to incite most resistance in women is its *values*, implicit and explicit. Indeed, it's reasonable to question whether this managerialism has any 'values' at all: if values of social justice are perceived as irrelevant to marketization; and if values of equity, collegiality and cooperation are seen as anathema to efficiency, individualism and competition, where and how can social inequalities be acknowledged? (Morley, 1999). Unfortunately, in the narrowly focused equal opportunities culture of the 1990s, the strong emphasis on the 'values' of performance, standards, and improvement in the discourses of new managerialism became *fused* – incongruently – with social justice values and issues (Salisbury and Riddell, 2000). Therefore, the absorption of equal opportunities into new managerialism's structures and processes effectively sanctioned the increasing demise of 'equality' and the diminishing of the social justice roots from which EO has grown (David *et al.*, 2000). So, while the incorporation of EO into personnel reduced the *complexity* of equal opportunities to a general notion of 'functions', Walsh (2002: 33) asserts, 'the *politics* of equal opportunities was sidelined, as EO became a new PR mechanism, torn from its liberatory and oppositional roots, and appropriated into the rhetoric of new managerialism'. In short, 'new managerialism' has been held responsible for effectively 'handcuffing' equal opportunities in the academy.

For the future, those policy-makers and institutional leaders responsible for quickening the massification and managerialism of UK HE should recognize and attempt to reconcile the basic anomaly that 'values about markets, business, enterprise, efficient management, individualism and competition sit uneasily with those which emphasize public service on the basis of need, social justice, collective ideas, human development of the aesthetic and the emotional as well as the cognitive' (Deem, 2000: 204). Equal opportunities, therefore, need to be somehow 'freed' from the excesses of marketization, re-connected to their social justice roots and re-calibrated into a 'valuable' and *meaningful* element of the way in which UK HEIs are run. This will only be achieved with major re-visioning, restructuring and recalibration of the ways, attitudes and processes by which academic women and men are recruited, professionalized and progressed/promoted; and the ways in which their productivity and 'value' are measured and remunerated. Some of this now appears to be in progress. In the wider context also, the new Women and Work Commission set up to champion 'Women into Work' – a key New Labour economic strategy – will submit its report in Autumn 2005 on issues affecting women's employment, discussed below in the UK HE context.

The issues: academic women's position in UK HE

The numerical representation, pay rates, contractual terms and conditions, and positions of seniority of female academics, as a group, continue to lag behind those of males, and show lamentable progress, given some thirty-five years of an Equal Pay Act, thirty years of a Sex Discrimination Act, and a decade of trumpeting on-the-ground EO policies in UK universities. At the end of the 1980s, our universities were described as being 'bastions of male power and privilege' (Hansard Society, 1990); and at the end of the 1990s: 'amongst the least equal of British institutions in terms of gender equity' (Bett, 1999). In 2004, seemingly unabated, such assertions persisted: 'Women suffer 5K pay gap' (Johnston, 2004), and 'Serious lack of women in academia' (Smithers, 2004). The Athena Survey of Science, Engineering and Technology spurred the heading, 'Universities rife with institutional sexism' (Curtis, 2004a); the AUT's (2004b) report *Gender and Research Activity in the 2001 RAE* prompted 'Sex bias limits women in the RAE' (Baty, 2004a); the AUT's (2004c) report *The Unequal Academy* incited 'Women academics continue to get a raw deal' (AUT, 2004f); and the AUT's (2004d) commissioned report *Working to the Limit* prompted the heading, 'Cracks in the ivory towers'

(Curtis and Crace, 2004). Further, academic papers such as Acker and Armenti (2004), and Simpson and Cohen (2004), reinforce evidence of a new rise in levels of stress and bullying felt by many female academics.

Despite the rhetoric of a large number of UK HEIs claiming their championing and upholding of equal opportunities policy and practice, the most recent research and statistics lack evidence for such claims. Without a duty of rigorous monitoring of their claims – or a statutory duty to implement systematic and comprehensive EO procedures and practice – such rhetoric can continue uncurbed, confirming EO as a nebulous concept. Equal opportunities issues relating to gender equality concentrate around four main areas: recruitment and representation, contractual status, progression and promotion, and pay.

Recruitment and representation

Despite the 'serious and worsening problems' of recruitment and retention of academic staff in UK HE reported by IRS Research in 2001, an overall steady average annual rise of 2 per cent was sustained from 1995/6 to 2002/3, albeit through HEIs being net importers of staff. The fairly constant number of staff leaving UK HEIs is about half the number of new entrants, mainly from the EU (AUT, 2004c: 8). Of the 145,510 academic staff employed in 122 HEIs, 39 per cent (56,480) are women (AUT, 2004c). This reflects a sharp increase of 43 per cent in female recruitment (almost 20,000 people) between 1995/6 to 2002/3; and compares with a mere 4 per cent increase (3500 people) in male recruitment over the same period, bringing the total number of male academics to just over 89,000 (AUT, 2004c: 10).

On the face of it, this is good news, since this surge of female recruitment is tipping the see-saw of academic women's numerical under-representation. However, these increasing numbers of female recruits are disproportionately concentrated in more junior and more casualized posts. Further, the 39 per cent female staff minority shows a stark gender imbalance with the student population, now nearing a 60 per cent female majority. Perhaps the most interesting aspect of recent statistics is the falling numbers of male academics entering the profession, and achieving promotion. Although the 61 per cent overall male majority continues to form the majority at all staff grades (Curtis, 2004b), the number of new male recruits in 2002/3 increased by only 0.7 per cent (compared with 5.7 per cent for females); and the number of male lecturers fell by 625 that year and by 715 in 2001/02. This has prompted claims that men are being deterred by a decline in the perceived status of HE, fuelled by low pay and increased regulation (Hill, 2004).

If these trends continue, then there may result a paradoxical situation where more vacancies exist for women and, 'if the status continues to go out of the profession, more opportunities open up for women' (Morley, 2004). Are we witnessing the beginnings of a feminization of the 'new' university sector? Ironic, indeed. Or are we observing some sort of 'academic nemesis' – a retribution by potential or established (previously autonomous) male academics, for the increasingly unacceptable and unfamiliar massification and managerialism of our universities (and, by default, the creation of 'space' for women)? Or, are we seeing the beginnings of the process of equality of opportunity? As HEIs become more aware of their obligations to comply with equality legislation, are more women being given a fair chance, and so are more women being appointed and being promoted? Answers are elusive.

Contractual status

While the sharp increase in the recruitment of female academics has raised their share of the sector to 39 per cent, it has also disproportionately swelled the ranks of more junior level and casualized posts. Increasingly, we hear of universities being propped up by armies of women on temporary contracts, being paid less on average than men and facing unequal promotion prospects (Sanders, 2004a). Almost half (48 per cent) of all female academics are now employed on fixed-term contracts, compared to just 38 per cent of men (AUT, 2004c). We also increasingly hear about the plight of part-time workers in our universities: low pay, 'hidden' hours of unpaid work, hanging around departments in the hope of a full-time post, and general lack of support, facilities, resources and status – or as a recent report was titled: *A Rich Contract: The 'Ragged-Trousered Philanthropy' of Part-Time Staff* (LSDA, 2004). Women comprise over half (56 per cent) of those working part time in UK HEIs; and twice as many women (26 per cent) as men (13 per cent) are working on part-time contracts (HESA, 2004).

The UK HE sector now qualifies as one of the most casualized industries in the UK, likened to the building trade, burger bars (NATFHE, 2004a) and pub work (Bunting, C., 2004); and second only to catering, as reported by a House of Commons Select Committee (Canovan, 2001). However, new legislation, *The Fixed-Term Employees (Prevention of Less Favourable Treatment) Regulations*, was finally enacted in October 2002, backdated to take effect from 30 July 2002. The regulations state that following a maximum continuous four-year period on two or more consecutive contracts, a fixed-term contract (FTC) must revert to a permanent contract unless the employer can prove 'objective justification' to the contrary. But despite this new legislation, and despite UK universities signing an agreement to reduce their use of such contracts, 'very few universities have actually reduced their use of FTCs' (Hunt, 2004).

The future, in terms of casualization, eagerly points to 30 July 2006 when the first cases arise, and very much depends on holding to account the HEIs' use of 'objective justification' to retain FTCs. Already universities are ridding themselves of staff on casual contracts, in preparation (Sanders, 2004b). Worse still, one university is moving all its casual staff on to permanent contracts, but not guaranteeing any work for them – maximizing its own flexibility but removing any commitment to provide work (Baty, 2004b). At worst, as has happened in Germany, we may witness FTC research staff being forced to take breaks between 'slightly different' contracts; or being 'horse-traded' between HEIs running collaborative projects (Tanner, 2004). Certainly, for academic women working on fixed-term contracts and wishing to remain at the same institution, the 'single contract' culture that will inevitably emerge will arguably leave them worse off than at present. For the time being though, almost half of all academic women remain on short-term contracts. FTCs shatter job security, stifle career progression, stymie pensions planning, erode academic freedom and increase vulnerability and the risk of exploitation (AUT, 2004e). FTCs clearly fly in the face of equal opportunities for academic women (Bryson, 2004).

Progression and promotion

Academic women appear to be at last 'cracking the glass ceiling' (Hill, 2004). The situation as recently as 2002 (Saunderson, 2002) was that: 'academic men are securing professorships at more than three times the rate of academic women' (NATFHE, 2002: 13). The 2004 HESA figures show an about-turn. In the year to 2002/03, there was a 10.4 per cent leap in the number of women professors: the biggest single change in the figures; and almost seven times the percentage increase of male professors (1.5 per cent). The second largest increase in staff was amongst women senior lecturers – a 6.4 per cent rise on the previous year, compared to a 1.1 per cent rise for men. However, the 'ceiling is cracked, not shattered' (Ross, 2004). Men continue to dominate the higher echelons of UK HEIs, where women remain poorly represented. Only 8 per cent of vice-chancellors are women; only 14 per cent of professors, and just 26 per cent of all senior lecturers (HESA, 2004).

In terms of equal opportunities for career progression and promotion, new evidence of discrimination in the RAE has elicited accusations of institutionalized sexism. The AUT's (2004b) research revealed that of the 43,000 staff recorded as 'research active' in the 2001 RAE, only 25 per cent were women. A total of just 19 per cent of all female academics were included in the 2001 RAE (compared with 37 per cent of men), so male academics were almost twice as likely to be counted as research active (Baty, 2004a). This 'massive systematic discrimination against women throughout their careers' (Cottrell, 2004) constitutes fundamental and direct discrimination, since inclusion in the RAE is a key determinant in career progression and promotion.

For the future, there is no particular indication that women will change their tendency to take on more teaching and administration if asked, and more 'emotional labour' (Ogbonna and Harris, 2004), student involvement and pastoral care. As 'massification' of UK HE speeds into the 'universal' category, women are likely to take *more* – not less – of the strain. Work–life balance becomes even more about struggling; less about 'juggling'. For the

RAE in 2008, HEFCE insists that EO will be a 'fundamental principle' underlying its design and conduct (just as they were in 2001?) though the briefing to panels (HEFCE, 2005) is more about meeting legislative requirements. An important point for the future concerns the wider implications of 'stunted' career progression in our universities, since few women in senior positions means few women qualified to join outside bodies. According to the chief executive of UUK, 'this produces a spin-off effect which leads to unbalanced royal commissions and representation on governing bodies of public service providers' (cited in Smithers, 2004).

Pay

The gender pay gap is possibly the most invidious of the 'issues', given that it arises largely from the impact of gender differences in educational levels and length of work experience – including part-time working and career breaks – often dictated by women's caring roles and responsibilities.

In international terms, UK academic pay comes close to the bottom of the scale when compared with other Commonwealth countries. Only lecturers in Malaysia earn less than UK lecturers; and senior lecturers in the UK are at the bottom of the earnings table (Sanders, 2004c). Further, with UK academic salaries increasing at just half the rate of the UK public sector average since the mid-1990s, the AUT's analysis, based on figures from the Government's New Earnings Survey, show that while academic pay increased by just 6.6 per cent, schoolteachers' pay increased by 12.3 per cent, medics' by 26.6 per cent and managers' by 31.6 per cent (Sanders, 2004c). Vice-chancellors enjoyed pay increases of between 42 per cent and 80 per cent between 1994/5 and 2001/2 (Fenton, 2004).

For women academics in the UK, these already low academic salaries and relatively slow pay increases are further compounded by the gender pay deficit. Female full-time academics earn, on average, just 85 per cent of the salaries of their male counterparts. This pay gap translates into women's average salary of £30,500 being over £5000 less per year than the average for male academics. At individual HEIs across the UK, the differential ranges from as much as 42 per cent to −0.6 per cent (AUT, 2004a: 2). The gap is slightly less in England, at 14.7 per cent; but more in Northern Ireland (16.9 per cent) and Scotland (17.5 per cent); with Wales (18 per cent) equalling the overall 18 per cent average national pay gap (EOC, 2004) in the UK. Back in 1999, NATFHE estimated a cost of £188 million to dissolve the disparity (NATFHE, 1999); while the Bett Report (1999) reckoned that it would swallow a 2.5 per cent share of the sector's total costs – £283 million in 1997/8 (AUT, 1999). The rise in female recruitment since the late 1990s will, of course, substantially increase the cost to UK HEIs of meeting their equal pay obligations.

The most dependable and robust route to redress will be via systematic and comprehensive equal pay audits. However, despite JNCHES's 2002 publication of the sector's own targeted equal pay review guidelines – and UCEA's equal pay audit 'computer tool' – the majority of HEIs have not done this (AUT, 2004a): an all-too-common feature of 'guiding' change as opposed to regulating for it. The EOC have issued a Code of Practice on Equal Pay and, although the code is not statutory, according to the ECU (2004b), a tribunal or court would take account of the guidance in it. Further, two amendments written into *The Equal Pay Act 1970 (Amendment) Regulations 2003*, allowing an extension of the six-month time limit for bringing an equal pay case, and extending the two-year arrears period up to a possible six years of back pay for long-standing cases of pay discrimination, suggest obvious benefits to women bringing equal pay cases in the university sector. The effects remain to be seen of the October 2004 legislative changes to the tribunal procedure (likely to prolong cases since the institution's disciplinary procedures must be exhausted before going to tribunal); and changes to the procedure in equal value claims (which removes the employer's ability to argue 'no reasonable grounds'). Of course, it is anticipated that in August 2006 the Framework Agreement (FA) for the Modernization of Pay Structures, supporting the achievement of equal pay for equal work of equal value, will address much of the gender pay gap issue. This depends on the FA's comprehensive and rigorous implementation – and does not weaken the necessity for systematic and comprehensive equal pay audits.

The empirical evidence: 'vulnerable' academic identities

A flurry of research and commentary since the late 1990s has lamented the often capricious nature and revolutionizing effects of the new managerialist approach of UK HE, and its concomitant shackling of effective equal opportunities. Less research has focused on its impact at the institutional micro-level of individual academic identities – surprising, since we might suppose that individual academic identities (Henkel, 2000) would be a necessarily critical starting point for constructing the new corporate 'imaging' of the collective identities of departments, faculties, research centres and their respective university institutions. Work by Saunderson elicited idiographic profiles of academic staff's values, beliefs and identifications relating to salient aspects of their academic lives. By 'anchoring' such identifications in their own individual value systems, using a custom-designed 'Identity Structure Analysis' Identity Instrument, a classification of 'identity variants' was generated (Saunderson, 2002; Weinreich and Saunderson, 2003; Saunderson, 2004).

The UK HE system's *institutional* structures and processes were found to be impacting upon academic women's *identity* structures and processes in ways that create 'vulnerable' academic identities. The findings revealed two distinct 'variants' of vulnerable identity, with quite different orientations to EO and the new regime, which appeared to produce a 'two-track' effect in terms of academic women's identity and orientation within their HEI.

1 'Diffused' academic identities, 'Corporate Outsiders': These academics carry many and diverse identification conflicts with the HE system (particularly with promotion, related to tensions between RAE and teaching loads), often paralleled by low self-evaluation: EO is mainly perceived as PR and 'spin'.

Academic identities on the 'outside track' are compromised, challenged and laid vulnerable through varying feelings of being undervalued, overlooked, overburdened, and/or being the subjects of unequal treatment in a 'masculinized' and often alienating academic climate where, as one woman said, 'output is privileged over process'. 'Diffused' identities are in an arena of conflict, often paralleled by low self-regard, virtually negating the women's personally-held values, and resulting in a 'crisis' identity state. This is an 'unhealthy' and 'uncomfortable' psychological state. Some academic women experienced this crisis identity state only in their academic-self, whilst perfectly 'healthy' identity states were maintained in their female/personal-self and their past self-image. This 'diffused' vulnerability in academic identity appeared to be strongly linked to negatively-perceived and experienced aspects of the new management practices, performance expectations and equal treatment and, in turn, to a lack of redress through accessible and transparent equal opportunities practice.

2 'Foreclosed' academic identities, 'Corporate Insiders': These academics respond to the system with a defensive denial of conflict, often with inflated self-evaluation: EO policy and practice is defensively championed.

Academic identities on the 'inside track' appear to have mounted a defensive response to the 'fear' of such identity alienation and identification conflicts with aspects of their university lives – adopting, absorbing and championing the new managerialism in their unrealistically rigid and equally vulnerable identity states. In a somewhat unreflective and unreflexive embracing of change, managerialism and the current system, these academic women evaluated both their 'past-self' and 'female-self' more negatively than their 'academic self'. EO policy and efforts, like all the central tenets of the corporate bureaucracy, were championed.

The findings do not suggest that *all* academic women have vulnerable identities, nor do they imply that all academic men have *non*-vulnerable identities. Using identity as a powerful sensitizing concept, and an effective 'measuring tool', findings were produced about academic women's perceptions, feelings, positions and responses to their working lives in the UK university sector. The level of vulnerabilities in their identities – and the 'extreme' identity positions they had adopted as coping responses – stand as a clear indictment of the current system, and hold potentially serious implications for HEIs' duty of care and statutory responsibility to uphold the psychosocial well-being of their employees. The 'diffused' vulnerable identity stance of the 'corporate outsiders', involving all the issues discussed earlier in this chapter, suggests a clear indication that EO policies are not being translated into accessible and effective EO practice. The 'corporate insiders' readily adopt and exemplify the new corporatist values, but in a defensive 'tunnel-visioned' rigidity that renders their identities vulnerable and problematic. The central tension is between, on the one hand, the individual academic's capacity to construct and reconstruct self, identifications and academic identity, resisting the penalties, constraints and imperatives of the corporate academic structure; and, on the other, the individual academic's *dependence* on that very corporate academic structure as the source of who they experience themselves to be as academics.

The future: towards EOs as a *meaningful* concept in UK HE

This chapter would appear to confirm EO as a 'nebulous concept' for many academic women in UK HE. The raft of evidence presented represents a serious 'wake-up call' and warrants urgent attention by policy-makers, senior managers and involved staff to *activate* EO policy statements: to *substantiate* 'empty shell' EO policies (Hoque and Noon, 2004) with supporting EO practice. The empirical evidence of increasingly polarized and 'vulnerable' identity responses of female staff to the impact of the current system carries potentially serious implications for the HE sector's duty of care and statutory responsibility to uphold the psychosocial well-being of its employees. Significant in terms of EO, all these gender issues appear to mirror racial issues for staff from black and minority ethnic (BME) groups: not a single black vice-chancellor; only nine black women professors (NATFHE, 2004b); and constituting just 9.2 per cent of full-time academics (AUT, 2004g) – serious considerations since over 20 per cent of home student entrants are from BME groups. The crucial questions towards *meaningful* EO for academic women – 'what needs to be done?'; 'who is responsible?' and 'how can they be held accountable?' – point to the need for firm legislation from policy-makers, bold leadership from institutional senior managers, and sustained demand and support for EO from staff.

Policy-makers

They should be responsible for reinforcing statutory minimum requirements for 'evidenced' EO practice in HEIs, particularly in research and RAE-related promotion principles and procedures, and for imposing penalties where breaches occur: accountability should be clearly designated from HEI level, through the funding councils, to government level. An upper limit should be imposed on the number of fixed-term contracts (FTEs) permitted in HEIs, for example, at school or faculty level, as a percentage of staff grade. Systematic and comprehensive equal pay audits across the sector are urgently required to expose the detail of the gender pay deficit. They will help to clarify the picture for the implementation of the Framework Agreement's pay and grading procedures in August 2006. The government's work–life balance campaign (launched in March 2000) appears to have largely by-passed the university sector: efforts to facilitate the regulation of academic working time will greatly improve EOs for women.

Senior managers

Senior managers should implement equal pay audits at faculty level across their institutions. They should reduce the use of fixed-term contracts; guard against 'strategic hiring and firing' of fixed-term contract staff approaching 30 July 2006 to 'beat' the legislation; and should exercise a principled use of the 'objective justification' clause. Subsequent 'horse-trading' of contract staff across collaborative project centres will encourage the rise of a 'single contract' culture and is against the spirit of EO and the agreement to reduce FTCs. If senior managers, staff and their trades unions adopt a partnership approach to produce an 'enabling' context within which EO strategies can be refined and implemented, the quality of the strategies and commitment to implementing them will be enhanced. An 'enabling' context necessitates practical efforts through staff training to change the often sexist (and racist) institutional culture. Senior managers should set up an 'Equal Opportunities Monitoring Group' (as in Aston) and 'Equal Opportunities Officers' (as in Loughborough) to mediate the gap between on-the-ground staff and the often 'distant' advisory and implementation units at the centre. Transparency should dominate the 2008 RAE and any associated hastily-formed 'hot-housing' research institutes: precisely who is included, and why? Excessive demands of academic careers are systemic problems requiring institutional remedies: work–life balance can only be achieved by work-time limits (Jacobs, 2004), particularly for academic mothers. Towards respecting work-time limits, micro-level 'surveillance', unnecessary form-filling, meetings and committees should be kept to a minimum. A staff EO attitude survey or online self-assessment can provide a valuable overview of staff motivation and performance and be used as the basis for action planning.

Staff

The best, and the most, that staff can do is to staunchly uphold, and hold to account, the principles laid out in the Gender Equality PSA (Public Sector

Agreement) Objective 2003–2006; to encourage and support fellow staff in upholding those principles; and to individually and collectively uphold the spirit of EO policies and their practical application in our UK HEIs. And, to strive wherever and whenever possible to enforce accountability at all levels – from fellow staff, line managers, senior managers, and policy-makers.

References

Acker, S. and Armenti, C. (2004) Sleepless in academia, *Gender and Education*, 16 (1): 3–24.

AUT (Association of University Teachers) (1999) *Pay Gaps and Casual Jobs: An Analysis of the Gender, Pay and Employment of UK Academic Staff*. London: AUT.

AUT (2004a) *The Gender Pay Gap in UK HE 2001*. London: AUT.

AUT (2004b) *Academic Staff 2002–03: Gender and Research Activity in the 2001 RAE*. London: AUT.

AUT (2004c) *The Unequal Academy*. London: AUT.

AUT (2004d) *Working to the Limit*. London: AUT.

AUT (2004e) The use of fixed-term contracts. Policies. www.aut.org.uk/index.cfm?articleid=398

AUT (2004f) Women academics continue to get a raw deal, *AUT News*, 30 September.

AUT (2004g) Employers' proposals could compound 'institutional racism', *AUT News*, 9 March.

Ball, S. (1994) *Education Reform – A Critical and Post-Structural Approach*. Milton Keynes: Open University Press.

Baty, P. (2004a) Sex bias limits women in the RAE, *THES*, 16 July.

Baty, P. (2004b) Contract guarantees post but not pay, *THES*, 30 July.

Bett, M. (1999) *Independent Review of Higher Education Pay and Conditions*. Report of a Committee Chaired by Sir Michael Bett. London: The Stationery Office.

Bryson, C. (2004) The consequences for women in the academic profession of the widespread use of fixed term contracts, *Gender, Work and Organization*, 11 (2): 187–206.

Bunting, M. (2004) Why inequality matters, *Guardian*, 19 October.

Bunting, C. (2004) Young losers in the generation game, *THES*, 10 September.

Canovan, E. (2001) Short-term and short-changed? *THES*, 27 April.

Cottrell, P. (2004) Quoted in P. Curtis, Women suffer in research ratings, *Guardian*, 15 July.

Curtis, P. (2004a) Universities rife with institutional sexism, *Guardian*, 28 April.

Curtis, P. (2004b) University gender gap narrows, *Guardian*, 14 June.

Curtis, P. and Crace, J. (2004) Cracks in the ivory towers, *Guardian*, 16 November.

David, M., Weiner, G. and Arnot, M. (2000) Gender equality and schooling, education policy-making and feminist research in England and Wales in the 1990s, in J. Salisbury and S. Riddell (eds) *Gender, Policy and Educational Change: Shifting Agendas in the UK and Europe*. London: Routledge.

Deem, R. (2000) Gendered governance: education reform and lay involvement in the local management of schools, in J. Salisbury and S. Riddell (eds) *Gender, Policy and Educational Change: Shifting Agendas in the UK and Europe*. London: Routledge.

ECU (Equality Challenge Unit) (2004a) *About ECU: Vision, Mission and Aims.* Equality Challenge Unit website. www.ecu.ac.uk/vision/ (accessed 17 December 2004).

ECU (2004b) *Women and Men Guidance Sources: Legislation UK.* 10 September. See: http://www.eoc.org.uk/cseng/legislation/law_code_of_practice.pdf

EOC (Equal Opportunities Commission) (2004) *Britain's Competitive Edge: Women Unlocking the Potential.* London: EOC.

Fenton, N. (2004) Why I want to see vice-chancellors on the picket line, *THES*, 20 February 2004.

Hansard Society Commission (1990) *Women at the Top.* London: The Hansard Society for Parliamentary Government.

Hansson, S. O. (2004) What are opportunities and why should they be equal? *Social Change and Welfare*, 22: 305–16.

HEFCE (Higher Education Funding Council for England) (2005) *RAE 2008: Equality briefing for panel chairs, members and secretaries*, Bristol, HEFCE for the funding agencies.

Henkel, M. (2000) *Academic Identities and Policy Change in Higher Education.* London: Jessica Kingsley.

HESA (Higher Education Statistics Agency) (2004) *Resources of Higher Education Institutions.* 2002/03. Cheltenham: Higher Education Statistics Agency.

Hill, P. (2004) Women crack glass ceiling, *THES*, 25 June.

Hoque, K. and Noon, M. (2004) Equal opportunities policy and practice in Britain: evaluating the 'empty shell' hypothesis, *Work, Employment and Society*, 18 (3): 481–506.

Hunt, S. (2004) AUT attacks scandal of job insecurity, *AUT News*, 4 October.

IRS research (2001) *Recruitment and Retention of Staff in UK Higher Education 2001: A Survey and Case Studies.* Report commissioned by HEFCE, SCOP, UCES and UUK. London: IRS Research.

Jackson, B. and Segal, P. (2004) *Why Inequality Matters.* London: Catalyst.

Jacobs, J. A. (2004) The faculty time divide. *Sociological Forum*, 19 (1): 3–27.

Johnston, C. (2004) Women suffer 5K pay gap, *Guardian*, 3 September.

LSDA (The Learning and Skills Development Agency) (2004) *A Rich Contract: The 'Ragged-Trousered' Philanthropy of Part-Time Staff.* London: The Learning and Skills Development Agency.

Morley, L. (1999) *Organising Feminisms: The Micropolitics of the Academy.* Basingstoke: Macmillan.

Morley, L. (2004) Quoted in P. Hill, Women crack glass ceiling, *THES*, 25 June.

NATFHE (National Association of Teachers in Further and Higher Education) (1999) Natfhe analysis of HESA data reported in the *Independent*, 11 November, in AUT (1999) *Pay Gaps and Casualised Jobs.* AUT Research, November.

NATFHE (2002) *The Price of Equality: Comprehensive Spending Review 2003/4–2005/6*, Higher Education Submission, January 2002. London: NATFHE.

NATFHE (2004a) University withdraws 'burger bar' contracts after union action. Natfhe Press Release: www.natfhe.org.uk/rels2004/2004pr070.shtml

NATFHE (2004b) Help and advice: Equality. www.natfhe.org.uk/help/help0005.html

Ogbonna, E. and Harris, L.C. (2004) Work intensification and emotional labour among UK university lecturers: an exploratory study, *Organisation Studies*, 25 (7): 1185–1203.

Ross, K. (2004) Ceiling cracked not shattered, *THES*, 2 July.

Salisbury, J. and Riddell, S. (eds) (2000) *Gender, Policy and Educational Change: Shifting Agendas in the UK and Europe.* London: Routledge.

Sanders, C. (2004a) Casual culture props up academe, *THES*, 1 October.

Sanders, C. (2004b) Contract staff laid off in preparation for EU Law, *THES*, 8 October.

Sanders, C. (2004c) Academic pay rises lag behind teachers', *THES*, 15 October.

Saunderson, W. (2002) Women, academia and identity: constructions of equal opportunities in the 'new managerialism' – a case of 'lipstick on the gorilla'? *Higher Education Quarterly*, 56 (4): 376–406.

Saunderson, W. (2004) 'Lipstick on the gorilla': Identity and EO issues in UK HE. Paper for the ESRC/SRHE seminar Series, 'From Mass to Universal Higher Education: Building on Experience'. Seminar 5b: 'Changing Systems, Changing Roles: Expectations and Experiences of Staff'. CISHE, UCL, 8 January.

Simpson, R. and Cohen, C. (2004) Dangerous work: the gendered nature of bullying in the context of higher education, *Gender, Work and Organisation*, 11 (2): 163–86.

Smithers, R. (2004) 'Serious lack' of women in academia, *Guardian*, 18 March.

Stedward, G. (2003) Education as industrial policy: New Labour's marriage of the social and economic, *Policy and Politics*, 31 (2): 139–52.

Tanner, R. (2004) Open end could spell dead end, *THES*, 16 April.

Walsh, V. (2002) Equal opportunities without 'equality': redeeming the irredeemable, in G. Howie and A. Tauchert (eds) *Gender, Teaching and Research in Higher Education: Challenges for the 21st Century*. Aldershot: Ashgate.

Weinreich, P. and Saunderson, W. (eds) (2003) *Analysing Identity: Cross-cultural, Societal and Clinical Contexts*. London: Routledge.

15

Administrators or Managers? The Shifting Roles and Identities of Professional Administrators and Managers in UK Higher Education

Celia Whitchurch

Introduction

This chapter focuses on shifts in the roles and identities of professional administrators and managers in UK universities, in particular movements around understandings of the terms 'administration' and 'management'. It builds on earlier work (Whitchurch, 2004) on a repositioning of professional administrators and managers as a result of changes in the higher education environment, in particular the impact of larger institutions, devolved organizational structures, and multi-functional team working. It is suggested that while professional administrators and managers increasingly regard themselves as 'managers' rather than 'administrators', elements of a service ethos remain. Not only have administrative and management functions become blurred, but the boundaries between professional administrators and managers, academic managers, and rank and file academic staff have become less clear-cut, and their activities interlinked in increasingly complex ways. The analysis that follows is based on doctoral work at the University of London Institute of Education. It draws on interviews with ten heads of administration and three heads of institutions from a representative sample of UK higher education institutions.

Are universities 'different'?

The move from an elite to a mass higher education system has had a significant impact on institutional identities, not least in terms of agendas such as wealth creation and widening participation (Scott, 1995), and government accountability and audit requirements. In some ways this has brought them closer to other sectors. However, when asked whether there was a quintessential difference between working in universities and working in other public or private sector organizations, all of those interviewed felt that there *was* something distinctive, even if they thought that, on the whole, the skills and knowledge involved were transferable. This went beyond the concept of 'service' that might also exist in, for instance, schools and hospitals. It was described as something to do with being a *member* of an institution rather than an *employee* of an organization, as well as with having the headroom to create new and innovative pathways. It meant subscribing to institutional values and having empathy for academic activity, as described by one vice-chancellor:

> . . . no-one, however pure their administrative role, can somehow opt out of the kind of core values of the institution, 'I'm just working here' kind of thing . . .

It was likely to involve doing something that is groundbreaking:

> enabling people (students and staff) to achieve their potential

and something that has a social purpose:

> I always just genuinely believe that university education changes people's lives.

Ideologically, these reasons may not be so far removed from the factors that motivate the 'idealists' among academic staff (Henkel, 2000: 148, 256).

There was also a pragmatic difference about managing a university, which was that, despite a seemingly higher profile for 'management', managers (academic or administrative) cannot simply 'give orders' and expect them to be implemented. As one head of administration, who had experience of both the pre-1992 and the post-1992 sectors, put it:

> I do think they (universities) are unique . . . because even now you can't say to anyone 'you will go out and do this'. You've got to negotiate your whole life into getting people to follow university policy . . . In a similar situation in a commercial company you could go out and say 'you will do this'. And you know there's no point in doing that.

Translating strategy into practice, therefore, requires the ability to contextualize and argue a case, taking account of a range of factors (market, legal, reputational), through an intelligent reading of the environment:

> You do have to have someone who is very good at . . . scanning the horizon and understanding where the system as a whole is moving, where your institution might reasonably fit in that system.

The sense, therefore, is that professional administrators and managers have membership of the university as a community, and that this is something beyond the operation of conventional organizational structures and boundaries.

Administrators or managers?

The administrative function in the pre-1992 universities has its origins in the traditions of public administration, and has been encapsulated as 'a sort of academic civil service' (Sloman, 1964). Until the government funding cuts of the early 1980s, this was facilitated by predictable quinquennial funding arrangements, in which the university's super-ordinate purposes of teaching and research were unlikely to be disturbed by the hard choices that characterized later decades. While career professionals were expected to operate within well-defined and formal boundaries

> . . . to be seen and not heard, not to speak at a committee, except perhaps the Registrar, and then only when asked to give an opinion, you know, 'Registrar, can you remind us of the Regulations' or something, that kind of thing . . .

their influence in 'leading from behind', in civil service mode, could be considerable. Arrangements in the post-1992 sector were drawn from the traditions of local government, and there was variability, depending on the local authority, in the modus operandi of officer-level staff. Some operated within a very prescribed roles, effectively as local government clerks, while others had the freedom and flexibility to develop higher profiles. The influence of earlier traditions from both sectors can be seen in contemporary institutions today.

As government and market imperatives impacted upon the UK higher education system, the idea of 'academic administration' expanded and diversified. Organizational arrangements whereby academic activity is served or serviced by a discrete 'administration' have been superseded by more complex, multi-dimensional models. One major impact of the increase in size and geographical spread of institutions is that it is no longer possible for individuals such as the head of administration to be known personally to a majority of staff. Furthermore, flatter, devolved structures mean that lateral communication between, say, schools and faculties, increasingly becomes an issue, in terms of maximizing the synergy of academic, physical and financial resources. The use of multi-functional teams, for instance, in relation to a quality or Investors in People initiative, can foster the development of matrix structures with lateral and vertical lines of communication. The idea of a well understood caucus of administrative staff thus breaks down as new, hybrid identities emerge.

In common with their institutions, professional administrators' and managers' work is characterized by increasing permeability with other sectors and knowledges (Gibbons *et al.*, 1994). At the same time understandings around the terms 'administration' and 'management' have become more fluid, and there has been a drift away from the traditional functions of a regulatory administration, with well defined rules and procedures, towards a focus on the provision of 'expert' opinion to aid decision-making about institutional futures (Whitchurch, 2004). New concepts of service, directed towards institutional stakeholders, have emerged, as described by one head of administration:

> When we started, I think we regarded our bosses as our customers. Now, actually, people regard the real customers as the customers . . . You can see it when you walk in [to Student Services]. They'll turn away from me to deal with the customers, and that's absolutely right.

The administration/management nexus is characterized by the difficulty of naming and framing professional staff. This is noted in the Lambert Report (2003: 94), which points out that they are, in some institutions, being subsumed under the generic title 'professional services', which are becoming increasingly visible. For instance, estates and facilities have become significant factors in the bid to attract high quality students. Defining the boundaries of 'administration', 'management' and 'professional services' is complicated because the terms have different meanings for different sections of the institutional community, and there is considerable movement by individuals between them. Similar difficulties have been identified in the US and Europe; Rhoades and Sporn (2002) made a distinction between 'administrators' and 'academic managers', and coined the term 'managerial professionals' to describe staff who might cross these categories. For the purpose of this chapter, however, the staff under discussion correspond broadly to staff in the 'managers and administrators' category (HESDA, 2002), and represent around 8 per cent of the total workforce in UK higher education. They do not, therefore, include teaching and learning professionals, such as library and IT staff.

An equivocation around 'administration' and 'management' is reflected in the various ways in which institutions define their professional staff as a collective. One head of administration's institution had re-launched its service structure, and stated 'We call[ed] them the Administration because we couldn't think of anything better'. Another had taken a formal step to 're-brand' a broad range of functions under the heading 'professional services'. This encompassed, for instance, areas such as teaching and learning support and information services, whose staff 'would never allow themselves to be called administrators'. While an extension of this kind of conceptual restructuring may cause the term 'administration', de facto, to wither, the study suggests that, at the very least, an idea of service continues, although it is a more client-oriented form of service. Significantly, both the Association of Heads of University Administration and the Association of University Administrators still use it as part of their titles, reflecting possible sensitivities vis-à-vis their academic colleagues about who is 'managing' the institution.

It will be interesting to see whether the increasing traffic of senior appointments between pre- and post-1992 sectors, and a stronger tradition of 'management' in the post-1992 sector, via directorate structures, has an influence in this regard. Preliminary indications from the study suggest that in the latter there may be a clearer gap between process-oriented, 'clerical' functions and middle management functions, and that there are fewer 'no go' areas for professional managers, who are freer to comment on academic matters, which in the pre-1992 sector would be regarded as the sole preserve of academic managers.

Beyond 'administration' and 'management'?

Notwithstanding lingering legacies of 'administration', all the heads of administration interviewed, whilst acknowledging the administrative trad-ition from which they came, regarded themselves as managers. This was partly a function of seniority, partly of personality and approach, but also a result of generic changes in the working environment. There was consensus that a watershed had occurred at the beginning of the 1980s:

> . . . any time after about 1980, you really couldn't be a strong academic institution if you weren't either stinking rich or . . . sufficiently well-managed to . . . stay the right side of the line.

Their status as managers was seen principally as a function of their involve-ment in the handling of resources, in increasingly risk-laden decision-making, and in the choices arising therefrom. While some felt that 'administration' and 'management' coexisted along a continuum, and that each shaded into the other, others felt that a gap had opened up between them, leaving a vacuum at times:

> The risk is that you end up with these rather diffuse, fuzzy systems which we now have, that you have people at the bottom, relatively junior, who operate within a fairly clearly defined role, and then you have people who have the self-confidence to navigate this rather, sort of, political environment, as I would call it, but in between you've got a *bit of a gap* really (emphasis added).

There was difficulty in pinpointing precisely where 'administration' and 'management' might overlap, or what, if anything, had filled any gap that had opened up. While there was a consistent view that roles and functions had moved on to being reinforcing of, rather than subordinate to, academic activity, individuals struggled to define the essential nature of this activity:

> I have difficulty [with the word 'administration'] because I think it gives the wrong impression of what we do. And it has a touch of the old-fashioned about it . . . I do see some strong elements of administration as being important in the overall management role. But I'd hate to think that it could be used as a term of disparagement.

Others found it easier to define 'administration' by making a distinction between 'the grunt-and-grind stuff' where you 'oiled the machine', and the creativity (a word that frequently recurred) involved in management. Thus administrators 'just do the same things better' whereas managers are 'grabbing hold of things and creatively changing them and turning them around'. One head of administration saw a distinction between managing individual projects at an operational level (administration), and managing a corporate entity at institutional level (management). They went on to say that much of what they did was 'somewhere in the middle between management and administration . . . I can't quite put into words what that "something other" is'. Defining that 'something other', at the interstices of administration and management, and whether it is something embedded in or independent of both, is at the heart of the conundrum.

While the tide of opinion may have turned against using 'administration' to represent functions, or what administrative staff do, it might, however, remain as a descriptor for values, standards, and the maintenance of communicative relationships. Roles involving guardianship of regulatory processes may provide a clue as to why 'administration' might continue to exist, as a counterweight to 'management':

> You have to be careful that in creating a very empowered situation you don't lose the standards and the values.

Thus 'administrative' ways of being might underpin the ethos on which academic and institutional reputations are built, while the activity of management strives to maximize the resource that underpins the institution's competitive position. Administration-within-management might continue to exist in terms of:

> advice and solutions . . . and I would say that's hopefully what administration contributes . . . that you're told what you can do in terms of the regulations, and the good administrator tells you, *despite that*, we can do this by doing x, y and z . . . (emphasis added)

Thus professional managers would seem to have a capability for ensuring that controls are in place, whilst simultaneously enabling progress to be made. What is significant about this duality is that it is not simply two complementary aspects of the same function, but a facility to contain and enact seemingly contradictory functions, of saying yes and no at the same time.

One legacy of 'administration' is the fact that professional administrators are often regarded as a repository of information, 'keeper of the conscience', providing the collective memory of an institution, which is passed on from one generation to the next. They are, therefore, seen as a source of continuity, an anchoring that links the institution to its organizational history, particularly when academic managers have limited terms of office. While the balance has tipped in favour of 'management', there remain different levels of visibility, in a civil service tradition. This can be advantageous for all parties, for instance when a restraining policy was being pursued and one group uses the other to shield it from the fallout of unpopular decisions. Profiles may, therefore, vary according to circumstances:

It's this notion of partnership, that we're working in this together; . . . you know, 'I am perfectly happy for you to get all the kudos for that, but I'm not necessarily going to hide completely behind.'

Again there is a duality in that professional managers need to be able to lead both from behind and in front, and be sensitive enough, personally and politically, to know what is appropriate for the occasion.

The interface with academia

There was a consensus that a key distinguishing feature about universities was:

> a particular issue about the relationship [with] the academic body which is driving the academic agenda, which is ultimately the purpose of the institution, and those who are actually working with them.

This was further characterized as 'a delicate social contract', something that was critical and dynamic, and more than simply a managerial or employer-employee relationship. Words used to describe it included 'partnership', 'mutual respect', 'empathy', 'parity of esteem' and 'sensitivity', all conveying the idea of belonging to a super-ordinate community, as well as something that was symbiotic rather than hierarchical. At its best the relationship would appear to have a tautness that is genuinely creative:

> . . . being an administrator you need . . . to be very sharp in order to be able to push back where necessary against . . . some often very cogent and sharp criticism.

The relationship was also a pragmatic one, based on the knowledge of where individual interests lie, and the exchange value of what each had to offer:

> . . . people who work on quality or research grants are now seen very much as allies of the academics in helping them to get what they want . . .

The partnership was reflected in the composition of senior management teams where heads of administration, and other senior managers such as directors of finance and human resources, were likely to be represented. At its most positive, therefore, joint working between academic and professional managers appeared to involve the two groups getting under each other's skin:

> You have got academics who are financially literate, and educated in university policy, and you've got administrators who bring certain technical skills but actually think in academic terms. And it is that inter-reaction of academic and managerial, which creates the sort of top team which is really successful.

Under this scenario, professional administrators and managers would bring expertise to bear on academic decisions and act as interpreters, translating academic policy into real-time outcomes. Despite the potential for genuine symbiosis, however, the partnership with academic colleagues was undoubtedly subject to the vagaries of circumstance, and had to be nurtured. In the ebb and flow of dialogue, professional administrators and managers were obliged to (re)-define, and on occasion defend their territory, about which no assumptions could be made.

While they had secured a place in overall strategy making, therefore, there was an awareness of a balance to be struck:

> They [academic staff] don't like somebody who's too powerful, and particularly ... if they feel that the Registrar is not somebody who is constantly supportive of what they want to do ... and you can't be because you have to balance up the overall long term interests of the institution.

The relationship was, therefore, subject to continual negotiation and renewal. Thus, despite evidence of (and some excitement about) the positive effects of collaborating in teams of professional and academic staff, there was caution about taking anything for granted.

Moving targets and complex futures

The movements around professional administrative and management roles suggest that, as one head of administration put it, 'all bets are off' with respect to future identities. Nevertheless, the influence of these groups is unlikely to decline, especially when students paying tuition fees are likely to expect higher standards of academic services, infrastructure and welfare. There are, therefore, issues for consideration and development, not only at institutional level, but also by agencies such as the Leadership Foundation and Higher Education Academy, with respect to, for instance:

- How the potential of professional administrators and managers might be optimized, in terms of the added value they can offer to their institution's academic direction;
- How they might best achieve the balancing act required to maintain threshold standards and accountability, while maximizing institutional potentials and competitive advantage;
- How they might best achieve common purpose with other constituencies of the university in fulfilling the academic vision of their institution;
- How they might be prepared for future hybrid roles, and for joint working with academic colleagues, for instance in multi-functional teams in relation to 'third stream' activity;
- How they might best promote what they have to offer and contextualize their work;

- How academic staff, in turn, might best articulate their needs, and derive benefit from the contributions of professional administrators and managers.

Conclusion

The project has enabled preliminary understandings to be established in relation to the concepts of 'administration' and 'management', and of the meanings associated with them. While the idea of a discrete 'administration' would appear to be in retreat, it is not clear whether or how it has been replaced. Where it is retained it would seem to provide a reference point for the maintenance of standards and values, and to retain elements of a public service ethos. Despite a shift towards 'management', there remain sensitivities around its use, and it requires some qualification, not least because of the interface with the roles of academic managers. Although there does not seem to be a consensus about precisely how this might be achieved, a start has been made in building a picture of an increasingly multi-faceted and multi-layered pattern of relationships. While professional administrators and managers occupy critical border territories between the values of administration and the pragmatics of management, there may also be places where there is potential for them to define their own territory.

Acknowledgement

The author wishes to acknowledge the support of King's College London in her undertaking of this project.

References

Gibbons, M., Limoges, C., Nowotny, H., Scott, P. and Trow, M. (1994) *The New Production of Knowledge: The Dynamics of Science and Research in Contemporary Societies.* London: Sage.
Henkel, M. (2000) *Academic Identities and Policy Change in Higher Education.* London: Jessica Kingsley.
HESDA (Higher Education Staff Development Agency) (2002) *Higher Education: The Second Skills Foresight Report.* Sheffield: HESDA.
Lambert, R. (2003) *Lambert Review of Business-University Collaboration. Final Report.* London: TSO.
Rhoades, G. and Sporn, B. (2002) New models of management and shifting modes and costs of production: Europe and the United States, *Tertiary Education and Management,* 8(1): 3–28.
Scott, P. (1995) *The Meanings of Mass Higher Education.* Buckingham: SRHE/Open University Press.

Sloman, A. (1964) *A University in the Making* (Reith Lectures 1963). London: British Broadcasting Corporation.

Whitchurch, C. (2004) Administrative managers in UK higher education: a critical link, *Higher Education Quarterly*, 58(4): 280–98.

16

University Governance and the Role of the State

Michael Shattock

It is a truism that as higher education has become larger it has become a greater cost to the state. The state has become more interested in how its money is spent and more concerned about corporate failure. Modern thinking about the importance of research and the production of qualified manpower as contributors to the growth of regional and national economies, and about the role of higher education in improving social inclusion, has also encouraged the state to adopt a much more proactive, not to say interventionist, policy towards higher education and, in consequence, a much more dirigiste attitude to its funding. If the state has adopted a more positive steering role than in the past it is not surprising that it is interested in what mechanisms exist to ensure that institutions are responsive to its policy drivers. The state can, and has, created a quasi (and sometimes self-contradictory) market which is intended to incentivize institutional behaviour to be consonant with national policy, but it has also developed an interest in governance structures, believing, understandably, that these should steer institutions. In addition, and for the most part quite separately, concerns about transparency and accountability to shareholders in public companies and the potential economic impact of large private sector corporate failures have prompted the state, as higher education's largest stakeholder, to wish to import the mechanisms being put in place in the private sector to safeguard the state's interests in higher education.

The purpose of this chapter is not to question the legitimacy of the state's interest in these issues. It asks whether its approach to realizing that interest is effective. The concern is prompted by the Lambert proposals on university governance (Lambert, 2003) but also reflects a more longstanding trend in government thinking that safeguards against corporate failure and control over institutional steering (the determination of strategy) should be located primarily, if not exclusively, in the governing body.

The Lambert Review (Lambert, 2003) was commissioned by the Chancellor of the Exchequer to look at business-university collaboration; governance issues were added to the remit at a later date. Lambert reports that 'Business told the Review that universities could be more dynamic in their approach to collaboration. The perception is of a sector that can be slow-moving, bureaucratic and risk averse' (para. 7.3). We are not told who the Review asked and how representative or reliable the responses were. However, the Review takes the position that a situation where universities are 'run as communities of scholars' with 'participatory' governance and management structures is not 'fit for modern times' (para. 7.3). It commends the delegation of business away from committees to academic and administrative managers which it says produces 'more rapid decision-making and more dynamic management' (para. 7.4). It sees a need therefore 'to plainly differentiate management from governance' (para. 6) as is provided for in the constitution of the new universities and concludes that 'the sector has reached a point where a voluntary code of governance should be developed' (para. 6). It then offers a draft 'as the starting point' for drawing one up (para. 7.1). The Review accepts that the code should be voluntary: it recommends that where institutional governance does not conform to the agreed code universities should explain in their annual report 'why their particular governance arrangements are more effective' (para. 6). The government in its response to the Review 'fully supports a code that challenges the sector to meet best practice . . . [but] recognises, however, that good practice exists in structures or processes outside that of the proposed code'. It states that 'The code should not become a national prescription' accepting that where institutional practice was not consistent with the code, an explanatory note should be published in the corporate governance sector of the audited financial statements. It recommends that the code be revised regularly 'to ensure it remains at the forefront of the best practice' (HM Treasury, DTI, DfES, 2004: 77).

The Lambert recommendations and the government's response represent staging posts in a long-running process of government trying to make university governance conform more closely to the established norms or to best practice in business. The process began with the Jarratt Committee recommendation that the role of governing bodies should be reinforced vis-à-vis that of senates (CVCP, 1985), exemplified in the provisions laid down in the 1988 and 1992 legislation as to the constitutions of the polytechnics and the post-1992 universities. The weaknesses of the latter have been explored by Knight (2002) and less directly in Shattock (2002). The 1992 legislation did not apply to the pre-1992 universities and the Dearing Committee's recommendations, designed to make governing bodies more effective and to reduce their membership to no more than 25, could be seen as an attempt to bring them into line (Shattock, 1998).

The model that Dearing (1997) and Lambert have in mind is based in great part on the reforms in company board structures, beginning with Cadbury (Committee on Corporate Governance, 1992) and continuing through Hampel (Committee on Corporate Governance, 1998) and Higgs (2003). The essence of all these reports is the enhancement of the role of non-executive directors to monitor and exercise control over board decisions in the interest of the shareholders. The result of the reforms has been the creation of the Combined Code in Corporate Governance, adherence to which is monitored by the Financial Reporting Council, which public companies must accept to gain admission to the Stock Exchange. The Higgs Review updated the Code to ensure that corporate governance provided 'an architecture of accountability' (para. 1.5) and that non-executive directors were 'the custodians of the governance process' (Higgs, 2003, para. 1.6).

Lying behind Higgs was the belief that 'Governance shortcomings have contributed to falling markets. The combination of the two has in some cases been the trigger for corporate collapse' (Higgs 2003, para. 1.3). A good illustration of such shortcomings can be found in the Report commissioned by the DTI into the collapse of TransTec PLC (Aldous and Kaye, 2003). Essentially the collapse was triggered by financial obligations incurred by decisions of the managing director and director of finance which were not reported to the board. The DTI Report went further than this in commenting on the culture and operational effectiveness of the board in relation to the conduct of business of the company. The Report provides a vivid textbook account of what corporate governance in public companies is about and what can go wrong. The Report found that:

> TransTec was a company whose board did not direct the business effectively and whose senior management participated in the board yet misled the board. It was a company whose corporate governance failed ... primarily ... through a lack of openness about, and grip of events. Rather than being open and frank, its governance and management was closed and dysfunctional.
>
> (Aldous and Kaye, 2003, para. 5.170)

and that 'Rather than challenge management, the non-executive directors chose to rely on the auditors for assurance. They did not appreciate that the auditors were, like them, unwilling to challenge management and unwilling also to express a robust opinion' (para. 5.176).

Perhaps we should not be so surprised at the defectiveness of TransTec's non-executive directors. At one of the many conferences held in the City to consider the implications of the Enron collapse in the USA, the Chairman of the Treasury Select Committee was quoted as saying:

> I've been on boards where I have a non-executive role – I've always found it hard to understand what the executives are up to and to be up with their thinking. And when someone is at work five, six, seven days a week and is responsible for the strategic focus and direction of the company and somebody flits in once a week or once a month I doubt that the latter person has a chance against a real professional.
>
> (McFall, 2002)

Universities are entitled to ask how true this statement is of some of the lay members of their own governing bodies, particularly as the DTI Report emphasizes the expertise which board members are expected to bring to the table:

It goes without saying that directors must understand the company's business, understand the decision-making processes in the business and must think about what is happening in the company and how best to predict opportunities, risks and the future position and profitability of the business. The board should, in particular, ensure that it is monitoring the underlying health of the business rather than just the latest financial reports.

(Aldous and Kaye, 2003, para. 5.17)

Understanding the business of the institution, including 'the underlying health' is clearly a critical criterion for effective board membership and, it could be argued, for any unicameral board of an HEI which has responsibility, not just for the overall management of the institution, but for determining its educational character and mission. Both Dearing and Lambert argue that in order to be more effective membership of governing bodies in the pre-1992 universities, where the average is about 33, should be reduced to no more than 25. There are two problems about this. First, the company model of non-executive directors envisages essentially the non-execs adding value and a measure of control over a similar number, if not a majority, of executive directors. But in the pre-1992 universities the internal (academic) members comprise only a third of the governing body, and much less in the post-1992 institutions. It could be argued that the vice-chancellor is the only executive director on the board. If governing boards are to become smaller, consideration needs to be given to a changed balance of executive and non-executive members, not least to ensure that the board is adequately equipped to do its job. Second, there is no research evidence that connects size of board with company performance. If one translates this to the world of higher education it could be argued on the basis of the published league tables that in the UK there is an inverse ratio between size of governing body, and associated proportion of academic representation, and the performance of the institution. Edwards (2003: 53) concludes that 'There is a considerable body of research emerging that the size of [university] boards or Councils is not related to either Council or institutional performance'. She quotes Chait *et al.* (1996) on governing board effectiveness in US universities who found that 'these data safely allowed only one generalisation: large boards wished they were smaller and small boards wished they were larger'.

Both Dearing and Lambert want to see a Code of Governance introduced. Their ostensible reasons for arguing this are difficult to fathom from their published statements. Universities already have legal instruments laid down by the Privy Council (in the case of most pre-1992 universities) and legislation (in respect to the higher education corporations); and the Committee of University Chairmen has issued a Guide on governance (CUC 2000), which is widely used.

Dearing argued for a code:

- to ensure that governing bodies took decisions in a way that was 'effective, transparent and timely';
- to make governance arrangements familiar within institutions;
- to ensure that the governing body had an appropriate membership;
- to ensure that governing bodies met 'their obligations inside and outside the institution'.

(Dearing, 1997, para. 15.38)

Lambert's justifications are even less clear cut. On the one hand he points to the need for ways to be found 'to encourage managers to take more responsibility without referring decisions to the safety blanket of committees' (Lambert 2003, para. 7.18); on another he says that a key role of a governing body 'is to approve management's strategy and measure performance against plan' (para. 7.19). A code would be more 'concise than guidance' and would 'act as a catalyst to spread best practice' (para. 7.20). The only argument that is not mentioned but which seems to underlie both sets of ideas is the parallel with the Combined Code applied to public companies. In 2004 the Committee of University Chairmen bowed to pressure and published a Code along the lines Lambert recommended (CUC 2004). It adds nothing to the Guide.

However, Dearing and Lambert go beyond seeing such mechanisms in terms of propriety and good governance but take a proactive view of governing bodies and their role in determining institutional strategy. Lambert, it is true, refers to 'approving management's strategy' but in a situation where the governing body may not have a strong 'executive director' component this leaves a governing body significantly at risk if its membership is not sufficiently expert in the institution's underlying business. At Lancaster, for example, after the governing body were persuaded by management to sign a debenture bond, which was to plunge the University into a cash flow crisis and cause it to back out of an agreed merger with another institution, the subsequent investigation concluded:

> We consider that Council has not been able to properly perform its role as the governing body . . . and are concerned that its members and especially its officers may not have acted with sufficient frequency and firmness to test the proposals laid before it . . . it is a body that must rely on recommendations that are soundly based, well supported with accurate information, cogently argued and clearly presented, with a range of options from which members can make a choice.
>
> (Rowe, 1997: 207)

It went on to suggest that 'key strategic decisions to be decided by Council are first brought to the Senate so that its views are known' (Rowe, 1997: 215). One study of governing bodies operating under the 1988 and 1992 legislation concluded that they:

> could be said to be very efficient but passive bodies in that they deal with a large number of items at board meetings but mostly without discussion

or debate. They could be said to be rather ineffective bodies, not appearing to have any major impact on the strategic plans and major governance matters of their institutions or overly involved with the monitoring of executive performance.

(Bennett, 2002: 298)

In other words they have not developed the kind of 'open and responsive culture' (para. 5.17) which the DTI Report on TransTec commends and do not 'challenge management' or 'monitor the performance of the chief executive and the competence of senior management', which DTI sees as characteristics of 'the effective board' (Aldous and Kaye, 2003, para. 5.18).

These examples are not quoted to suggest that governing bodies do not fulfil important and enormously necessary functions in universities. Elsewhere I have outlined the hugely important contribution they make to university life (Shattock, 2003: 103–6) but the state risks overestimating the extent to which they can provide direction to their institutions' affairs other than in partnership with representative academic bodies, as well as the institutions' senior managements. In other words, unless the academics who deliver the institutional performance in research, teaching, the recruitment of home and overseas students, the regional economic commitment, are themselves represented, like executive directors, on the board, the board is unlikely to be connected to the underlying drivers of success or failure, and will lack the critical expertise in understanding the business beyond simply the equivalent of 'the latest financial reports'. This is not an argument for a return to a traditional simplified senate and council diarchy with measured interchanges between two constitutionally separate bodies. Clark (2004: 173) in his follow-up study on entrepreneurial universities makes the point that: 'Entrepreneurialism works when it is significantly collegial. Management teams cannot do the job alone, old academic senates cannot dominate, new forms of academic-administrative relations have to be worked out.' And again:

> Entrepreneurial universities become based on entrepreneurial departments – dynamic places attractive to faculty, students and resource providers. Heartland departments do not fade away. What they are willing to do gets done; what they set their face against is slowed down or eliminated along the way.
>
> (p. 176)

The state is taking a superficial view of how HEIs work if it believes that it can influence their direction without directly engaging with and convincing the academic community, and without involving the academic community in the fundamental questions of governance and accountability. One world league table of universities (Shanghai Jiao Tong University, 2004] suggests that by far the two most successful universities in the UK are Cambridge (ranked third after Harvard and Stanford) and Oxford (eighth). Those universities have minimal lay involvement in governance (Oxford) or none at all (Cambridge) and strategic policy decisions are taken by 'executive directors' who are front line leaders in their academic fields rather than by non-executive directors from outside. We can acknowledge historical factors as contributing to Oxbridge's success without exaggerating the importance of imposed governance mechanisms on institutional importance. As the Hampel Report says of the private sector: 'People, teamwork, leadership, enterprise and skills are what really produce prosperity. There is no single formula to weld these together and it is dangerous to encourage the belief that rules and regulations about structure will deliver success' (Hampel 1998, para. 1.2).

If we were to formulate a response to government thinking it might therefore encapsulate the following propositions:

1 The tasks of safeguarding fiduciary propriety, managing assets effectively and determining institutional strategy cannot be the responsibility of governing bodies alone, nor of governing bodies whose only advice comes from management, narrowly defined.
2 There is a danger that the state, as the largest stakeholder, has exaggerated the ability of governing bodies to deliver what it may be seeking from higher education. It needs to recognize that governing bodies not acting in concert and partnership with representative academic bodies such as senates or academic boards may lack connectivity with the essential drivers of institutional performance.
3 Governance structures need to be adapted to institutional mission and context, not arbitrarily arrived at by analogy with private sector companies or through overarching codes.

References

Aldous, H. and Kaye, R. for DTI (2003) *TransTec PLC: Investigation under Section 432 (2) of the Companies Act 1985*. London: The Stationery Office.

Bennett, B. (2002) The new style boards of governors – are they working?, *Higher Education Quarterly*, 56(3).

Chait, R. P., Holland, T. P., Taylor, B. E. (1996) *Improving the Performance of Governing Boards*. Phoenix: AZ Onyx Press.

Clark, B. R. (2004) *Sustaining Change in Universities*. Maidenhead: SRHE/Open University Press.

CUC (Committee of University Chairmen) (2000) *Guide for Members of Governing Bodies of Universities and Colleges in England, Wales and Northern Ireland*. Sheffield: CUC.

Committee on Corporate Governance (1992) *The Financial Aspects of Corporate Governance* (Cadbury Report). London: Gee Publishing.

Committee on Corporate Governance (1998) *Financial Report* (Hampel Report). London: Gee Publishing.

CUC (2004) *Guide for Members of Higher Education Governing Bodies in the UK*. Sheffield: CUC.

CVCP Committee of Vice-Chancellors and Principals (1985) *Report of the Steering Group on University Efficiency* (Jarratt Report). London: CVCP.

Economist (2004) Economic and financial indicators: top universities, 4 September.

Edwards, M. (2003) *Review of New Zealand Tertiary Education Governance.* New Zealand: Ministry of Education.

Higgs, D. (2003) *Review of the Role and Effectiveness of Non-executive Directors.* London: HMSO.

HM Treasury, DTI, DfES (2004) *Science and Innovation Investment Framework, 2004–2014,* Appendix C 'The Government's response to the Lambert Review'. London: The Stationery Office.

Knight, M. (2002) Governance in Higher Education Corporations: a consideration of the constitution created by the 1992 Act, *Higher Education Quarterly,* 56(3): 276–86.

Lambert, R. (2003) *Lambert Review of Business–University Collaboration. Final Report.* London: The Stationery Office.

McFall, J. (2002) Scope and purpose of the Treasury Select Committee Inquiry. Paper presented at Enron and Auditor Independence: the implications for the UK, London, 26 April.

NCIHE (The National Committee of Inquiry into Higher Education) (1997) *Higher Education in the Learning Society* (The Dearing Report). London: The Stationery Office.

Rowe, P. (ed.) (1997) *The University of Lancaster. Review of Institutional Lessons to be Learned 1994–1996.* Lancaster: University of Lancaster.

Shanghai Jiao Tong University (2004) *Academic Ranking of World Universities 2004.*

Shattock, M. L. (1998) Dearing on governance: the wrong prescription, *Higher Education Quarterly,* 52 (1): 35–48.

Shattock, M. L. (2002) Re-balancing modern concepts of university governance, *Higher Education Quarterly,* 56(3): 235–45.

Shattock, M. L. (2003) *Managing Successful Universities.* Maidenhead: SRHE/Open University Press.

Part Five

Looking forward, moving on

17

The Agenda Ahead: Building on Experience

Ian McNay

Introduction

In trying to develop future strategy, there are, as Donald Rumsfeld has noted, 'known knowns', 'known unknowns', and 'unknown unknowns'. We know what the fee regimes in different UK countries will be in the next period. We do not know what impact there will be on any moves to higher levels of participation – 'universal' in Trow's terms, nor on cross-border flows between different fee and student support regimes, even within the UK. My work suggests that there is a fourth category to complete the set – 'unknown knowns'. Many staff with whom I work, who have strategic responsibilities, or who need at least to have strategic awareness, do not have a developed appreciation of the stream of events, or the pattern of trends in the environment, that affect their professional context. That is true, even where knowledge is in the public domain, or at least the wider professional domain. They may have a focused analysis, but not linked laterally – a criticism by HEFCE (2001) of institutional strategic plans. Many are concentrating on survival day to day and any strategy emerges operationally, through action, and is made sense of retrospectively (Weick, 1995).

In this chapter I draw first on work with HE staff on scenario development. Then I look back on the preceding chapters, on the final, residential seminar in the ESRC series, and on the consultative colloquium on the survey reported in Chapters 1 and 12. From these emerge several key, complex themes to set an agenda for policy and research over the coming period, since the 2005 general election has given New Labour a third term in which to further improve higher education.

Scenario development

Scenario development is an established element in strategic planning in business and commerce. Van der Heiden (1996; van der Heiden *et al.*, 2002) sees it as provoking 'strategic conversation', which is an aim of this book. There are a number of advantages to the approach:

• It allows escape from rationalistic confines, which lead to conclusions that 'there is no alternative'. By encouraging a starting point detached from the present, it reverses the direction of thinking;
• It, therefore, widens and enhances perception and frees the creative imagination;
• It acknowledges complexity and uncertainty;
• It promotes integration across portfolios;
• It provides a safe context for thinking teams, because of the distance from today's reality; and so,
• it encourages an open dialogue, conversation and communication between those who might not engage otherwise and in a different climate.

The conversation can then progress from 'what if?' to 'so what?', and that second stage can lead to pro-activity to affect the future or to anticipate it in developing a new sense of place, of identity, within it, filtered through the values that underpin the policy perspective. Our power to create our own futures may be limited but it is not completely eliminated. The plangent determinism of some in HE may be a tribute to their analytical skills, but needs to be counterbalanced with a disposition to action. The analysis without the action is sterile; the action without the analysis may be futile.

Possible futures in higher education

This section draws on work with staff based mainly in two institutions, one a member of the Russell group of elite universities, one committed to employment as a strapline mission statement (McNay, 2004a, b), but with some additional respondents from outside those two. The process uses an instrument (McNay, 2003) listing statements about the future of HE provision and asks respondents to rate these as to how likely they are to be true, within a ten-year perspective. Collated replies are then converted into a 'perceived probability percentage rating' and fed back to provoke discussion – 'conversation' – in line with Delphi technique. If time allows, there can be several iterations. The suggestion is that items getting a rating of 70 per cent or more can be used as a basis for a next stage – considering the implications for a particular institution or department or even individual (Becher and Kogan, 1992).

What emerged from the two exercises at the end of 2004 confirmed some of the findings reported above (Chapter 1). There is a scepticism about government policy. There is also a lack of preparedness for other developments in the policy and operating context of HE.

The scepticism was most apparent on issues of funding. The statement that 'the cap on fees (in England) will be removed after 2010' got a rating of 75 per cent, and there was a 74 per cent rating for the probability that the unit of funding for teaching from HEFCE would fall after top-up fees were introduced. Both of those developments run counter to espoused policy and strong ministerial denials. The view of the immediate future (81 per cent) was that 'more than 90 per cent of full-time HE-based undergraduate degrees will charge £3000 after 2006'. That has now been borne out by the access agreements submitted to OFFA. They undermine any expectation that universities might differentiate themselves by 'ticket price', though 'cash back' and bursaries will be elements in marketing. Longer term, respondents expected even more emphasis on 'payment by results' with funding conditional upon completion rates (70 per cent).

The second group of highly rated items covered study patterns:

- study will be more flexible with regard to intensity and to levels of attendance required (77 per cent);
- most students will study at least 25 per cent of their course through packaged/independent learning (72 per cent);
- a personal laptop will be essential for HE study (71 per cent).

They support the arguments of Conole (Chapter 7). The first poses problems for student funding. In the UK there is a bipolar distinction – full-time and part-time – and fees and student support can be starkly different depending on which side the course followed falls, no matter how many hours of contact are required. There is no spectrum of support depending on study pattern, no gradient of funding. In the USA, fees are charged by credit, and can differ even by time of study, with those offered in unsocial hours having lower fees. Note that unsocial in that context is after 3.30 pm; the traditional image of UK students suggests that they would see anything *before* that time as a challenge! Respondents did not (52 per cent rating) see fragmentation of fees as likely, with charges by service usage levels of the library, or computing facilities; nor by levels of academic engagement – enrolment, materials, tutor contact, assessment, though some Open University courses have already experimented with such an approach.

The final cluster treated here is of items with low ratings:

- (growth in student numbers) will be almost exclusively in foundation degrees (47 per cent);
- Education Maintenance Allowances (EMAs) will increase the staying-on rate until 18, and so increase the proportion of an age group getting HE entry qualifications (52 per cent);
- strategic planning for FE and HE will be done at regional level, coordinated by Regional Development Agencies (51 per cent);
- degree classifications will go, and be replaced by 'skills profiles' (50 per cent).

However, the first and third of those are stated policy in the 2003 White Paper (DfES, 2003); and the rating for the first ignores trends in Scotland and Northern Ireland (Gallacher and Osborne, this volume) about growth of HE in FE, which is also an English government policy. The second is a keystone of policy in England to increase demand, and the last rating was given despite a working party report recommending it at the time that views were sought (UUK/SCOP, 2004). The chapters by Pearson, Knight and Yorke (this volume) are relevant to the link between assessment, skills and employment.

The groups were also less than fully familiar with patterns of participation and shifts in the profile of students – the diversity agenda treated in Part 2 above.

The ratings were given on a scale of 1–10 and 11 items out of 26 had scores covering the whole scale; the others all covered 8 points on the scale. So, there is no collective, shared understanding, or agreement in analysis. Debating the reasons for these different perceptions would be a good first stage of the 'strategic conversation' so absent in processes at all levels.

Diversity and equity

Those two concepts provide one of the recurrent themes of this book. Their reconciliation, according to one insider, was a constant topic for debate on education within the policy unit reporting to the prime minister in the 2001–5 government (Hyman, 2005). There are issues for national policy, for the missions and management of institutions, for teaching and learning, for assessment and the nature of graduateness, for research and development, and for staff.

Leathwood argues that challenging social and economic inequalities must be a central plank of widening participation, informing not only student access and funding, but also institutional cultures, curriculum inclusivity, and staffing. Gallacher shares her concern that differentiation has meant stratification, and argues that systems must be in place to counter the negative effects of stratification and to reconcile differentiation with goals of social justice and equity. Osborne sets the debate in the particular context of the 'fractured society' of Northern Ireland. Lucas underlines the rank order in research funding and argues for a more diverse interpretation of quality in research. Wedgwood provides a model for a similar broad interpretation of knowledge transfer and the diverse roles of HEIs in supporting their communities. McNay's first chapter argues for recognition of different excellences, and for parity of funding for the diverse missions that government charges HEIs to pursue. That would allow a more values based choice of institutional profile rather than a resource based one.

Knight, Yorke and Conole treat the themes within the pedagogy of mass higher education provision. They argue that there is now a diversity of sources of knowledge and learning, that students bring diverse previous experiences, and that their achievements cannot be assessed in simple standard ways that fail to recognize the complexity of processes and outcomes. There needs to be a blend and balance of face-to-face learning and those using new technology. Assessment needs to be aligned with learning and the needs of the 'real world' from which the academy is no longer separated in an elite privileged enclave. Little is concerned that the higher education experience widens inequalities in social capital, which affects graduate entry to the job market. Pearson considers the issue of possible oversupply of graduates to that market, and the need for a more diverse conceptualization of a graduate and of a graduate job. Within the rapidly changing world of employment, even traditional graduate jobs are changing from within. Graduates are making jobs 'graduate' in what they bring to interpreting roles and extending job descriptions, fulfilled at high levels. What needs attention is the attitude of employers, who have perennially lamented standards, but done little to invest in further staff development.

Roles are changing within higher education, too, and staff need to change, as Whitchurch suggests is happening with administrative staff. Court is concerned with widening inequalities between academic staff salaries and previous comparator groups. Saunderson illustrates the internal inequalities by gender that need redressing. Similar cases could be made for other staff groups. The proportions of women students and of those from ethnic monority groups are consistently underestimated by those working on scenario development. Yet, on present trends, their proportion of the student population will continue to increase. The time lag before this is reflected in staff profiles should now have elapsed. HEIs need to be more diverse and inclusive in staffing policies.

There is also a need for research on those outside the traditional mainstream. The student experience is no longer, if it ever was, a dominantly full-time, campus based one. Learning communities are no longer exclusively intra-mural. Work is needed on the diversity of life experience brought by diverse students and their diverse expectations and interpretations of success. We need to know more about part-time students, home-based students, those on professional postgraduate courses, and those without a white, middle-class hinterland. The same is true of staff with a diversity of contracts. The full-time tenured academic is no longer a norm. And not only academics – half the staff in HEIs are not academics in any traditional sense. There are very, very few studies of those in a diversity of support and service roles who are essential to the student experience and the culture of an organization.

Individual and collective identity

That leads to a second theme. The colloquium believed strongly that mass provision was in danger of losing sight of the individual, and of losing the essential humanity that should imbue higher education. The survey for the colloquium revealed that academic staff are aware of an increasing anomie, as they see provision dominated by system requirements, which require a Procrustean approach to fitness for purpose. The purpose, in this case, is the corporate one, and staff and students are cut or stretched to the one size that fits all. Challenge to received wisdom is seen as dissent, not a healthy diversity of opinion. The RAE encourages staff to stick to the mainstream of knowledge (McNay, forthcoming), not to challenge it, since it is the domain of the powerful.

The draft strategic plan for 2003–2008 from HEFCE referred to lifelong learning as leading to a bespoke educational experience for every student. The final version removed such a revolutionary idea (no doubt for resource reasons), but we need to recapture that spirit. Paradoxically, it may be that the provisions of the mass media are part of the solution within mass higher education. The diversity of learning sources and resources needs recognition, and credit given for learning 'otherwise' than as prescribed in student and course handbooks.

Individual institutions also need to find a secure identity, and to be assertive in proclaiming it. Equity of esteem and of funding will create a freedom to do this, which means a change to the present elite preference funding. That collective identity needs to be collectively arrived at, and the assertive autonomy of institutions embraced as a strength with incentives offered to individual identities and distinctive roles.

Freedom and trust

The present hierarchy of power and of provision has a negative impact on the development of higher education for the next stage of provision. There is a lack of trust between levels in the development of policy and the organization of provision. Too much control is held at levels above the effective level. People in those higher levels need to learn to let go, rather than micromanaging, badly, provision that is functionally and structurally distant. That will allow for more diversity of provision as recommended above, and a better fit with a diversity of local situations within which learning should be situated. The regulatory regimes stressing compliance and conformity have had a similar negative effect on creativity and innovation, and, in the case of teaching quality, have not justified their existence by finding significant levels of poor provision.

That greater self-determination in a culture of professional confidence, then, linked with equity of esteem and reward, can allow individuals more freedom to explore and experiment: for students through self-actuated learning, beyond the boundaries as prescribed (and in territories sometimes proscribed), and for staff in a diversity of roles that are recognized as essential parts of the collective. It can release the continuing commitment to learning for liberation and transformation revealed in the colloquium survey.

That collective identity then emerges from collective decision-making, Shattock's 'shared governance', with significant devolution, where heads of department are key leaders, together with their programme/project leaders for teaching and research where the key organizing unit is the *team*, a more adaptive entity than any others in traditional structures. Again, there has been little research on how such teams work within higher education and the factors that make for success.

Such approaches cannot thrive in institutions with a corporate culture. The needs for openness and trust are as great at institutional level as at system level. Institutions need to become reflexive as anticipated by Scott (1995). They need to develop as learning organizations (McNay, Chapter 12, this volume), where success is shared and mistakes are opportunities for learning, not for lambasting those at lower levels. Senior staff need to accept responsibility for training and supporting those for whom they are responsible.

Collaboration and community commitment

The final element in planning for progression to universal levels of provision, emerging from the diversity of roles, and the recognition of diversities of learning sites and situations, is one of partnership. The barriers erected by some institutions have been more seditious than the barricades of 1960s students. Yet universal access means that the community of place that has defined, physically and visually, the 'university' needs to see itself as part of a university of life, within lifelong learning. Some specialist colleges are excellent in involving those from the communities of practice for which they are preparing students. Others have significant continuing professional development (CPD) provision for those who bring experiential learning to test the rigour of cognitive skill development against operational skills, tested and tempered in the workplace. Arrangement for third stream work (Wedgwood, this volume) must be predicated on an 'equal but different' contribution from partners. The quality of performance in boundary spanning roles will be crucial to such activity.

The same must be true of partnerships for progression by learners, and the significant emergent role for FE colleges in extending provision. Those partnerships must recognize equity and diversity as organizing values to avoid the academic drift that has been the fate of first the civics, then the Colleges of Advanced Technology, and then the polytechnics and central institutions. The renewed links between town and gown may have been driven by the need for political partners and economic magnets and investment of resources. In a system of universal provision, the deeper needs of personal development of citizens and the value added beyond the earnings premium, must emerge and inform policy and practice.

References

Becher, T. and Kogan, M. (1992) *Process and Structure in Higher Education.* London: Routledge.

DfES (Department for Education and Skills) (2003) *The Future of Higher Education.* Norwich: The Stationery Office.

HEFCE (Higher Education Funding Council for England) (2001) *Review of Strategic Plans and Financial Forecasts.* Bristol: HEFCE.

Hyman, P. (2005) *1 out of 10: From Downing Street Vision to Classroom Reality.* London: Vintage.

McNay, I. (2003) *Developing Higher Education Senior Managers Strategically.* Sheffield: HESDA and Universities Scotland.

McNay, I. (2004a) The university learning community: challenge and change, Conference on '*Education in a Changing Environment*', Higher Education Research Centre, University of Salford. Now published in Coates, N. (ed.) (2005) *Education in a Changing Environment,* University of Salford.

McNay, I. (2004b) Scenario development and strategic planning: possible futures in higher education, seminar presentation, EDP Debates, University College, London, 25 November.

McNay, I. (forthcoming) Research assessment; researcher autonomy in C. Kayrooz, M. Tight and G.S. Åkerlind (eds) *Autonomy in Social Science Research.* Maidenhead: Open University Press.

Scott, P. (1995) *The Meaning of Mass Higher Education.* Buckingham: SRHE/Open University Press.

UUK/SCOP (Universities UK and Standing Conference of Principals) (2004) *Measuring and Recording Student Achievement.* Report of a group chaired by Professor Robert Burgess. London: UUK/SCOP.

van der Heiden, K. (1996) *Scenarios: The Art of Strategic Conversation.* Chichester: John Wiley.

van der Heiden, K., Bradfield, R., Burt, G., Cairns, G. and Wright, G. (eds) (2002) *The Sixth Sense: Accelerating Organisational Learning with Scenarios.* Chichester: John Wiley.

Weick, K. (1995) *Sensemaking in Organizations.* London: Sage.

Index

Page references in *italics* indicate diagrams and tables.

The Society for Research into Higher Education

The Society for Research into Higher Education (SRHE), an international body, exists to stimulate and coordinate research into all aspects of higher education. It aims to improve the quality of higher education through the encouragement of debate and publication on issues of policy, on the organization and management of higher education institutions, and on the curriculum, teaching and learning methods.

The Society is entirely independent and receives no subsidies, although individual events often receive sponsorship from business or industry. The Society is financed through corporate and individual subscriptions and has members from many parts of the world. It is an NGO of UNESCO.

Under the imprint *SRHE & Open University Press*, the Society is a specialist publisher of research, having over 80 titles in print. In addition to *SRHE News*, the Society's newsletter, the Society publishes three journals: *Studies in Higher Education* (three issues a year), *Higher Education Quarterly* and *Research into Higher Education Abstracts* (three issues a year).

The Society runs frequent conferences, consultations, seminars and other events. The annual conference in December is organized at and with a higher education institution. There are a growing number of networks which focus on particular areas of interest, including:

Access	FE/HE
Assessment	Graduate Employment
Consultants	New Technology for Learning
Curriculum Development	Postgraduate Issues
Eastern European	Quantitative Studies
Educational Development Research	Student Development

Benefits to members

Individual

- The opportunity to participate in the Society's networks
- Reduced rates for the annual conferences
- Free copies of *Research into Higher Education Abstracts*
- Reduced rates for *Studies in Higher Education*

- Reduced rates for *Higher Education Quarterly*
- Free online access to *Register of Members' Research Interests* – includes valuable reference material on research being pursued by the Society's members
- Free copy of occasional in-house publications, e.g. *The Thirtieth Anniversary Seminars Presented by the Vice-Presidents*
- Free copies of *SRHE News* and *International News* which inform members of the Society's activities and provides a calendar of events, with additional material provided in regular mailings
- A 35 per cent discount on all SRHE/Open University Press books
- The opportunity for you to apply for the annual research grants
- Inclusion of your research in the *Register of Members' Research Interests*

Corporate

- Reduced rates for the annual conference
- The opportunity for members of the Institution to attend SRHE's network events at reduced rates
- Free copies of *Research into Higher Education Abstracts*
- Free copies of *Studies in Higher Education*
- Free online access to *Register of Members' Research Interests* – includes valuable reference material on research being pursued by the Society's members
- Free copy of occasional in-house publications
- Free copies of *SRHE News* and *International News*
- A 35 per cent discount on all SRHE/Open University Press books
- The opportunity for members of the Institution to submit applications for the Society's research grants
- The opportunity to work with the Society and co-host conferences
- The opportunity to include in the *Register of Members' Research Interests* your Institution's research into aspects of higher education

Membership details: SRHE, 76 Portland Place, London W1B 1NT, UK Tel: 020 7637 2766. Fax: 020 7637 2781. email: srheoffice@srhe.ac.uk world wide web: http://www.srhe.ac.uk./srhe/ *Catalogue*: SRHE & Open University Press, McGraw-Hill Education, McGraw-Hill House, Shoppenhangers Road, Maidenhead, Berkshire SL6 2QL. Tel: 01628 502500. Fax: 01628 770224. email: enquiries@openup.co.uk – web: www.openup.co.uk